Effective MySQL
Replication Techniques in Depth

About the Authors

Ronald Bradford has worked in the relational database industry for over 20 years. His professional background began in 1989 with Ingres and Oracle RDBMS. His expertise includes a vast experience with database architecture, performance tuning, and management of large enterprise systems. Ronald has, for the past 13 years, worked primarily with MySQL, the world's most popular open source database. His previous employment has included Oracle Corporation (1996–1999) as an Oracle Consultant and MySQL, Inc. (2006–2008) as a senior MySQL Consultant.

His contributions to the MySQL community have included recognition as the all-time top individual MySQL blog contributor at Planet MySQL (2010), an Oracle ACE Director (2010), and MySQL Community Member of the Year (2009).

Ronald combines his extensive consulting expertise with a passion to share the knowledge and benefits of using MySQL. He is the author of four books on MySQL, and his many public speaking engagements have included presentations at conferences in over 25 countries. The Effective MySQL series of books and presentations aim to provide practical education for DBAs, developers, and architects in MySQL performance, scalability, and business continuity.

Chris Schneider is a long-time open source advocate and MySQL evangelist, administrator, and architect. Over the past decade Chris has devoted his professional career to open source technologies, with his primary focus being MySQL at scale. His previous employment has included GoDaddy, Facebook, and Ning.com, along with his own MySQL consulting company.

He has designed, implemented, and maintained small to large MySQL installations while training and mentoring teams of DBAs. This includes building architecture from the ground up and improving on those that are currently in place while emphasizing scalability, performance, and ease of use.

Chris has also shared his experiences and knowledge through the many speaking engagements he does, such as Oracle Open World, MySQL Connect, Percona Live, and the former O'Reilly MySQL Conference. Chris is also the technical editor of the second book in the Effective MySQL series, *Effective MySQL: Backup and Recovery.*

About the Technical Editors

Nelson Calero has been working with Oracle technology since 1996, and with MySQL since 2005, specializing in architecture, administration, and performance for very large databases (VLDBs) and highly available (HA) environments. His previous experience included being a teacher and researcher in the Computer Science Institute (InCo) of the Engineering University (UdelaR) in Uruguay. Nelson now focuses on providing industry consulting to both the private and public sectors throughout Latin America, from Argentina to Mexico.

In the past few years, Nelson has become a frequent speaker at user community events in the Americas, including Oracle Open World Latin America and Collaborate. Currently he is an independent consultant, an Oracle University instructor, and president of the Oracle User Group of Uruguay (UYOUG).

Giuseppe Maxia works as QA Director with Continuent, Inc. He is an active member of the MySQL community and long-time open source enthusiast. During the past decades he has worked in various IT related fields, with focus on databases, object oriented programming, and system administration. He is fluent in Italian, English, Perl, Python, SQL, Lua, C, and Bash, and a good speaker of C, French, Spanish, and Java. He works in cyberspace with a virtual team and a blog (http://datacharmer.blogspot.com). Giuseppe has twice been the recipient of the MySQL Community Award (2006 and 2011) and recognized as an Oracle ACE Director (2012).

Sheeri K. Cabral has a master's degree in computer science specializing in databases from Brandeis University and a background in systems administration. Unstoppable as a volunteer and activist since age 14, Cabral founded and organizes the Boston, Massachusetts, MySQL User Group and is the creator and co-host of OurSQLCast: The MySQL Database Community Podcast, available on iTunes. She was the first MySQL Oracle ACE Director, and is the founder (and current treasurer) of Technocation, Inc., a not-for-profit organization providing resources and educational grants for IT professionals. She wrote the *MySQL Administrator's Bible* (Wiley and Sons, 2009) and has been a technical editor for high-profile O'Reilly books such as *High Performance MySQL, 2nd Edition* (2012) and C.J. Date's *SQL and Relational Theory* (2009).

Hans Forbrich has been working with computers since the early 1970s, in particular with entity-relationship and relational databases, starting in 1979 using an engine on IBM mainframes called GERM (General Entity Relationship Model). Since that time, Hans has been a DBA, an operations architect for a number of organizations, and an Oracle University instructor but always heavily involved in high availability and recoverability.

As a fellow ACE Director, Hans is pleased and honored to have been a technical reviewer for this book. This topic is an important area of MySQL, and Ronald's expertise and experience in this area shine through.

Darren Cassar is a senior MySQL Database Administrator at Lithium Technologies. He holds a computer and communications engineering degree from the University of Malta and started his career doing systems administration in Malta, later moving on to database administration in Malta, London, New York, and San Francisco. Darren is the author of Securich, an open source security plugin for MySQL, a subject that he has presented at several conferences in both the United States and Europe.

ORACLE® Oracle Press™

Effective MySQL

Replication Techniques in Depth

Ronald Bradford
Chris Schneider

New York   Chicago   San Francisco
Lisbon   London   Madrid   Mexico City
Milan   New Delhi   San Juan
Seoul   Singapore   Sydney   Toronto

The McGraw·Hill Companies

Cataloging-in-Publication Data is on file with the Library of Congress

Effective MySQL: Replication Techniques in Depth

1 2 3 4 5 6 7 8 9 0   QFR QFR   1 0 9 8 7 6 5 4 3 2

ISBN   978-0-07-179186-1

MHID   0-07-179186-8

Sponsoring Editor	Giuseppe Maxia	**Production Supervisor**
Paul Carlstroem	Sheeri K. Cabral	Jean Bodeaux
Editorial Supervisor	Hans Forbrich	**Composition**
Patty Mon	Darren Cassar	Cenveo Publisher Services
Project Manager	**Copy Editor**	**Illustration**
Vastavikta Sharma, Cenveo Publisher Services	Lisa McCoy	Cenveo Publisher Services
Acquisitions Coordinator	**Proofreader**	**Art Director, Cover**
Ryan Willard	Claire Splan	Jeff Weeks
Technical Editors	**Indexer**	**Cover Designer**
Nelson Calero	Ted Laux	Pattie Lee

For MySQL culture, past, present, and future.
To those I know in the Oracle/MySQL community:
you are more than colleagues; you are, and
always will remain, great friends.

CONTENTS

ACKNOWLEDGMENTS

This book is the third of the Effective MySQL series published for the Oracle Press label. Without the commitment of the team at McGraw-Hill, this publication would not be available today.

Significant time, effort, and support are needed to create a book. This result would not be possible without the support of my wife, Cindy.

To Chris Schneider, thank you for your contributions as a co-author for this title. My technical editors, Sheeri, Giuseppe, Nelson, Hans, and Darren, have made this book a companion in quality and detail to the first two books of the series. This does not become a published book without the help, input, clarification, and discussion of these trusted and respected senior technical advisors and friends.

Several others have also contributed to making this a great reference. Thanks to Alexey Yurchenko and Seppo Jaakola from Codership for their assistance in explaining and triage of issues and reviewing information on Galera. Also to Shlomi Noach, Yoshinori Matsunobu, and Chuck Bell for the review of their respective companion products.

Several others in the Oracle/MySQL team have helped with answers during the writing of the book. Thank you, Rohit Kalhans, Lars Thalmann, Luis Soares, and Mats Kindahl for your time and input. Finally, to Keith Larson and Dave Stokes from the Oracle/MySQL community team, who have helped in the support, feedback, and evangelism for this Effective MySQL series, keep up the good work.

—*Ronald Bradford*

First and foremost I would like to thank my family for all of the support they gave me while writing this book. Keri, my wife, has been very understanding and encouraging during this whole process. Luke, my son, has been able to balance me out by inviting me to clear my mind and play soccer in the back yard. And Sadie, my daughter, has given me an endless amount of "I love yous" and hugs exactly when I need them the most.

To Ronald, thank you for this great opportunity to co-author. This has been a significant challenge, and I have learned a lot from the experience overall. My technical editors, Sheeri, Giuseppe, Nelson, Hans, and Darren, have done a fantastic job in ensuring that this book will be well received by the MySQL and Oracle communities. I would also like to thank each one of you for sharing your enormous amount of experience in MySQL and how to be a better author myself.

—*Chris Schneider*

INTRODUCTION

MySQL powers many of the largest high traffic websites on the Internet. All of these installations use MySQL replication extensively to provide a scalable and highly available database solution. This book is designed for the architect and DBA to help with understanding the foundation, features, and options for creating a successful and scalable MySQL solution.

This book describes the native MySQL asynchronous replication that is commonly used, detailing the relative strengths and limitations that can affect more advanced operations. There are many options available for improving native MySQL replication, including new features in MySQL 5.5 and MySQL 5.6 that are described in Chapter 3. The MySQL ecosystem has a large number of utilities and tools to support, manage, and enhance MySQL replication and help with data integrity. These include OpenArk, Percona Toolkit, MySQL Workbench Utilities, and MySQL HA, which are discussed in Chapter 5. Each is important to evaluate for the administration of the various approaches for creating a complex MySQL topology.

Also covered are details for understanding and using multi-master replication correctly and safely, and implementing MySQL semisynchronous replication. Additional products and add-ons are now available to support MySQL synchronous replication, automated failover, and more complex topologies. A detailed discussion and examples of Galera replication for MySQL and Continuent Tungsten Replicator are included in Chapter 6.

A working knowledge of MySQL replication is a primary skill for the MySQL DBA. Detailed in the appendix are the MySQL Sandbox and a virtualized environment using VirtualBox for running MySQL replication. This is an ideal and recommended approach for testing and evaluating the various options, features, and products that comprise a total MySQL solution.

In recent years there has been great advancement with MySQL replication, and this book aims to cover the leading products and features. While every attempt has been made to provide the most accurate information, commands, options, and operation, some software described is under development and should be carefully considered before use in a production environment.

Conventions

All code in this book is shown in a proportional font. For example:

```
mysql> SHOW MASTER STATUS\G
            File: log-bin.000006
        Position: 348043830
    Binlog_Do_DB:
Binlog_Ignore_DB:
1 row in set (0.01 sec)
```

SQL statements in code examples are prefixed with mysql> to indicate execution with the mysql command line client. This program is included with a full MySQL distribution. When using multiple servers with MySQL replication examples, the prefixes master> and slave> are used accordingly for clarification. For example:

```
master> SHOW MASTER STATUS;
slave>  SLAVE START;
```

All SQL statements listed with these prefixes can generally be performed in any alternative MySQL client graphical user interface (GUI) tool; however, the \G syntax for vertical display output is a mysql command line client-specific directive.

All SQL syntax within text or code examples is in uppercase. For example, the SHOW SLAVE STATUS statement provides important information on the state of replication on a slave. This SQL syntax is provided in the standard paragraph font. SQL statements in MySQL are case insensitive. This syntax is used only to easily distinguish SQL keywords from other database objects or variables in statements and is not required when using MySQL.

A specific syntax or value from a code example that is described in general text is provided in a monofont, for example, the Seconds_Behind_Master value.

For any Unix/Linux command, this is prefixed with a $ to indicate a shell prompt. For example:

```
$ mysqladmin extended-status
```

While this book does not describe the use of MySQL for Microsoft operating systems, MySQL is supported on this platform, and many of the standard MySQL commands detailed will also operate on Microsoft systems. The majority of scripts, utilities, and tools used to support MySQL replication that are described in this book will not operate natively with Microsoft; however, most administration can be performed remotely on a Linux/Unix client connecting to a MySQL instance on a Microsoft operating system.

About MySQL

The MySQL database server is an open source product released under the GPL V2 license. More information about this license can be found at http:// www.mysql.com/about/legal/licensing/index.html. The copyright owner of MySQL at the time of this publication is Oracle Corporation. Oracle Corporation provides product development, commercial licenses for OEM providers, and comprehensive subscription services that includes commercial support and additional product features.

More information about MySQL can be found at the official MySQL website at http://mysql.com and the MySQL developer zone at http://dev .mysql.com.

The current generally available (GA) version of MySQL is version 5.5. This book is written to support MySQL versions 5.0 and later, with specific version differences noted when applicable. The current development milestone release (DMR) and next version of MySQL is version 5.6. Documented in this book are many new MySQL replication features that are in this current 5.6 development version. These are subject to the Oracle Safe Harbor statement that is included here for reference.

Oracle Safe Harbor Statement for MySQL 5.6 Features

The following is intended to outline our general product direction. It is intended for information purposes only, and may not be incorporated into any contract. It is not a commitment to deliver any material, code, or functionality, and should not be relied upon in making purchasing decisions. The development, release, and timing of any features or functionality described for Oracle's products remains at the sole discretion of Oracle.

Open Source Licenses

Products detailed in this book are covered under various different open source licenses and may have different conditions for use. These include the following:

- **GPL**   The GNU General Public License (GPL) may be version 2 or version 3. More information can be found at http://www.gnu.org/copyleft/gpl.html.

- **LGPL**   The GNU Lesser General Public License (LGPL) can be found at http://www.gnu.org/copyleft/lesser.html.

- **BSD**   Information on the Berkeley Software Distribution (BSD) license can be found at http://www.linfo.org/bsdlicense.html. The New BSD License/Modified BSD license and the Simplified BSD License/Free BSD License are variants of this license.

- **Creative Commons (CC)**   Details of the various different CC licenses can be found at http://creativecommons.org/.

More information about various open source licenses can be found at the Open Source Initiative website at http://www.opensource.org/. A detailed list of the various licenses can also be found at http://www.gnu.org/licenses/license-list.html.

Common Technical Abbreviations

It is expected that the reader of this book have a basic understanding of SQL and relational databases. The following commonly used abbreviations are important and familiar terms when using MySQL and developing software with MySQL.

Relational Database Terms

RDBMS - Relational Database Management System
SQL - Structured Query Language
DBA - Database Administrator
DDL - Data Definition Language
DML - Data Manipulation Language
ACID - Atomicity, Consistency, Isolation, Durability

Hardware Terms

CPU - Central Processing Unit
RAID - Random Array of Independent Disks
SSD - Solid State Drive
I/O - Input/Output

Software Terms

SSL - Secure Sockets Layer
SSH - Secure Shell
IP - Internet Protocol
DNS - Domain Name Services
GNU - GNU's Not Unix!
BSD - Berkeley Software Distribution
GPL - GNU Public License

Common MySQL Terms

GA - Generally Available
RC - Release Candidate
DMR - Development Milestone Release

Additional terms that the reader may not be familiar with are described at the appropriate time.

Code Examples

All examples detailed in this book are available for download from the Effective MySQL site at http://effectivemysql.com/book/replication-techniques/. Code, scripts, and sample data are also available on GitHub at https://github .com/effectiveMySQL/ReplicationTechniques.

A separate text document of all URLs used is also included on the website to enable quick access to these references.

References

The MySQL Reference Manual at the MySQL developer zone is an invaluable resource. This can be found at http://dev.mysql.com/doc/refman/5.5/ en/index.html. Access to manuals for both older and newer MySQL versions can be found at http://dev.mysql.com/doc.

The Planet MySQL website at http://planet.mysql.com provides an aggregation of thousands of MySQL bloggers detailing everything about MySQL. This is excellent resource for information on MySQL replication examples, experiences, and use cases.

1

The Five Minute DBA

MySQL replication has stopped on a slave server with an error message. What is the impact of this error on your application users, your scale-out architecture, and your backup and recovery strategy? You have to make a choice between skipping the SQL statement and correcting your information to enable the SQL statement to succeed successfully. What is the impact on data consistency for each choice? What could the downstream effects be?

As a *DBA*, you need to use the information from various tools to determine if a problem exists, find exactly what has gone wrong, and then fix the underlying issue in order to ensure this does not happen again.

In this chapter we will be discussing:

- Essential information to diagnose a replication issue
- Options for correcting stopped replication
- Understanding causes of replication problems

The 2 A.M. Alert Notification

You receive an alert that MySQL replication has stopped on your production slave server that is running MySQL 5.5. This rarely happens during work hours or at an appropriate time.

SHOW SLAVE STATUS

The first action is to look at the current replication status on the applicable server. You achieve this with the following SQL statement:

```
slave> SHOW SLAVE STATUS\G
*************************** 1. row ***************************
               Slave_IO_State: Waiting for master to send event
                  Master_Host: 10.0.0.48
                  Master_User: repl
                  Master_Port: 3306
                Connect_Retry: 60
              Master_Log_File: mysql-bin.001220
          Read_Master_Log_Pos: 3453586
               Relay_Log_File: relay-log.003586
                Relay_Log_Pos: 3452185
        Relay_Master_Log_File: mysql-bin.001220
             Slave_IO_Running: Yes
            Slave_SQL_Running: No
              Replicate_Do_DB:
          Replicate_Ignore_DB:
           Replicate_Do_Table:
       Replicate_Ignore_Table:
      Replicate_Wild_Do_Table:
  Replicate_Wild_Ignore_Table:
                   Last_Errno: 1062
                   Last_Error: Error 'Duplicate entry '42-2011-04-16 00:00:00'
for key 'user_id'' on query. Default database: 'book'. Query: 'INSERT INTO
product_comment(product_id,user_id,comment_dt,comment) VALUES
(20,42,'2011-04-16 00:00:00','I found this very useful with product Y')'
                 Skip_Counter: 0
          Exec_Master_Log_Pos: 3452040
              Relay_Log_Space: 3453930
              Until_Condition: None
               Until_Log_File:
                Until_Log_Pos: 0
```

```
              Master_SSL_Allowed: No
              Master_SSL_CA_File:
              Master_SSL_CA_Path:
                Master_SSL_Cert:
              Master_SSL_Cipher:
                 Master_SSL_Key:
           Seconds_Behind_Master: NULL
Master_SSL_Verify_Server_Cert: No
                  Last_IO_Errno: 0
                  Last_IO_Error:
                 Last_SQL_Errno: 1062
                 Last_SQL_Error: Error 'Duplicate entry '42-2011-04-16 00:00:00'
for key 'user_id'' on query. Default database: 'book'. Query: 'INSERT INTO
product_comment(product_id,user_id,comment_dt,comment) VALUES
(20,42,'2011-04-16 00:00:00','I found this very useful with product Y')'
      Replicate_Ignore_Server_Ids:
                 Master_Server_Id: 1
```

There are several indicators of a replication problem with this output.

- The SQL thread is not running, as indicated by `Slave_SQL_Running=No`

- Replication lag is unknown, indicated by `Seconds_Behind_Master=NULL`

- Error information identified in `Last_Errno` and `Last_Error`

At 2 A.M. in the morning, determining what caused this may not be as important as rectifying the problem to ensure your data is up to date for your application to use the slave server that has the reported error.

NOTE   *Columns in this output have not been ordered by importance. The convention of the MySQL product has been to add new columns to the end of the list—for example,* `Replicate_Ignore_Server_ids` *and* `Master_Server_Id` *are new columns for MySQL 5.5. In MySQL 5.1, individual error numbers and descriptions were added for the I/O and SQL threads at the end of the list rather than with existing error columns.*

TIP   *Many alerting systems use rules to determine an error condition. In this example, an alert was triggered by the rule* `Seconds_Behind_Master = NULL OR Seconds_Behind_Master > 30`. *Incorporating the output of the SHOW SLAVE STATUS command in the email alert is one further step toward improving the diagnosis. This saves time, and could enable some form of action without having to initially connect to the server.*

Identifying the Problem

Instead of automatically correcting the problem, it is important to first understand why MySQL replication is not running. Was this due to an error, or was replication stopped for some other purpose—for example, a backup process or software upgrade? The `Slave_SQL_Running=No` indicator is not solely the result of an unexpected error. The STOP SLAVE SQL_ THREAD statement produces the same situation. This is one reason why an alert on this condition is not always accurate. An alert should be in place for `Slave_SQL_Running=No`; however, you do not want to be alerted every morning when the backup process stops replication intentionally, but only when the backup process fails and replication is not restarted in an appropriate amount of time. MySQL replication includes two threads, as shown in the earlier SHOW SLAVE STATUS output, and the I/O thread is still running with `SLAVE_IO_Running=Yes`. It is important to monitor both thread states.

SHOW CREATE TABLE

The actual error message from the SHOW SLAVE STATUS output in the `Last_Error` column shows a duplicate key error occurred. This can be confirmed with a review of the structure of the underlying database table, and then looking at the current data:

```
slave> SHOW CREATE TABLE product_comment\G
*************************** 1. row ***************************
       Table: product_comment
Create Table: CREATE TABLE `product_comment` (
  `comment_id` int(10) unsigned NOT NULL AUTO_INCREMENT,
  `product_id` int(10) unsigned NOT NULL,
  `user_id` int(10) unsigned NOT NULL,
  `comment_dt` datetime NOT NULL,
  `comment` varchar(1000) NOT NULL,
  PRIMARY KEY (`comment_id`),
  UNIQUE KEY `user_id` (`user_id`,`comment_dt`)
) ENGINE=InnoDB AUTO_INCREMENT=2 DEFAULT CHARSET=latin1
```

As you can see, there is a UNIQUE KEY called `user_id` on the `user_id` and `comment_dt` columns, which corresponds with the index name in the error message. MySQL can only produce a duplicate entry message for a UNIQUE KEY or the PRIMARY KEY. The value from the `Last_Error` column can be used to determine the actual values that were being inserted. The following SQL statement can be constructed to verify the data causing the error:

```
slave> SELECT * FROM product_comment
    -> WHERE user_id = 42
    -> AND comment_dt = '2011-04-16 00:00:00'\G
*************************** 1. row ***************************
comment_id: 1
product_id: 10
   user_id: 42
comment_dt: 2011-04-16 00:00:00
   comment: The packaging does not state this requires X
(1 row in set (0.01 sec)
```

Indeed, the SQL statement reported by MySQL replication that caused the duplicate key violation was correct. Now what? Is this statement somehow invalid? Should we ignore it? Is the data that exists in the table incorrect? Should it be deleted? The product_id and comment values are actually different, indicating this statement is not an identical statement, only the unique key constraint columns of user_id and comment_dt are duplicated.

At this time there is insufficient information to make an informed decision. One option is to review the master MySQL database to look at the data for verification:

```
master> SELECT * FROM product_comment
     -> WHERE user_id = 42
     -> AND comment_dt = '2011-04-16 00:00:00'\G
*************************** 1. row ***************************
comment_id: 1
product_id: 10
   user_id: 42
comment_dt: 2011-04-16 00:00:00
   comment: The packaging does not state this requires X
*************************** 2. row ***************************
comment_id: 2
product_id: 20
   user_id: 42
comment_dt: 2011-04-16 00:00:00
   comment: I found this very useful when used with product Y
(2 rows in set (0.01 sec)
```

We find there is a discrepancy in the master and slave data. That was unexpected because this violates the defined unique key constraint. Verifying the table structure on the master database gives us:

```
master> SHOW CREATE TABLE product_comment\G
*************************** 1. row ***************************
        Table: product_comment
```

```
Create Table: CREATE TABLE `product_comment` (
  `comment_id` int(10) unsigned NOT NULL AUTO_INCREMENT,
  `product_id` int(10) unsigned NOT NULL,
  `user_id` int(10) unsigned NOT NULL,
  `comment_dt` datetime NOT NULL,
  `comment` varchar(1000) NOT NULL,
  PRIMARY KEY (`comment_id`),
  KEY `user_id` (`user_id`,`comment_dt`)
) ENGINE=InnoDB AUTO_INCREMENT=5 DEFAULT CHARSET=latin1
```

A key exists for the `user_id` and `comment_dt` columns; however, closer inspection shows this is no longer a unique constraint. As the MySQL slave is a copy of the master, you may ask how this happened. In MySQL, it is possible for a slave to have a different table structure and still operate normally. In this example, the difference has subsequently caused an error. There are several techniques and utilities for comparing database objects between MySQL instances to identify differences. These are discussed in Chapters 2 and 5.

Rectifying the Problem

We can see that the underlying data on the master is different from the data on the slave, and that the SQL statement would seem to bring the data toward a more consistent state. One option is to simply start the slave and see if some bizarre unexplained situation caused MySQL replication to stop unexpectedly, and now it will magically work. In this case, because we have reviewed the underlying table structure and table constraints, this is not going to result in a successful outcome.

SQL_SLAVE_SKIP_COUNTER

A common, although normally discouraged, approach is to simply skip over the SQL statement and move onto the next statement in the replication stream. This would be achieved by running the following SQL statements:

```
slave> SET GLOBAL SQL_SLAVE_SKIP_COUNTER = 1;
slave> START SLAVE SQL_THREAD;
```

Further verification of the replication status with SHOW SLAVE STATUS confirms that error has been skipped:

```
slave> SHOW SLAVE STATUS\G
*************************** 1. row ***************************
            Slave_IO_State: Waiting for master to send event
...
          Slave_IO_Running: Yes
```

```
            Slave_SQL_Running: Yes
...
                   Last_Errno: 0
                   Last_Error:
...
        Seconds_Behind_Master: 0
Master_SSL_Verify_Server_Cert: No
              Last_IO_Errno: 0
              Last_IO_Error:
             Last_SQL_Errno: 0
             Last_SQL_Error:
  Replicate_Ignore_Server_Ids:
            Master_Server_Id: 1
```

CAUTION   *It is important that you understand why a SQL statement failed before executing SQL_SLAVE_SKIP_COUNTER. This may only result in one error being ignored, and the following SQL statements may cause MySQL replication to stop again. How many SQL statements do you skip before considering if this was a good idea?*

As you can see, the error is now gone, MySQL replication is running, and you can return to sleep. This, however, is not the appropriate solution to this problem. What has happened is that you have now caused an inconsistency between the data in the master database table and the slave database table. For example:

```
master> SELECT COUNT(*) FROM product_comment WHERE user_id=42;
+----------+
| COUNT(*) |
+----------+
|        2 |
+----------+
slave> SELECT COUNT(*) FROM product_comment WHERE user_id=42;
+----------+
| COUNT(*) |
+----------+
|        1 |
+----------+
```

MySQL replication is an asynchronous process and does not perform a consistency checksum of the underlying data in the table. As long as a SQL statement completes without error, replication will report success regardless of the number of rows affected. In Chapter 2 we will discuss these design characteristics and the related issues in more detail.

When working with multiple MySQL instances in a large topology, you can change the default MySQL prompt as described in the previous examples. This was achieved in the `mysql` client with:

```
mysql> PROMPT slave>
```

TIP   For more complex topologies, it is advisable to use additional attributes, including the host, schema, and user, in the prompt for the MySQL command line client.

Addressing the Underlying Cause

There are many reasons why MySQL replication may stop with an error. In Chapter 2 we will discuss the most common causes and respective solutions. In this situation, we discovered that the table schema was different with both servers. How did this happen?

We can determine that the table was changed on the master, but not on the slave. There is insufficient auditing history to determine who or what performed this operation. This issue occurred because a software upgrade of the application schema objects on all MySQL databases was not completed correctly. The following statements were found to have occurred on the master database by reviewing the upgrade procedure:

```
master> SET SQL_LOG_BIN=0;
master> ALTER TABLE product_comment
    -> DROP INDEX user_id,
    -> ADD INDEX (user_id, comment_dt);
master> SET SQL_LOG_BIN=1;
```

Analysis to determine the cause of this problem required more work than reviewing MySQL schema and data. It was not possible to determine this precise syntax from any MySQL logs. It was necessary to review the business process that occurred and supporting system logs. This confirmed that an application upgrade with schema modifications was performed recently.

From this SQL, the underlying table structure of the `product_comment` table was modified to remove the uniqueness constraint for the `user_id`, `comment_dt` index. The reason why this was not applied on the slave database table is the `SET SQL_LOG_BIN=0` statement. This statement disables the MySQL binary log for the ALTER statement. The binary log is the communication channel used for replication events to a slave.

There is a perfectly valid reason for this syntax when executing an ALTER TABLE statement in a large replication environment. To maximize uptime of MySQL servers and to not block the MySQL slave SQL thread, which is a single thread, running ALTER TABLE commands manually on each server provides a means to bypass the MySQL replication single-thread limitation.

The management process for this software upgrade process has failed. First, not all servers have this modification, and second, slave servers should generally be upgraded first. Third, and more importantly, you as the on-call DBA may have not been notified of a software upgrade process occurring. It is also possible you were notified and this occurred some time ago, and only now an error situation has occurred.

Rectifying the Problem Correctly

The correct resolution for this problem is to find out why the table structures are different. In this situation, that is, applying the software upgrade to the slave server before restarting MySQL replication. You could have chosen to modify the structure of this table to be consistent with the master; however, understanding that a change happened does not inform you of other changes that may have occurred at the same time. This could be a process that involves a lot of work and significant downtime, depending on the time to execute schema changes.

The outcome of this problem highlights that having additional checks for schema object consistency is needed. MySQL tables, columns, triggers, and stored procedures can all have an effect on replication, as shown in this example. As described in *Effective MySQL: Backup and Recovery* (McGraw-Hill, 2012), it is important that your regular backup strategy collect metadata on objects and checks with previous versions for any detectable differences. In Chapter 5 we will discuss a number of tools that can help in determining and correcting problems, including this example.

TIP   *It is always important to keep a copy of your database objects for backup purposes. This process can also be used to perform additional validation checks between servers in your replication topology for any inconsistencies.*

Understanding Replication Issues

MySQL replication is an asynchronous operation that works by processing completed DDL and DML statements on the master that are recorded in the binary log. A MySQL slave can only have one MySQL master server. This limitation is subject to change in future MySQL versions, and is already possible when using Tungsten Replicator. The processing of binary log statements on individual slaves is via a pull process. In most situations, MySQL replication works just fine and without incident.

Some features of MySQL can complicate replication—for example, temporary table processing. While data on a MySQL slave can be identical to a MySQL master, there are also ways the data may differ. You may choose to use different storage engines, and these could result in the same data, or with the BLACKHOLE storage engine, different data. Different configuration options for replication can include or exclude specific tables, or act differently when handling SQL errors. Chapter 7 will discuss configuration options in more detail.

It is important to understand how replication works and how to use replication effectively in your environment for your business needs.

User Security

As seen by this example, a software upgrade was able to modify the expected results of the replication stream with a SQL command. Alternatively, does your application have sufficient permissions to do the same? The classic GRANT ALL ON *.* privilege for an application user is cause for great alarm in a number of situations, including the ability to disable binary logging as shown here, bypass slave read-only capabilities, and modify global system variables that can affect durability and consistency. Chapters 2 and 7 will discuss the SUPER privilege in more detail.

Configuration Options and Variables

The MySQL reference manual provides a good introduction and background on configuration and implementation options at http://dev.mysql .com/doc/refman/5.5/en/replication.html.

There are several important configuration variables that can directly affect replication operation. The change of `slave_exec_mode` variable from the default value of STRICT to IDEPOTENT would alter the result of the error reported in this chapter example. In addition to disabling the replication stream, rules on the master or the slave can change what SQL statements are executed. Chapter 7 will provide full details of important MySQL configuration options.

Conclusion

MySQL replication is the backbone of any production MySQL infrastructure. Replication can be used for read scalability, a failover strategy, a backup strategy, geographical support, software testing, and many other purposes. The flexibility in these choices show that MySQL replication is a technology feature that should be carefully understood, managed, and monitored.

MySQL replication is not without issues in more complicated situations. This chapter has indicated one potential issue. In Chapter 2 we will discuss more common replication problems, and in further chapters will show how to use replication effectively and what additional features, configuration, and third-party products can be used in providing advanced replication techniques to support any complex MySQL topology.

Examples and links in this chapter are available for download from http://EffectiveMySQL.com/book/replication-techniques.

2

Diagnosing Common Replication Problems

MySQL replication has detected an error condition and has stopped. While correction is necessary, why did this SQL statement failure occur? How would you avoid this situation in the future? What are the implications on your data consistency? Understanding replication conditions can help in designing preventive measures and monitoring for problem detection and management.

In this chapter we will be discussing:

- Detecting replication errors
- Managing consistency issues
- Addressing replication lag
- Ideal monitoring guidelines

MySQL Replication Architecture Review

To understand the features and limitations of MySQL replication, it is important to understand the basic mechanics between a MySQL master and slave.

As outlined in Figure 2-1, the following are the key steps in the successful execution of a transaction in a standard asynchronous MySQL replication environment. This is not an exhaustive list of all data, memory, and file I/O operations performed, rather a high level representation of important steps.

1. A MySQL transaction is initiated on the master (Point 1).

2. One or more SQL statements are applied on the master (Point 2). The true implementation of the physical result depends on the storage engine used. Generally, regardless of storage engine, the data change operation is first recorded within the applicable memory buffer. For InnoDB, the statement is recorded in the InnoDB transaction logs (note that InnoDB data is written to disk by a separate background thread). For MyISAM, the operation is written directly to the applicable table data file.

3. At the completion of the transaction, the master binary log records the result of the *DML* or *DDL* statement(s) applied (Point 3). MySQL supports varying modes that may record the statement(s) or the actual data changes.

4. A success indicator is returned to the calling client program to indicate the completion of the transaction (Point 4).

5. The slave server detects a change has occurred in the master binary log position (Point 5).

6. The changes are received (i.e., a pull process) by the slave server and written to the slave relay log by the slave I/O thread (Point 6).

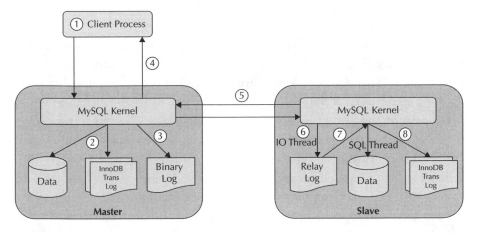

Figure 2-1 *MySQL replication workflow*

7. The slave SQL thread reads the new events from relay log (Point 7) and applies all statements in the transaction (Point 8). These changes may be recorded as a statement to be executed, or as a physical row modification.

8. A success indicator is returned to the slave replication management when the transaction completes.

In summary, SQL transactions are recorded in the master binary log, and the change of this log is used as a triggering event for the slave to pull the change. Throughout this book we will discuss different features that affect and can alter this default asynchronous behavior.

Interpreting Replication Information

Knowing what and where to look for replication information is a key component in the toolbox of a DBA; however, interpreting replication information can sometimes be challenging. Understanding the moving parts, how they act together, and how to view the state of replication are essential steps to administer MySQL. In the following sections we will outline the components of replication and how to use various commands and tools to make informed decisions about your replicated environment.

Binary Logs

Replicating data with MySQL default replication requires you to enable the binary log. This is specified with the `--log-bin=[base_name]` option when starting `mysqld` or with the MySQL configuration file (e.g., `my.cnf`). The default value for the `base_name` for the binary log is the hostname of the server where MySQL is running. Changing the `base_name` of the binary logs from the default can help you avoid confusion if the hostname of the server changes in the future. The actual binary logs will include the base name and a sequenced extension.

MySQL will also create a binary log index file. This will default to the location and `base_name` of the binary logs, and with an `.index` extension. The `log-bin-index` configuration option can be used to change this. The following code snippet lists these files based on a defined value in the configuration file that includes a full directory.

```
$ MYCNF="/etc/my.cnf"
$ BINLOG=`grep log-bin ${MYCNF} | cut -d'=' -f2`
$ echo ${BINLOG}
$ DIR=`dirname ${BINLOG}`
$ cd ${DIR}
$ ls -lh *
$ cat *.index
/opt/mysql/binlog/mysql-bin
-rw-rw---- 1 mysql mysql 49M  Apr 30  2011 mysql-bin.000001
-rw-rw---- 1 mysql mysql 1.1G May 16 06:28 mysql-bin.000002
-rw-rw---- 1 mysql mysql 772M May 29 21:50 mysql-bin.000003
-rw-rw---- 1 mysql mysql 400M Jun  5 17:29 mysql-bin.000004
-rw-rw---- 1 mysql mysql  140 May 29 21:52 log-bin.index
/opt/mysql/binlog/mysql-bin.000001
/opt/mysql/binlog/mysql-bin.000002
/opt/mysql/binlog/mysql-bin.000003
/opt/mysql/binlog/mysql-bin.000004
```

TIP *It is recommended that you always specify the `base_name` for `log-bin`. The general recommendation is to provide a generic name without including details of the specific host.*

The binary log contains all write activity applied to the MySQL server, such as INSERT, UPDATE, DELETE, REPLACE, CREATE, ALTER, and DROP statements. Read activity is not recorded in the binary log. If you want to record all read and write activity, you can enable the general log using the `general_log` and `general_log_file` options.

NOTE *Historically, the general log was enabled with `--log`. This variable is deprecated as of MySQL 5.1.*

CAUTION   *While the general log provides details of all SQL statements executed, it is not recommended to enable this in a production environment due to the performance impact of logging a large number of statements.*

Binary Log Analysis

The binary log, as the name suggests, is an internal format. Using the `mysqlbinlog` client utility, you can view statements that are recorded in binary logs—for example:

NOTE   *The `mysqlbinlog` utility is the recommended tool for reading binary logs.*

```
$ mysqlbinlog `pwd`/mysql-bin.000001
# at 107
#111030 19:32:04 server id 1  end_log_pos 242   Query  thread_id=4
exec_time=0   error_code=0
USE book3/*!*/;
SET TIMESTAMP=1320003124/*!*/;
SET @@session.pseudo_thread_id=4/*!*/;
SET @@session.foreign_key_checks=1, @@session.sql_auto_is_null=0,
@@session.unique_checks=1, @@session.autocommit=1/*!*/;
SET @@session.sql_mode=0/*!*/;
SET @@session.auto_increment_increment=1, @@session.auto_increment_offset=1/*!*/;
/*!\C utf8 *//*!*/;
SET @@session.character_set_client=33,@@session.collation_connection=33,
@@session.collation_server=33/*!*/;
SET @@session.lc_time_names=0/*!*/;
SET @@session.collation_database=DEFAULT/*!*/;
CREATE TABLE repl_test ( ts INT, dt DATETIME)
/*!*/;
DELIMITER ;
# End of log file
ROLLBACK /* added by mysqlbinlog */;
/*!50003 SET COMPLETION_TYPE=@OLD_COMPLETION_TYPE*/;
...
```

An alternative way to gather all SQL information on a MySQL server is to use the slow query log and set the `long_query_time` to 0. Using the slow query log in this manner has the added benefit of being easier to parse with utilities, including `pt-query-digest` and `mysqldumpslow`.

TIP   *It is possible to record the slow query information into the `mysql.slow_log` table using the `log_format` configuration option. This can be of benefit if enabled for a few seconds to record all SQL statements, which then can be mined for additional information, including the read/write ratio and breakdown on a per-table basis.*

The two primary uses for the binary log are for replication and data recovery—more specifically, point in time recovery. These uses can be combined to assist in creating a clone of a production server with minimal downtime. Like other files in MySQL, the position of the file referenced in many SHOW commands represents the byte offset of the file itself. For example, the filesize can be found with the system tool stat:

```
$ stat mysql-bin.000001
  File: 'mysql-bin.000001'
  Size: 1052302  Blocks: 2064 IO Block: 4096 regular file
...
```

NOTE   *The command line tool* stat *has a different output depending on its origin. The code listing here is partial output from GNU* stat, *while the BSD* stat *looks more like a* ls -l *output.*

Alternatively, you could run the following:

```
$ ls -l mysql-bin.000001
-rw-rw---- 1 mysql mysql 1052302 Oct 30 18:47 mysql-bin.000001
```

The information about the binary log in MySQL can be found with the SHOW MASTER STATUS command:

```
$ mysql -uroot -p -e "SHOW MASTER STATUS\G"
             File: mysql-bin.000001
         Position: 1052302
     Binlog_Do_DB:
 Binlog_Ignore_DB:
Executed_Gtid_Set:
```

The file size in bytes for the mysql-bin.000001 file is 1052302. The position, shown in SHOW MASTER STATUS, is also 1052302. In a production system, the binary log can be changing constantly. The information here is shown on an idle server to demonstrate the verification steps.

As shown, the binary log names follow a base_name.nnnnnn convention, where nnnnnn represents a sequential file number. This number is incremented when the individual binary log reaches the size as specified by max_binlog_size, the server is restarted, or the FLUSH [BINARY] LOGS statement is issued.

While mysqlbinlog is the most common approach to review binary log files, several other options exist.

- The SHOW BINLOG EVENTS IN 'file' command can read the binary log events using an SQL interface.

- The MySQL replication listener includes the MySQL Binlog API. This can be used to read and process events in the MySQL binary log. This is discussed in Chapters 5 and 6.

- The various replication pre-fetch tools read and process the binary log. These tools can be used and modified to identify information. These tools are discussed in Chapter 5.

- Tungsten Replicator supports many different replication topologies. This product first reads and processes the MySQL binary log. This open source product can be used and modified appropriately to analyze binary logs. This is discussed in Chapter 6.

The binary log contains a wealth of data that can be mined to provide interesting information. The following command analyzes a binary log and provides DML statistics broken down by individual table. You can use this approach with various `mysqlbinlog` arguments to also determine statistics for any time duration. For example:

```
$ mysqlbinlog /path/to/mysql-bin.000999 | \
    grep -i -e "^update" -e "^insert" -e "^delete" -e "^replace" -e "^alter" | \
    cut -c1-100 | tr '[A-Z]' '[a-z]' | \
    sed -e "s/\t/ /g;s/\`//g;s/(.*$//;s/ set .*$//;s/ as .*$//" | \
    sed -e "s/ where .*$//" | sort | uniq -c | sort -nr

  33389 update e_acc
  17680 insert into r_b
  17680 insert into e_rec
  14332 insert into rcv_c
  13543 update e_rec
  10805 update loc
   3339 insert into r_att
   2781 insert into o_att
...
```

More information about this simple command can be found at http://ronaldbradford.com/blog/mysql-dml-stats-per-table-2009-09-09/.

Binary Log Management

By default, MySQL does not remove old inactive binary logs; however, you can enable automatic binary log removal with the `expire_logs_days` system variable. The default for `expire_logs_days` is 0, which means no automatic removal of binary logs. As the system variable suggests, assigning a value larger than 0 will remove binary logs older than the value specified, where "value" is measured in days.

Use caution with expire_logs_days, as MySQL will remove binary logs indiscriminately that are older than expire_logs_days. There are checks to ensure that all of the connected slaves are up to date; however, if a slave is broken or not connected to the master, the purge will occur anyway. For more information pertaining to binary log options, see Chapter 7.

Running the PURGE [BINARY|MASTER] LOGS command is a manual method to remove binary logs. In a production environment, removing binary logs is easy to automate based on your requirements as an alternative to using expire_logs_days. One reason you may need to automate the removal of binary logs yourself would be to coincide the purge with a point in time backup. There are two variations in which you can purge binary logs: by specifying the actual log to purge to, or by specifying a DATETIME using a BEFORE variant. The following are two examples for purging binary logs.

Example 1 (Purge to a specified file):

```
mysql> PURGE BINARY LOGS TO 'mysql-bin.000005';
```

Here, all of the binary logs prior to mysql-bin.000005 on the server would be removed, not including mysql-bin.000005 itself.

Example 2 (Purge to a specified date and time):

```
mysql> PURGE BINARY LOGS BEFORE '2011-10-31 09:00:00';
```

Here, all binary logs that were closed before the specified date would be removed.

NOTE   *PURGE MASTER LOGS and PURGE BINARY LOGS are synonymous variants.*

TIP   Effective MySQL: Backup and Recovery *(McGraw-Hill, 2012) covers the various options for managing binary logs in a production environment to ensure adequate redundancy for a disaster recovery situation.*

SHOW MASTER LOGS

The SHOW [MASTER|BINARY] LOGS command is used to see all of the binary logs and their respective file sizes on the server's host. Again, the terms MASTER and BINARY are synonymous variants.

In the following example you will notice that there are six files with different sequential log numbers and file sizes:

```
master> SHOW MASTER LOGS;
+------------------+-----------+
| Log_name         | File_size |
+------------------+-----------+
| mysql-bin.000009 |       150 |
| mysql-bin.000010 |    400567 |
| mysql-bin.000011 |     72534 |
| mysql-bin.000012 |    506830 |
| mysql-bin.000013 |    615407 |
| mysql-bin.000014 |    723937 |
+------------------+-----------+
```

It is important to mention that in the event a binary log is moved or removed from the file system directly, MySQL will still show a pointer to that file with a zero byte `File_size` even though the file no longer exists on the file system. Moving or removing binary logs from the file system directly is not a recommended technique. The following example highlights the impact of removing files physically:

```
$ rm -f mysql-bin.000009 mysql-bin.000010 mysql-bin.000011
master> SHOW MASTER LOGS;
+------------------+-----------+
| Log_name         | File_size |
+------------------+-----------+
| mysql-bin.000009 |         0 |
| mysql-bin.000010 |         0 |
| mysql-bin.000011 |         0 |
| mysql-bin.000012 |    506830 |
| mysql-bin.000013 |    615407 |
| mysql-bin.000014 |    723937 |
+------------------+-----------+
```

You will see the file sizes for physical binary logs that can no longer be found are zero bytes. When you run a subsequent PURGE MASTER LOGS command you will see the following warnings:

```
master> PURGE MASTER LOGS TO 'mysql-bin.000012';
Query OK, 0 rows affected, 3 warnings (0.01 sec)
master> SHOW WARNINGS\G
*********************** 1. row ***********************
  Level: Warning
   Code: 1612
Message: Being purged log ./mysql-bin.000009 was not found
*********************** 2. row ***********************
  Level: Warning
   Code: 1612
Message: Being purged log ./mysql-bin.000010 was not found
*********************** 3. row ***********************
  Level: Warning
   Code: 1612
Message: Being purged log ./mysql-bin.000011 was not found
3 rows in set (0.00 sec)
```

SHOW MASTER STATUS

As referenced earlier, you can use the SHOW MASTER STATUS command to view information about the current binary log. A user running SHOW MASTER STATUS needs the SUPER privilege. The current binary log is displayed as File: mysql-bin.000001, as in the following example, along with the Position: 107, which is a representation of the byte offset in the corresponding binary log:

```
master> SHOW MASTER STATUS\G
            File: mysql-bin.000001
        Position: 107
     Binlog_Do_DB:
 Binlog_Ignore_DB:
Executed_Gtid_Set:
```

There are three other pieces of information shown when running SHOW MASTER STATUS.

- Binlog_Do_DB is populated by listing databases in the system variable --binlog-do-db=[database name(s)].

- Binlog_Ignore_DB is populated by the system variable --binlog-ignore-db=[database names]. If no value exists in either setting, all write activity for all databases is being inserted into the binary log.

- Executed_Gtid_Set, new to MySQL 5.6.5, is used to show the set of Global Transaction Identifiers (GTIDs) executed on the master.

SHOW SLAVE STATUS

MySQL provides a view of all information pertaining to the status of replication with SHOW SLAVE STATUS.

NOTE   *The \G statement terminator for this statement is important for readability; \G will display the output of any SQL statement vertically in the* mysql *client.*

The following is an example of the SHOW SLAVE STATUS output from MySQL 5.5, the current *GA* version:

```
slave> SHOW SLAVE STATUS\G
            Slave_IO_State: Waiting for master to send event
               Master_Host: 10.0.0.1
               Master_User: repl
               Master_Port: 3306
```

```
              Connect_Retry: 10
            Master_Log_File: mysql-bin.000001
        Read_Master_Log_Pos: 525
             Relay_Log_File: mysqld-relay-bin.000002
              Relay_Log_Pos: 671
      Relay_Master_Log_File: mysql-bin.000001
           Slave_IO_Running: Yes
          Slave_SQL_Running: Yes
            Replicate_Do_DB:
        Replicate_Ignore_DB:
         Replicate_Do_Table:
     Replicate_Ignore_Table:
    Replicate_Wild_Do_Table:
Replicate_Wild_Ignore_Table:
                 Last_Errno: 0
                 Last_Error:
               Skip_Counter: 0
        Exec_Master_Log_Pos: 525
            Relay_Log_Space: 828
            Until_Condition: None
             Until_Log_File:
              Until_Log_Pos: 0
          Master_SSL_Allowed: No
          Master_SSL_CA_File:
          Master_SSL_CA_Path:
            Master_SSL_Cert:
          Master_SSL_Cipher:
             Master_SSL_Key:
      Seconds_Behind_Master: 0
Master_SSL_Verify_Server_Cert: No
              Last_IO_Errno: 0
              Last_IO_Error:
             Last_SQL_Errno: 0
             Last_SQL_Error:
  Replicate_Ignore_Server_Ids:
            Master_Server_Id: 1
```

SHOW SLAVE STATUS displays information about all aspects of replication for the given slave host. Reading the output earlier, you will be able to see what master server the slave is replicating from.

The most important components shown in SHOW SLAVE STATUS pertain to files and positions, along with the SQL and I/O slave thread. These two threads perform the physical work of writing and reading the relay log (the I/O thread) and applying the new events on the slave (the SQL thread).

- **Master_Log_File** The name of the current binary log the slave I/O thread is currently reading from.

- **Read_Master_Log_Pos** The position in the current master binary log the slave I/O thread has read up to.

- `Relay_Log_File`   The name of the current relay log where the slave SQL thread is reading from.

- `Relay_Log_Position`   The position of the current relay log read and executed by the slave SQL thread.

- `Relay_Master_Log_File`   The binary log where the most recently executed event by the slave SQL thread resides.

- `Slave_IO_Running`   States if the slave server has connected to the master host. There are three values: Yes, No, and Connecting (since version 5.1.46). Checking the corresponding value of `Slave_running`, a system status variable, can also help you determine if the slave is connected to the master.

- `Slave_SQL_Running`   States if the SQL thread is running.

There can be, and probably will be, times when your slave host falls behind the master given the asynchronous nature of MySQL replication. Innovations in MySQL 5.5, including semisynchronous replication and features in the 5.6 version of MySQL, have led to many replication improvements. Multithreaded slaves, checksums, and crash-safe slaves are just a few of these new features that will continue to be enhanced in future releases. These are discussed in detail in Chapter 3.

Refer to the MySQL documentation at http://dev.mysql.com/doc/refman /5.5/en/show-slave-status.html for a full listing of SHOW SLAVE STATUS output. It is important you view the documentation for the specific version of MySQL in use.

New MySQL 5.1 Information   The following new columns were added in MySQL 5.1:

- `Master_SSL_Verify_Server_Cert`

- `Last_IO_Errno`

- `Last_IO_Error`

- `Last_SQL_Errno`

- `Last_SQL_Error`

New MySQL 5.5 Information   The following new columns were added in MySQL 5.5:

- `Replicate_Ignore_Server_Ids`
- `Master_Server_Id`

New MySQL 5.6 Information The following are new columns in MySQL 5.6.5 at the time of this publication and are subject to possible change before general availability:

- `Master_Info_File`
- `SQL_Delay`
- `SQL_Remaining_Delay`
- `Slave_SQL_Running_State`
- `Master_Retry_Count`
- `Master_Bind`
- `Last_IO_Error_Timestamp`
- `Last_SQL_Error_Timestamp`
- `Master_SSL_Crl`
- `Master_SSL_Crlpath`
- `Retrieved_Gtid_Set`
- `Executed_Gtid_Set`

Relay Logs

MySQL uses a numbered set of files on the slave, called relay logs, to hold replicated database changes before the SQL thread applies them to the slave. The relay log files are numbered in sequence, starting from 000001, and are accompanied by what is referred to as the relay index file, which contains the names of all relay files currently available. Relay log files are in the same format as MySQL binary logs, making them easy to read using the `mysqlbinlog` client utility.

NOTE   The `mysqlbinlog` utility is the recommended tool for reading the relay logs.

Like the binary log, a relay log position is a representation of a byte off-set in the file, so if the Relay_Log_Pos is 671 and the Relay_Log_File is mysqld-relay-bin.000002, then MySQL has read up to 671 bytes of the corresponding file. The naming conventions for the relay log file can be altered with the relay-log=[file_name] and the relay log index with relay-log-index=[file_name] options in the my.cnf file. If either of the preceding is absent in the my.cnf file, the relay logs will take their naming convention from the pid-file option if specified.

For example, when the pid-file option is specified in the my.cnf and the relay-log and relay-log-index are omitted, the relay logs will be mysql_3306-relay-bin.index and mysql_3306-relay-bin.000001. If relay-log, relay-log-index, and pid-file are not specified, the relay logs will default to host_name-relay-bin.nnnnnn and host_name-relay-bin.index, where host_name is the server host and nnnnnn represents the sequential file numbering.

All events are recorded in the relay log files from the slave I/O thread. The slave SQL thread will read these events and execute them on the slave host. For example, to examine the relay log using the mysqlbinlog client utility:

```
$ mysqlbinlog mysqld-relay-bin.000005
#111030 19:32:04 server id 1  end_log_pos 242    Query
        thread_id=4    exec_time=0    error_code=0
USE book3/*!*/;
SET TIMESTAMP=1320003124/*!*/;
SET @@session.pseudo_thread_id=4/*!*/;
SET @@session.foreign_key_checks=1, @@session.sql_auto_is_null=0,
@@session.unique_checks=1,
@@session.autocommit=1/*!*/;
SET @@session.sql_mode=0/*!*/;
SET @@session.auto_increment_increment=1,
@@session.auto_increment_offset=1/*!*/;
/*!\C utf8 *//*!*/;
SET @@session.character_set_client=33,@@session.
collation_connection=33,@@session.collation_server=33/*!*/;
SET @@session.lc_time_names=0/*!*/;
SET @@session.collation_database=DEFAULT/*!*/;
CREATE TABLE repl_test ( ts INT, dt DATETIME)
/*!*/;
DELIMITER ;
# End of log file
ROLLBACK /* added by mysqlbinlog */;
/*!50003 SET COMPLETION_TYPE=@OLD_COMPLETION_TYPE*/;
```

Shown in this output is the CREATE TABLE statement that was run and described in the output of the master binary log.

Replication Consistency

MySQL replication has improved over the years; however, there are still issues with data and schema consistency. One of the major concerns with replication is the lack of checksums from the master to the slave. There are two built-in types of binary logging configurable inside of MySQL. Statement-based replication (SBR) has been a feature of MySQL since 3.23 and logs SQL statements to the binary log. Row-based replication (RBR) is relatively new, implemented in version 5.1, and logs blocks of data instead of the statement itself to the binary log. You can manipulate this format with the configuration setting `binlog_format={ROW|STATEMENT|MIXED}`. You can also change the binary log format at run-time by using `SET GLOBAL|SESSION binlog_format={ROW|STATEMENT|MIXED}`. There are three settings for `binlog_format`:

- **ROW**   Causes logging to be row based.
- **STATEMENT**   Causes logging to be statement based.
- **MIXED**   Causes logging to be both row and statement based. In some cases, statements are logged in statement format and in others, row format. For more information on what statements cause statement logging versus row logging, please refer to http://dev.mysql .com/doc/refman/5.5/en/binary-log-mixed.html.

NOTE   *When changing the binary log format at run-time you will need to ensure that any slave host connected to the master has the proper* `binlog_ format` *enabled before you change the master host.*

NOTE   *The* `binlog_format` *for the* `mysqlbinlog` *example in the previous section was set to* `STATEMENT`.

In this section we will cover how to identify data integrity issues and some examples of their cause.

Identifying Data Inconsistencies

The most effective way to identify data inconsistencies caused by replication is to look at your data. There are three types of data inconsistencies that need to be identified and fixed:

- Incorrect data on the slave.
- The slave is missing a row.
- The slave has an extra row.

When using SBR, a slave can easily become out of sync with its master. In many cases data inconsistencies are caused by a crash of the `mysqld` process and/or by using nontransactional storage engines, including My-ISAM. Given that replication prior to MySQL 5.6 lacked checksum capabilities, an administrator may never know about inconsistent data from master to slave unless they use a third-party tool to check.

It can be difficult to identify when a slave server has become inconsistent with the master. There are, however, tools to aid MySQL database administrators in identifying such problems. The widely used Percona Toolkit, originally Maatkit, created by Baron Schwartz and now maintained by Percona, enables DBAs to identify and fix consistency issues within any given dataset. Refer to Chapter 5 for more information about Percona Toolkit.

Identifying Schema Inconsistencies

Identifying schema inconsistencies and detecting when schema changes occur can be accomplished in a few ways depending on your business needs and requirements.

MySQL has built-in status variables responsible for tracking if an `ALTER` statement was run. The `Com_alter_%` status variables are counters that could be tracked and recorded on a specified timetable for each server in a MySQL replication topology. As you can see in the following, there has been one `ALTER TABLE` statement issued on this host, given the value of `Com_alter_table`:

NOTE   The global `Com_alter_%` status variables are reset when `mysqld` is restarted or when FLUSH STATUS is issued.

```
master> SHOW GLOBAL STATUS LIKE 'Com_alter%';
+------------------------+-------+
| Variable_name          | Value |
+------------------------+-------+
| Com_alter_db           | 0     |
| Com_alter_db_upgrade   | 0     |
| Com_alter_event        | 0     |
| Com_alter_function     | 0     |
| Com_alter_procedure    | 0     |
| Com_alter_server       | 0     |
| Com_alter_table        | 1     |
| Com_alter_tablespace   | 0     |
| Com_change_master      | 0     |
| Com_show_master_status | 3     |
+------------------------+-------+
```

NOTE *All global status variables are reset after a server restart. Including the*
Uptime value with all output can help determine if the variables have been
reset.

Schemasync is an open source tool that will identify schema differences
and create the SQL statements needed to bring a schema up to date. This
tool can also create the SQL for an undo script just in case you need to revert the changes. For more information on schemasync, its capabilities,
and limitations please visit http://schemasync.org.

MySQL Workbench is a graphical user interface (GUI) tool provided by
Oracle. One of the features of this tool is schema synchronization. Anyone
with the proper access and/or a SQL file can run schema diffs from server
to server or compare a SQL file to a running MySQL server. An administrator would also be able to automatically update a workbench model or
SQL file in either direction; furthermore, workbench models and running
MySQL servers can automatically update each other in either direction.

The mysqldump client utility can also be used when comparing schemas
on different hosts. When mysqldump is used in conjunction with the --no-
data option, a diff can be used with the output files. An extension of this
technique is incorporating md5sum to quickly determine any schema differences between a master and slave(s). For example:

```
$ mysqldump -uuser –ppasswd –h[master] --no-data \
--skip-dump-date --databases [db]| md5sum
45fa52599346a4fab39634b69774301f   -
```

```
$ mysqldump -uuser -ppasswd -h[slave] --no-data \
--skip-dump-date --databases [db] | md5sum
45fa52599346a4fab39634b69774301f  -
```

NOTE *The options* `--no-data` *and* `--skip-dump-date` *are essential in using this* `mysqldump` *technique to compare database schemas.*

The problem with the example here is the definition of any primary key columns that are auto increment. For an active environment these values will change over time. You can address this data change by removing the specific syntax from `CREATE TABLE` statements. Here is an example:

```
$ mysqldump -uuser -ppasswd -h[hostname] --no-data \
--skip-dump-date --databases [db] | sed -e \
"s/AUTO_INCREMENT=[0-9]* //" | md5sum
```

In the event of a difference in `md5sum` values you can drill down further and check individual tables. The following script performs a more detailed table check:

```
$ cat pertablemd5.sh
#!/bin/sh
SCRIPT_NAME=`basename $0`
AUTH="-uroot -ppasswd"
OPTIONS="--no-data --skip-lock-tables --skip-dump-date --skip-comments"
[ $# -ne 3 ] && echo "USAGE: ${SCRIPT_NAME} <master> <slave> <schema>" \
 && exit 1
MASTER=$1
SLAVE=$2
DATABASE=$3

[ -z "${TMPDIR}" ] && TMPDIR="/tmp"
mkdir -p ${TMPDIR}

[ -z `which mysql 2>/dev/null` ] && echo "ERROR: mysql not found in the PATH" \

 && exit 1

HAVE_DIFF="FALSE"
for TABLE in `mysql ${AUTH} -h${MASTER} -e \
 "SELECT table_name FROM information_schema.tables WHERE table_schema " \

 " = '${DATABASE}'" |grep -vi "^TABLE_NAME" |uniq`
do
mysqldump ${AUTH} -h${MASTER} ${OPTIONS} --database ${DATABASE} --table $TABLE \
  --result-file=${TMPDIR}/master.${DATABASE}.${TABLE}.sql
MASTER_MD5=`cat ${TMPDIR}/master.${DATABASE}.${TABLE}.sql | md5sum`
mysqldump ${AUTH} -h${SLAVE} ${OPTIONS} --database ${DATABASE} --table $TABLE \
  --result-file=${TMPDIR}/slave.${DATABASE}.${TABLE}.sql
```

```
SLAVE_MD5=`cat ${TMPDIR}/slave.${DATABASE}.${TABLE}.sql | md5sum`
[ "${MASTER_MD5}" != "${SLAVE_MD5}" ] && \
  echo "${DATABASE}.${TABLE} is different" && HAVE_DIFF="TRUE"
done
[ "${HAVE_DIFF}" = "TRUE" ] && \
  echo "You can view individual differences with " \


      "$ diff ${TMPDIR}/*.DATABASE.TABLE.sql"
exit 0
```

This output includes lines that have been modified for display purposes. A copy of the script can be obtained from http://EffectiveMySQL.com/book/replication-techniques.

SBR Schema Validation

When using SBR, MySQL does not validate a schema difference between master and slave. Columns can be out of order and have different type characteristics, which can be beneficial, in some temporary cases, but can also lead to issues within the database or application itself. In RBR you can append columns to the end of a table on a slave; however, column ordinal position and datatype validation are enforced. For example:

```
master> SET SESSION binlog_format=ROW;
master> CREATE SCHEMA IF NOT EXISTS book3;
master> USE book3
master> CREATE TABLE rbr_test(
    ->    id INT UNSIGNED NOT NULL,
    ->    val CHAR(3) NOT NULL,
    ->    comment VARCHAR(55) DEFAULT NULL,
    ->    PRIMARY KEY(id)
    -> ) ENGINE=InnoDB;
master> INSERT INTO rbr_test (id,val,comment)
    -> VALUES (1,'aaa','hello test');
```

Now we modify the table on the slave:

```
slave> USE book3
slave> ALTER TABLE rbr_test MODIFY comment TEXT;
```

Now executing an INSERT on the master:

```
master> SET SESSION binlog_format=ROW;
master> USE book3
master> INSERT INTO rbr_test (id,val,comment)
    -> VALUES (3,'ccc','hello test');
```

And finally, on the slave, replication has failed with the following error:

```
slave> SHOW SLAVE STATUS\G
. . .
Last_Errno: 1677
Last_Error: Column 2 of table 'book3.rbr_test' cannot be
 converted from type 'varchar(55)' to type 'text'
. . .
```

Causes of Data Inconsistency

Data inconsistency can be caused by a number of factors. The most common reason is human intervention. Other common reasons for inconsistent data can be attributed to configuration settings, a bug, feature, or crash within mysqld itself.

Deactivating the binary log within a session can be extremely useful but potentially dangerous. Changing the session variable SQL_LOG_BIN with SET SESSION SQL_LOG_BIN = 0 may precede an ALTER table statement in a planned schema change; however, if not reenabled within the same session, all future statements are not replicated. Automation is the key to avoiding a human error event like the one described earlier. The only time an administrator should use this technique is when a schema change would take too long for a normal maintenance window.

Setting the system variable, read_only, to 1 or ON is highly recommended to ensure no data modification can occur on a slave. Unfortunately, if a user has been granted the SUPER privilege (which is also enabled with GRANT ALL ON *.*), this user can bypass the read_only setting on the slave. This is an avoidable problem that is solved by using discretion when creating application user privileges.

Running replication while skipping databases and/or tables with --replicate-ignore-db or --replicate-ignore-table can also prove to be a problem. Session data, for example, stored in a database does not generally require replication in most cases; however, if you are ignoring the database or table and need to fail over or rebuild a node, you introduce additional complications. RBR has improved replicated data consistency issues and will be covered in detail in Chapter 3.

Common Replication Errors

There are many common replication errors that occur on slave servers.

MySQL Server ID

If, for instance, an administrator set up a new slave manually, the following 1593 error may occur:

```
slave> SHOW SLAVE STATUS\G
...
Slave_IO_Running: No
Slave_SQL_Running: Yes
...
    Last_IO_Errno: 1593
    Last_IO_Error: Fatal error: The slave I/O thread stops
 because master and slave have equal MySQL server ids; these ids must be
different for replication to work (or the --replicate-same-server-id option
must be used on slave but this does not always make sense; please check the
manual before using it).
...
```

A 1593 error is when both the master and slave have equal MySQL server IDs, and is easy to run into without proper automation and provisioning. Fortunately, this is also a very easy problem to fix by simply changing the `server_id` system variable on the slave server to be unique within the cluster. Notice that this error stops the I/O thread from connecting to the master server.

Missing Schema Objects

When running into schema differences, you may notice the 1146 replication error. Regardless of how the schema became different, there is a simple fix for the example shown here:

```
slave> SHOW SLAVE STATUS\G
...
    Slave_IO_State: Waiting for master to send event
 Slave_IO_Running: Yes
Slave_SQL_Running: No
...
        Last_Errno: 1146
        Last_Error: Error 'Table 'book3.no_tbl_on_slave' doesn't
exist' on query. Default database: 'book3'. Query: 'INSERT INTO
no_tbl_on_slave(id) VALUES(1)'
...
    Last_SQL_Errno: 1146
```

```
    Last_SQL_Error: Error 'Table 'book3.no_tbl_on_slave' doesn't
exist' on query. Default database: 'book3'. Query: 'INSERT INTO
no_tbl_on_slave(id) VALUES(1)'
...
```

Fixing this error is as simple as creating the table on the slave host and starting the slave. Keep in mind that although the specified fix works, there could be records in the table that may not be present on the slave by simply adding the table. An additional check of the number of rows on the master is more complex, as there may be subsequent SQL statements that create this data. In the event of this error steps should be undertaken to understand why this occurred.

Ignoring Duplicate Rows

An observed practice that is not recommended is to skip duplicate key errors by default when setting up a slave using the `--slave-skip-errors=1062` configuration variable. In a production system this can lead to data drift from master to slave. In this example you will see the impact of enabling the skipping of duplicate replication errors:

```
master> USE book3
master> CREATE TABLE uniq_test (
  id INT UNSIGNED NOT NULL
) ENGINE=InnoDB;
```

On the slave we modify the table structure:

```
slave> USE book3
slave> ALTER TABLE uniq_test ADD UNIQUE KEY (id);
```

Insert data on the master:

```
master> USE book3
master> INSERT INTO uniq_test(id) VALUES(1);
master> INSERT INTO uniq_test(id) VALUES(1),(2),(3);
master> SELECT * FROM uniq_test;
+-----------+
|        id |
+-----------+
|         1 |
|         1 |
|         2 |
|         3 |
+-----------+
4 rows in set (0.00 sec)
```

Review data and replication status on the slave:

```
slave> SELECT * FROM uniq_test;
+-----------+
|        id |
+-----------+
|         1 |
+-----------+
1 row in set (0.00 sec)
slave> SHOW SLAVE STATUS\G
...
Slave_IO_Running: Yes
Slave_SQL_Running: No
```

While there is no replication error, the data is now inconsistent. This represents a silent replication failure leading to an inconsistent slave host.

Under normal operations, without the `--slave-skip-errors=1062` option, the following replication error would occur:

```
slave> SHOW SLAVE STATUS\G
...
     Slave_IO_Running: Yes
    Slave_SQL_Running: No
...
          Last_Errno: 1062
          Last_Error: Error 'Duplicate entry '1' for key
'id' on query. Default database: 'book3'. Query: 'INSERT
INTO uniq_test(id) VALUES(1),(2),(3)'
...
Seconds_Behind_Master: NULL
...
       Last_SQL_Errno: 1062
       Last_SQL_Error: Error 'Duplicate entry '1' for key
 'id' on query. Default database: 'book3'. Query: 'INSERT
 INTO uniq_test(id) VALUES(1),(2),(3)'
```

In this section we covered just three of the most common replication errors. There are many more errors and scenarios where replication may produce an error. There are some very specific replication errors that can occur when using RBR. RBR will be covered in greater detail in Chapter 3.

Understanding Replication Lag

Replication lag can occur for many different reasons in many different scenarios. Finding the root cause may not always be apparent; however, in this section we will cover the primary reasons for replication lag along with other system aspects to check when diagnosing lag.

Primary Causes of Lag

Replication lag primarily occurs due to the asynchronous design and single-threaded application of replication events. Starting in MySQL 5.5, the implementation of semisynchronous replication is one step toward more replication capabilities. Replication lag has been further improved in MySQL 5.6 with multithreaded slave capabilities using the `slave_parallel_workers` configuration option. More information can be found at http://dev.mysql.com/doc/refman/5.6/en/replication-options-slave .html#sysvar_slave_parallel_workers.

Running a backup or an upgrade is another reason to stop replication, which will also cause replication lag. To obtain a consistent `mysqldump` backup on a slave instance, a DBA will typically run `STOP SLAVE SQL_THREAD` before running `mysqldump` in order to obtain the correct corresponding master binary log and byte offset/position found in `SHOW SLAVE STATUS`.

NOTE In MySQL 5.5 it is possible to obtain the master binary log position on the slave in `mysqldump` *with the* `--slave-data` *option.*

Stopping the slave during a backup is not always the best solution, especially if this is used as a read server or for failover purposes.

There are different replication errors that cause either the SQL or I/O slave thread to stop. Running a `CHANGE MASTER TO` statement and assigning the incorrect master credentials can cause a simple I/O thread error. Replication errors can be as complex as trying to solve a split-brain, primary key issue using multiple masters in a complex replication topology. Given all of the causes of replication lag, you should consider the following when starting to troubleshoot:

- Replication stopped intentionally (e.g., backup/upgrade)
- Replication stopped from an error (e.g., slave I/O or SQL thread or both)
- Master load
- Slave load
- Network latency and connectivity issues

After you have considered what the problem could be, the next step is to check the MySQL error log.

The MySQL Error Log

All of the errors covered in the previous section can also be seen and monitored in the MySQL error log. For example, if you are monitoring the error log, and you should be, you would see the following entries in your error log when a 1062 error occurs:

```
120602  5:56:44 [ERROR] Slave SQL: Could not execute Write_rows event on
 table book3.uniq_test; Duplicate entry '1' for key 'id', Error_code: 1062;
 handler error HA_ERR_FOUND_DUPP_KEY; the event's master log binary-
logs.000003, end_log_pos 1065, Error_code: 1062
120602  5:56:44 [Warning] Slave: Duplicate entry '1' for key 'id'
Error_code: 1062
120602  5:56:44 [ERROR] Error running query, slave SQL thread aborted. Fix
the problem, and restart the slave SQL thread with "SLAVE START". We stopped
 at log 'binary-logs.000003' position 905
```

If you were to run STOP SLAVE, `mysqld` would also record this in the error log. For example:

```
120611 13:39:42 [Note] Error reading relay log event: slave SQL thread was
 killed
120611 13:39:42 [ERROR] Error reading packet from server: Lost connection
to MySQL server during query ( server_errno=2013)
120611 13:39:42 [Note] Slave I/O thread killed while reading event
120611 13:39:42 [Note] Slave I/O thread exiting, read up to log
'mysql-bin.000003', position 107
```

The same behavior occurs when starting the slave with START SLAVE:

```
120611 13:41:36 [Note] Slave SQL thread initialized, starting replication
 in log 'mysql-bin.000003' at position 107, relay log
'./relay-bin.000008' position: 253
120611 13:41:36 [Note] Slave I/O thread: connected to master,
replication started in log 'mysql-bin.000003' at position 107
```

TIP   *The error log is one of the best sources of information you can use to gain insight on what might be happening or has happened on a server. It is usually the first place an administrator should look.*

Simple Techniques to Improve and Minimize Lag

The simplest way to improve replication lag is to improve SQL performance that blocks the single-threaded SQL execution on the slave. Reducing the execution time of UPDATE and DELETE statements can greatly improve replication lag. Effective MySQL: Optimizing SQL Statements (McGraw-Hill, 2011) provides many examples for improving SQL performance including techniques to reduce the number of, and complexity of,

SQL statements that are executed. Improving the schema design to remove excessive and duplicate indexes will improve the performance of applying DML statements on a slave.

In some cases you may not need to replicate certain databases or tables. Excluding certain databases and/or tables will reduce SQL execution on the slave host. MySQL replication has the ability to ignore specific databases and/or tables through the system variables `--replicate-ignore-db=[database   name]` and `--replicate-ignore-table=[table name]`, respectively. The logic behind this is that if you do not replicate certain databases or tables, there will be less relay log processing, and there will be fewer writes running to the slave host. That said, recovery of these databases or tables will have to considered in detail as to not affect production traffic in the event of a failover.

You should avoid using the `--replicate-ignore-db` option if you are using cross-database updates. For example, if the slave host was started with `--replicate-ignore-db=app` and you run the following SQL, the statement will be replicated to the slave:

```
master> USE book3;
master> UPDATE app.test_tbl
    -> SET val1 = 5 WHERE val1 = 1;
```

The update to the table succeeds on the master and is replicated because `--replicate-ignore-db` only applies to the default database set by the preceding USE statement. The solution is to use `--replicate-wild*` options.

NOTE   *The* `--replicate-*` *options do not accept multiple values in one line. To specify multiple databases or tables, add multiple* `--replicate-*-db` *or* `--replicate-*-table` *options to your* `my.cnf` *file.*

Choosing an alternate filesystem type—for example, ext4 or xfs—may provide additional benefits for your production workload. Tuning the filesystem configuration appropriately with `noatime` and `nobarrier` attributes can also assist in disk I/O performance. Appropriate hardware is also an essential part of any database architecture. If the system you are working with has a heavy write workload or a mixed read/write workload, consider using faster disks, more *CPUs*, and always more memory. Using the best *RAID* configuration and considering *SSDs* are discussed in the following section.

Your MySQL topology is only as good as the weakest link in your infra-structure. If you have well-configured hardware running your master, your slave also requires appropriate hardware choices. Recognizing the weakest link can lead to better system design in the future and higher availability in the event of an emergency. For all MySQL slave replication configuration options, visit http://dev.mysql.com/doc/refman/5.5/en/replication-options-slave.html.

Advanced Techniques to Improve and Minimize Lag

MySQL can be configured to behave differently in replication by changing certain system variables:

CAUTION   *Altering the MySQL configuration on a slave may impact your production failover or backup strategy. Use caution when altering the configuration between servers in any MySQL replication topology, now and in the future. At a later time, the requirements and the purpose for the slave may alter.*

- `innodb_flush_log_at_trx_commit`   By default, the value of `innodb_flush_log_at_trx_commit` is 1. This means that the log buffer is written after every commit and a flush disk operation is performed on the log file. You would normally change the default setting of `innodb_flush_log_at_trx_commit` when your system has an I/O bottleneck. Setting the value of `innodb_flush_log_at_trx_commit` to 2 will write every transaction to the log buffer; however, the flush to disk is only a loose interval of once per second. Although the default value of 1 is required for ACID compliance, it would be easy to automate and recognize when a slave may be lagging behind and change this global dynamic value from 1 to 2 during times of lag.

CAUTION   *Setting* `innodb_flush_log_at_trx_commit` *to 1 will ensure full ACID compliance. However, setting this variable to 1 also will hinder replication performance. For more information please see, http://dev.mysql.com/doc/refman/5.5/en/innodb-parameters.html#sysvar_innodb_flush_log_at_trx_commit.*

- **sync_binlog** The default value of 0 means that mysqld does not control synchronization to disk, but leaves synchronization up to the operating system. The system variable, sync_binlog, is another server tunable used to speed up replication when there is an I/O bottleneck on the system. When the value of sync_binlog is set to 1, the safest setting, events sync to the binary log after every commit, which provides, at most, one transaction lost in the event of a mysqld crash if autocommit is enabled. Setting sync_binlog to a value greater than the default, 0, allows MySQL to sync events at a much slower rate (allowing the disk to not work as much). Although setting sync_binlog to 1 is the slowest setting, it can also be sped up with the use of a battery-backed write cache.

In the event replication falls behind the master, an administrator can set sync_binlog to 30 and innodb_flush_log_at_trx_commit to 2 to help assist with replication catch-up. The action of changing these two variables may cause different problems in a disaster recovery situation.

You may also gain performance if you store your data and binary logs on separate storage partitions. This may affect your backup and recovery strategy if you use this slave for that purpose.

Using the correct RAID configuration within your hardware is another way to ensure minimal replication lag. RAID 1 + 0, or RAID 10, is the best configuration for database write throughput, whereas the more common RAID 5 is optimized for read workloads. Although more disk space is used when using RAID 10, the gain in write throughput can prove to be worth it. In a RAID 10 configuration, which requires a minimum of four disks, the addition of two disks can also make a significant improvement. Popular 1U servers generally support the installation of six drives.

If the writes of the system cause normal spinning disks to run with too much I/O wait, you may want to consider running SSD or a flash disk solution.

Prefetching data on the slave host is another possible optimization technique that is designed to read the relay log slightly ahead of the SQL thread. The SQL statement is then converted into a SELECT statement, and executed in a different thread. This has the benefit of performing the disk I/O of the read independently, and will result in increasing the speed of the write when it is executed. Chapter 5 will discuss this advanced feature in more detail.

Upgrading the version of MySQL can also provide benefits. There are new features in MySQL 5.6 that provide performance improvements for reducing lag. The binlog group commit (BGC) addition, discussed in Chapter 3, is one feature for considering the upgrade of your MySQL version in a high volume environment. MySQL replication can also support using a newer version on a slave, i.e., a MySQL master may be running MySQL 5.1 or MySQL 5.5, and a slave can be using MySQL 5.6. Some new features may be limited as they require MySQL 5.6 on the master.

Multiple companies are working to improve on the native MySQL replication implementation. While many products require a custom MySQL binary to be installed and configured, Tungsten Replicator can be installed and configured with an existing MySQL topology, including multiple MySQL versions, and can be used to take over native replication to improve replication performance and correct lag. Tungsten Replicator will be covered in more detail in Chapter 6.

It may be time to shard your environment. Sharding is a way to segment data into multiple vertical silos or partitions. Typically, sharding is needed to scale write activity in an environment, meaning expanding the number of master servers you have vertically. If an environment is made up of a master/slave topology where replication lag is prevalent, you may need to move some of the operations to a new master/slave topology. From a data and schema perspective, this is relatively easy; however, the application accessing this data may need to be modified to find the appropriate data in multiple locations.

Monitoring Replication

It has been stated that `Seconds_Behind_Master` in the output of `SHOW SLAVE STATUS` is poorly named, given the implication of its name. `Seconds_Behind_Master` really measures the latency in seconds the slave SQL thread is in relation to the slave I/O thread, or the quantity of relay log events not applied on the slave in relation to committed events on the master. If you see values higher than 0, you may be dealing with network latency or high server loads.

If you want a more accurate measurement of `Seconds_Behind_Master`, consider running your own heartbeat through the master from the slave server. A simple example can be found at http://datacharmer.blogspot .com/2006/04/measuring-replication-speed.html. The Percona Toolkit heartbeat utility `pt-heatbeat` is another example available at http://www.percona.com/.

`SHOW SLAVE STATUS` shows a great deal of information needed for replication monitoring and will be covered more in depth in Chapter 8. Another consideration is disk space utilization, both of the master and slave hosts. By default, the size of a binary log is ~1GB, and if you do not have a mechanism to remove older files, it could potentially fill up the entire disk. Chapter 5 provides some utilities to assist with disk management of binary logs.

Conclusion

Knowing some of the common issues you may find in a replicated environment will ensure you are better prepared to administer MySQL. Having a solid understanding of the moving parts in replication will help you diagnose issues faster when they arise. Every replication installation has different load and data manipulation characteristics. It is essential to benchmark and test different replication configurations to fit your unique business requirements. Armed with the information in this chapter you will be able to avoid common replication issues and hopefully avoid potential data disasters.

Examples and links in this chapter are available for download from http://EffectiveMySQL.com/book/replication-techniques.

3

Improving Standard Replication Features

In the past, improving replication involved implementing different replication topologies and increasing throughput with faster servers and networks. While these methods are still important today, MySQL replication is becoming more feature rich, and third party software products have been developed to break the asynchronous replication mold. Data drift and single threaded asynchronous replication are two of the important issues with the current implementation of MySQL replication, but there is hope for the future on multiple fronts.

In this chapter we will be discussing:

- Improving on asynchronous replication
- Securing MySQL replication
- New replication features in MySQL 5.6

Extending Asynchronous Behavior

A common complaint with traditional MySQL replication is that it is asynchronous. This means that a write operation has to complete on the master host before it is replicated and applied to the slave host. What if something happens to the data written on the master before this is replicated to the slave? There are many new capabilities, both in and outside the MySQL server that provide better data integrity and synchronization.

Semisynchronous Replication

In addition to the performance improvements in MySQL 5.5, one major new feature is semisynchronous replication. This new replication method is an intermediate mechanism when compared to asynchronous replication and synchronous replication. You can think of semisynchronous replication as a step in the right direction toward full synchronous replication.

Asynchronous replication in MySQL means that events are written to the binary log on the master host, and the slave I/O thread independently records the event on the slave. There is no guarantee to the master that events reach, or have been committed, to the slave host.

On the other side of the replication spectrum is synchronous replication where all transactions are acknowledged and committed on all slaves before returning to the session that initiated the transaction. Semisynchronous, in this case, means that after a commit on the master host, a wait will occur until one of the configured slave hosts has logged the event to disk. There is a drawback implied here, but we will cover this in more detail later in this section.

Semisynchronous Plugin Installation

Semisynchronous replication is installed using plugins on MySQL 5.5 and higher. This type of replication can be used as an alternative to traditional asynchronous replication. A best practice is to load the semisynchronous plugin with the INSTALL PLUGIN command on the master and slave hosts. Ensuring the MySQL server supports dynamic loading on both the master and slave host is a requirement if you want to install semisynchronous replication with these SQL statements. To see if dynamic loading is enabled on your MySQL master and slave server, run the following command:

```
master> SHOW VARIABLES LIKE 'have_dynamic_loading';
+----------------------+-------+
| Variable_name        | Value |
+----------------------+-------+
| have_dynamic_loading | YES   |
+----------------------+-------+
```

NOTE   *To install semisynchronous replication dynamically, both the master and slave hosts require the system variable* have_dynamic_loading *to be YES.*

There are two separate plugins used for semisynchronous replication, one for the master host and one for the slave host.

NOTE   *You should use the root account, or at least a user that has SUPER privilege and INSERT privilege on the* mysql.plugin *table when installing these plugins.*

On the master host:

```
master> INSTALL PLUGIN rpl_semi_sync_master SONAME 'semisync_master.so';
master> SHOW PLUGINS\G
...
*************************** 21. row ***************************
    Name: rpl_semi_sync_master
  Status: ACTIVE
    Type: REPLICATION
 Library: semisync_master.so
 License: GPL
```

On the slave host:

```
slave> INSTALL PLUGIN rpl_semi_sync_slave SONAME 'semisync_slave.so';
slave> SHOW PLUGINS\G
...
*************************** 21. row ***************************
    Name: rpl_semi_sync_slave
  Status: ACTIVE
    Type: REPLICATION
 Library: semisync_slave.so
 License: GPL
```

The system variables that toggle the use of semisynchronous replication are similar on the master and slave host. A zero (0) value for both `rpl_semi_sync_master_enabled` and `rpl_semi_sync_slave_enabled` system variables disables semisynchronous replication where a value of one (1) will enable it. Semisynchronous replication is a dynamic process which you can toggle at runtime, for example.

On the master host:

```
master> SET GLOBAL rpl_semi_sync_master_enabled = 1;
master> SHOW GLOBAL VARIABLES LIKE 'rpl_semi_sync_master_enabled'\G
*************************** 1. row ***************************
Variable_name: rpl_semi_sync_master_enabled
        Value: ON
```

On the slave host:

```
slave> SET GLOBAL rpl_semi_sync_slave_enabled = 1;
slave> SHOW GLOBAL VARIABLES LIKE 'rpl_semi_sync_slave_enabled'\G
*************************** 1. row ***************************
Variable_name: rpl_semi_sync_slave_enabled
        Value: ON
```

When enabled, this will be reported as a note in the MySQL error log:

```
120617 18:51:08 [Note] Semi-sync replication initialized for transactions.
120617 18:51:08 [Note] Semi-sync replication enabled on the master.
```

Another system variable you will need to consider is `rpl_semi_sync_master_timeout`. This variable represents the time in milliseconds the master will wait on a commit acknowledgement from a slave host before timing out and switching to asynchronous replication. The default value is 10,000, or 10 seconds, which is too high for many installations. In the example below the value has been changed from 10 seconds to 1 second:

```
master> SET GLOBAL rpl_semi_sync_master_timeout = 1000;
```

To ensure these dynamic semisynchronous replication settings are enabled after a server restart, you will need to add the following to your configuration files.

In the master configuration file:

```
[mysqld]
rpl_semi_sync_master_enabled = 1
rpl_semi_sync_master_timeout = 1000
```

In the slave configuration file:

```
[mysqld]
rpl_semi_sync_slave_enabled = 1
```

Semisynchronous replication currently includes four additional system variables. The full list is:

```
master> SHOW GLOBAL VARIABLES LIKE 'rpl_semi%';
+------------------------------------+-------+
| Variable_name                      | Value |
+------------------------------------+-------+
| rpl_semi_sync_master_enabled       | ON    |
| rpl_semi_sync_master_timeout       | 1000  |
| rpl_semi_sync_master_trace_level   | 32    |
| rpl_semi_sync_master_wait_no_slave | ON    |
+------------------------------------+-------+
```

Monitoring the operations of semisynchronous replication is possible with a number of MySQL status variables:

```
master> SHOW GLOBAL STATUS LIKE 'rpl%';
+-------------------------------------------+-------+
| Variable_name                             | Value |
+-------------------------------------------+-------+
| Rpl_semi_sync_master_clients              | 0     |
| Rpl_semi_sync_master_net_avg_wait_time    | 0     |
| Rpl_semi_sync_master_net_wait_time        | 0     |
| Rpl_semi_sync_master_net_waits            | 0     |
| Rpl_semi_sync_master_no_times             | 0     |
| Rpl_semi_sync_master_no_tx                | 0     |
| Rpl_semi_sync_master_status               | ON    |
| Rpl_semi_sync_master_timefunc_failures    | 0     |
| Rpl_semi_sync_master_tx_avg_wait_time     | 0     |
| Rpl_semi_sync_master_tx_wait_time         | 0     |
| Rpl_semi_sync_master_tx_waits             | 0     |
| Rpl_semi_sync_master_wait_pos_backtraverse| 0     |
| Rpl_semi_sync_master_wait_sessions        | 0     |
| Rpl_semi_sync_master_yes_tx               | 0     |
+-------------------------------------------+-------+
```

Semisynchronous replication can be disabled at any time when a timeout occurs. The `Rpl_semi_sync_master_status` status variable is important to monitor:

```
master> SHOW GLOBAL STATUS LIKE 'rpl%status';
+-------------------------------+--------+
| Variable_name                 | Value  |
+-------------------------------+--------+
| Rpl_semi_sync_master_status   | OFF    |
+-------------------------------+--------+
```

In the event this occurs, the MySQL error log will report the situation, but not as an error:

```
120617 18:53:09 [Warning] Timeout waiting for reply of binlog (file:
alpha-bin.000004, pos: 357), semi-sync up to file , position 0.
120617 18:53:09 [Note] Semi-sync replication switched OFF.
```

Semisynchronous Operation

Understanding the flow of a semisynchronous transaction will help in understanding some of the drawbacks when using this feature. The primary steps are as follows:

1. A slave connects to the master host.

2. The slave declares to the master if it is using semisynchronous replication or not (in this case, we are).

3. If both the master and at least one slave have semisynchronous replication enabled, transactions from the master to the slave will start using semisynchronous replication.

4. A thread on the master runs a commit on a transaction.

5. A wait occurs on the master while at least one semisynchronous slave acknowledges the transaction, or a timeout occurs if the wait on the master exceeds `rpl_semi_sync_master_timeout`.

NOTE If a timeout occurs the master automatically reverts to asynchronous replication for future transactions. The master will automatically switch back to semisynchronous replication when the slave is caught up to the master host.

6. On the slave, the transaction event is written to the relay log and flushed to disk.

7. The slave acknowledges to the master that the transaction is recorded.

8. The master releases the thread that performed the transaction.

9. The thread can execute the next transaction.

As you may have seen in the process there are a few drawbacks when using semisynchronous replication. In the case where a system has more than one slave server, there is no confirmation all of the slaves have acknowledged the receipt of the event; only one slave has to acknowledge the event. On top of not waiting for all slave hosts to acknowledge receipt of events, semisynchronous replication does not require those events to be fully executed and committed on the slave host. Thus, it is still possible to see replication lag (Seconds_Behind_Master > 0) on the slave host and have the rpl_semi_sync_master_status variable set to ON in the master host.

There are performance implications, as a commit has the overhead of slave acknowledgement for transactions. Network latency is an important factor when determining if semisynchronous replication is right for your installation and transaction throughput needs. It is still possible for replication to revert back to asynchronous replication in the event of a slave error or slow network connection. Semisynchronous replication is a positive step toward better data integrity, and like other technologies there are tradeoffs that need to be considered specifically for your installation. In a more complex MySQL topology it is possible to have both semisynchronous and asynchronous replication between different MySQL instances. For example, in a multi-master topology, this may be semisynchronous replication, while additional attached slaves could use asynchronous replication.

Synchronous Replication

The standard MySQL server distribution does not currently support synchronous replication. MySQL does provide a different product called MySQL Cluster that does support this functionality. It is important to understand that MySQL Cluster is a different product than MySQL server. An overview of MySQL Cluster is provided in Chapter 6.

Third party products, including Galera, Tungsten, and Schooner Tech, are now offering MySQL synchronous replication features. The cloud offerings of Amazon RDS with a Multi-AZ deployment and Google Cloud SQL also provide proprietary synchronous replication features. These will be discussed in detail in Chapter 6.

Securing Replication with SSL

Securing MySQL communication and MySQL replication with *SSL* has been around for a very long time; however, this is generally not implemented. With more organizations implementing cloud services, this additional security consideration is very significant for using replication. Setting up MySQL replication using an SSL connection for encryption will make it difficult for third parties to sniff out data transferred between the master and slave.

Making MySQL SSL Ready

You need to ensure SSL is enabled on both the master and slave host. To see if SSL is enabled, run the following command on both hosts:

```
master> SHOW VARIABLES LIKE '%ssl%';
+---------------+-------+
| Variable_name | Value |
+---------------+-------+
| have_openssl  | YES   |
| have_ssl      | YES   |
| ssl_ca        |       |
| ssl_capath    |       |
| ssl_cert      |       |
| ssl_cipher    |       |
| ssl_key       |       |
+---------------+-------+

slave> SHOW VARIABLES LIKE '%ssl%';
+---------------+-------+
| Variable_name | Value |
+---------------+-------+
| have_openssl  | YES   |
| have_ssl      | YES   |
| ssl_ca        |       |
| ssl_capath    |       |
| ssl_cert      |       |
| ssl_cipher    |       |
| ssl_key       |       |
+---------------+-------+
```

If either `have_openssl` or `have_ssl` is set to DISABLED, you will need to add the `ssl` option to the `my.cnf` file and restart the MySQL server.

Creating the Necessary Security Certificates

The next step is to create and store three types of certificates, the Certificate Authority (CA), server, and client. In this example we will create the certificates on the master host first in the `/usr/local/mysql/certs` directory that we will also create.

On the master host:

```
$ sudo mkdir -p /usr/local/mysql/certs
$ openssl genrsa 2048 > ca-key.pem
Generating RSA private key, 2048 bit long modulus
....................+++
..+++
e is 65537 (0x10001)

$ openssl req -new -x509 -nodes -days 9999 \
 -key ca-key.pem > ca-cert.pem
You are about to be asked to enter information that will be incorporated
into your certificate request.
What you are about to enter is what is called a Distinguished Name or a DN.
There are quite a few fields but you can leave some blank
For some fields there will be a default value,
If you enter '.', the field will be left blank.
-----
Country Name (2 letter code) [GB]:US
State or Province Name (full name) [Berkshire]:CA
Locality Name (eg, city) [Newbury]:Sunnyvale
Organization Name (eg, company) [My Company Ltd]:EffectiveMySQL
Organizational Unit Name (eg, section) []:SSL Replication
Common Name (eg, your name or your server's hostname) []:
Email Address []:
You can see the two files created for the CA certificate below:
$ ls *.pem
ca-cert.pem   ca-key.pem
```

Next we need to create the server certificates:

```
$ openssl req -newkey rsa:2048 -days 1000 -nodes -keyout \
server-key.pem > server-req.pem
Generating a 2048 bit RSA private key
..........+++
.....................................................+++
writing new private key to 'server-key.pem'
-----
You are about to be asked to enter information that will be incorporated
into your certificate request.
What you are about to enter is what is called a Distinguished Name or a DN.
```

```
There are quite a few fields but you can leave some blank
For some fields there will be a default value,
If you enter '.', the field will be left blank.
-----
Country Name (2 letter code) [GB]:US
State or Province Name (full name) [Berkshire]:CA
Locality Name (eg, city) [Newbury]:Sunnyvale
Organization Name (eg, company) [My Company Ltd]:EffectiveMySQL
Organizational Unit Name (eg, section) []:SSL Replication
Common Name (eg, your name or your server's hostname) []:
Email Address []:

Please enter the following 'extra' attributes
to be sent with your certificate request
A challenge password []:
An optional company name []:
```

Leave the challenge password empty in the previous example.

```
$ openssl x509 -req -in server-req.pem -days 9999 -CA ca-cert.pem \
 -CAkey ca-key.pem -set_serial 01 > server-cert.pem
Signature ok
subject=/C=US/ST=CA/L=Sunnyvale/O=EffectiveMySQL/OU=SSL Replication
Getting CA Private Key
```

You can see on the file system that three new files have been created:

```
$ ls server-*.pem
server-cert.pem   server-key.pem   server-req.pem
```

The last set of certificates is the client certificates, which are created as follows:

```
$ openssl req -newkey rsa:2048 -days 9999 -nodes -keyout \
client-key.pem > client-req.pem
Generating a 2048 bit RSA private key
............+++
...........................+++
writing new private key to 'client-key.pem'
-----
You are about to be asked to enter information that will be incorporated
into your certificate request.
What you are about to enter is what is called a Distinguished Name or a DN.
There are quite a few fields but you can leave some blank
For some fields there will be a default value,
If you enter '.', the field will be left blank.
-----
Country Name (2 letter code) [GB]:US
State or Province Name (full name) [Berkshire]:CA
Locality Name (eg, city) [Newbury]:Sunnyvale
Organization Name (eg, company) [My Company Ltd]:EffectiveMySQL
Organizational Unit Name (eg, section) []:SSL Replication
Common Name (eg, your name or your server's hostname) []:
Email Address []:
```

```
Please enter the following 'extra' attributes
to be sent with your certificate request
A challenge password []:
An optional company name []:
```

Leave the challenge password empty in the preceding example.

```
$ openssl x509 -req -in client-req.pem -days 9999 -CA ca-cert.pem -CAkey \
  ca-key.pem -set_serial 01 > client-cert.pem
Signature ok
subject=/C=US/ST=CA/L=Sunnyvale/O=EffectiveMySQL/OU=SSL Replication
Getting CA Private Key
```

All of the certificates we just created are listed here:

```
$ sudo mv *.pem /usr/local/mysql/certs/
$ ls -l /usr/local/mysql/certs
total 32
-rw-rw-r-- 1 uid gid 1229 Jun 11 16:23 ca-cert.pem
-rw-rw-r-- 1 uid gid 1679 Jun 11 16:23 ca-key.pem
-rw-rw-r-- 1 uid gid 1099 Jun 11 16:25 client-cert.pem
-rw-rw-r-- 1 uid gid 1704 Jun 11 16:24 client-key.pem
-rw-rw-r-- 1 uid gid  956 Jun 11 16:24 client-req.pem
-rw-rw-r-- 1 uid gid 1099 Jun 11 16:24 server-cert.pem
-rw-rw-r-- 1 uid gid 1700 Jun 11 16:21 server-key.pem
-rw-rw-r-- 1 uid gid  956 Jun 11 16:23 server-req.pem
```

You will need to create the `/usr/local/mysql/certs` directory on the slave host and copy the newly created `ca-cert.pem client-cert.pem client-key.pem` files to the slave.

Slave:

```
$ sudo mkdir -p /usr/local/mysql/certs
```

Master:

```
$ scp ca-cert.pem client-cert.pem client-key.pem \
  root@slave.example.com:/usr/local/mysql/certs
```

In the event the slave host is promoted to master, you will need to have all of the server SSL keys on the slave host. You can copy all files to the slave server. The previous `scp` syntax is to illustrate the minimum number of files needed.

MySQL SSL Configuration Requirements

The final step is to define these certifications in the master and slave `my.cnf` configuration file:

NOTE   *It is important to add the following configuration settings to both the master and the slave for failover purposes.*

Add the following variables to the `[mysqld]` section of the `my.cnf` file:

```
$ vi /etc/my.cnf
[mysqld]
ssl
ssl-ca=/usr/local/mysql/certs/ca-cert.pem
ssl-cert=/usr/local/mysql/certs/server-cert.pem
ssl-key=/usr/local/mysql/certs/server-key.pem
```

A MySQL restart is needed on both the master and slave host for the SSL changes to take effect. The following example verifies the new configuration is operational:

```
$ service mysql restart
$ mysql -uroot -p -e "SHOW VARIABLES LIKE '%ssl%'"
+---------------+-----------------------------------------+
| Variable_name | Value                                   |
+---------------+-----------------------------------------+
| have_openssl  | YES                                     |
| have_ssl      | YES                                     |
| ssl_ca        | /usr/local/mysql/certs/ca-cert.pem      |
| ssl_capath    |                                         |
| ssl_cert      | /usr/local/mysql/certs/server-cert.pem  |
| ssl_cipher    |                                         |
| ssl_key       | /usr/local/mysql/certs/server-key.pem   |
+---------------+-----------------------------------------+
```

MySQL User Privileges Requirements

Replication requires a MySQL user account with the appropriate REPLICATION SLAVE permission. To use SSL, the REQUIRE SSL attribute is also necessary.

NOTE   *Setting up a replication user with the requirement to use SSL is important. If you include REQUIRE SSL in your GRANT statement, only encrypted SSL slave threads will be allowed. In the following example, this means the user "repl" from % (everywhere) will only be able to connect to the master host with SSL encryption. If REQUIRE SSL is omitted, then both SSL encrypted and normal replication threads will be allowed with the same user. Here is a GRANT statement that illustrates how to enable a replication user, with SSL required for connections:*

```
master> GRANT REPLICATION SLAVE ON *.* TO 'repl@'%'
     -> IDENTIFIED BY 'some_password' REQUIRE SSL;
```

It is also important to mention that if you have more than one GRANT set up for replication, you will need to modify these users to also use REQUIRE SSL. This would be the case if you have specifically added multiple "repl" accounts from a specific IP, IP range, or hostname. For example, if you have three slave hosts that connect to this master and have specified the slave's IP address to connect from, all specified "repl" users would need to have REQUIRE SSL added:

```
master> SELECT user,host,password
    -> FROM mysql.user
    -> WHERE user = 'repl'
    -> ORDER BY host\G
*********************** 1. row ***********************
    user: repl
    host: %
password: *48924CC1D59E9904D72265EFD60FB3C5C88BBEB5
*********************** 2. row ***********************
    user: repl
    host: 192.168.1.101
password: *48924CC1D59E9904D72265EFD60FB3C5C88BBEB5
*********************** 3. row ***********************
    user: repl
    host: 192.168.1.102
password: *48924CC1D59E9904D72265EFD60FB3C5C88BBEB5
*********************** 4. row ***********************
    user: repl
    host: 192.168.1.103
password: *48924CC1D59E9904D72265EFD60FB3C5C88BBEB5
4 rows in set (0.00 sec)
```

Limiting replication connectivity to a specific IP is something you may want to implement in your environment when using SSL encrypted replication. When implementing this you should also consider removing "repl" users with broader access credentials. Doing this can add a more granular level of security to your system.

Adding the REQUIRE SSL option to any user can be accomplished by running the GRANT line shown earlier with the username and host modified to fit our needs. In the following example the new privilege is defined for one user. The process would need to be repeated for all "repl" users that require SSL encryption.

Before:

```
master> SHOW GRANTS FOR repl@192.168.1.102\G
*********************** 1. row ***********************
GRANT REPLICATION SLAVE ON *.* TO repl@192.168.1.102
IDENTIFIED BY PASSWORD
'*48924CC1D59E9904D72265EFD60FB3C5C88BBEB5'
```

Adding the REQUIRE SSL option:

```
master> GRANT REPLICATION SLAVE ON *.* TO
repl@192.168.1.102
   -> IDENTIFIED BY 'some_password' REQUIRE SSL;
```

After:

```
master> SHOW GRANTS FOR repl@192.168.1.102\G
*********************** 1. row ***********************
GRANT REPLICATION SLAVE ON *.* TO
repl@192.168.1.102 IDENTIFIED BY PASSWORD
'*48924CC1D59E9904D72265EFD60FB3C5C88BBEB5' REQUIRE SSL
```

On the slave host you have two options to start using SSL replication. You can either add the slave certificates to the [client] section in the slave my.cnf file, or you can explicitly specify the SSL information using the CHANGE MASTER TO statement. Remember, we copied the ca-cert .pem, client-cert.pem, and client-key.pem over to the slave host and these are located in the /usr/local/mysql/certs directory on the slave. The following are examples of both methods:

NOTE *If you choose to implement the SSL changes in the* [client] *section of the* my.cnf *file you should also add these options to the master* my.cnf *file in the event the master is demoted to slave.*

Master and slave my.cnf file change:

```
[client]
ssl
ssl-ca=/usr/local/mysql/certs/ca-cert.pem
ssl-cert=/usr/local/mysql/certs/client-cert.pem
ssl-key=/usr/local/mysql/certs/client-key.pem
```

You then need to restart the slave host with --skip-slave-start and then run a CHANGE MASTER TO statement with the MASTER_SSL = 1 option:

```
slave> CHANGE MASTER TO
  MASTER_HOST='master.example.com'',
  MASTER_USER='repl',
  MASTER_PASSWORD='some_password',
  MASTER_PORT=3306,
  MASTER_LOG_FILE='binary-logs.000001',
  MASTER_LOG_POS=106,
  MASTER_CONNECT_RETRY=10,
  MASTER_SSL = 1;
```

The second option is to specify all of the certificates within the CHANGE MASTER TO statement:

```
slave> CHANGE MASTER TO
  MASTER_HOST='master.example.com',
  MASTER_USER='repl',
  MASTER_PASSWORD='some_password',
  MASTER_PORT=3306,
  MASTER_LOG_FILE='binary-logs.000001',
  MASTER_LOG_POS=106,
  MASTER_CONNECT_RETRY=10,
  MASTER_SSL = 1,
  MASTER_SSL_CA = '/usr/local/mysql/certs/ca-cert.pem',
  MASTER_SSL_CERT = '/usr/local/mysql/certs/client-cert.pem',
  MASTER_SSL_KEY = '/usr/local/mysql/certs/client-key.pem';
```

After you have your new SSL options in place, remember to run START SLAVE on the slave host and check that replication is running as it should be:

```
slave> START SLAVE;
slave> SHOW SLAVE STATUS\G
*************************** 1. row ***************************
               Slave_IO_State: Waiting for master to send event
                  Master_Host: master.example.com
                  Master_User: repl
                  Master_Port: 3306
                Connect_Retry: 10
              Master_Log_File: binary-logs.000001
          Read_Master_Log_Pos: 106
               Relay_Log_File: mysqld-relay-bin.000001
                Relay_Log_Pos: 4
        Relay_Master_Log_File: binary-logs.000001
             Slave_IO_Running: Yes
            Slave_SQL_Running: Yes
...
            Master_SSL_Allowed: Yes
            Master_SSL_CA_File: /usr/local/mysql/certs/ca-cert.pem
            Master_SSL_CA_Path:
               Master_SSL_Cert: /usr/local/mysql/certs/client-cert.pem
             Master_SSL_Cipher:
                Master_SSL_Key: /usr/local/mysql/certs/client-key.pem
...
```

SSL replication is a long process and is difficult to diagnose if you mistype something or miss a step. Anyone who is looking for added security, especially within a cloud service like Amazon Web Services (AWS), should consider running SSL replication for MySQL. More information can be found at http://dev.mysql.com/doc/refman/5.5/en/replication-solutions-ssl.html.

New Replication Features

Starting with MySQL 5.5, there have been major performance and scalability improvements added to the MySQL server. With MySQL 5.6 there are many new additions to replication specifically focused on data integrity, performance, and usability.

New and Improved Data Integrity

Data integrity is very important to a business and should not be taken lightly by database administrators. When data integrity issues are identified, it usually takes operational time to remedy and engineering time to fix moving forward. With MySQL 5.6 less administration time is needed if a slave crashes, a human or application error occurs with a destructive SQL statement on a master, or you are suffering from data drift.

Crash-Safe Slaves

Traditionally, runtime replication information has been stored on the slave host in two files found in the data directory, `master.info` and `relay-log.info`. While this is still the default method in MySQL 5.6, MySQL now supports logging replication information to tables located in the `mysql` database. There are two new configuration variables that control how the master connection information and slave relay log information are stored:

- **`master-info-repository`**   When the value of this option is set to TABLE the master info log information will be stored in the `mysql.slave_master_info` table. When the value of this option is set to FILE the default filename `master.info` will be created on the file system to store the appropriate connection information.

- **relay-log-info-repository** When the value of this option is set to TABLE the relay log information will be stored in the mysql .slave_relay_log_info table. When the value of this option is set to FILE the default filename relay-log.info will be created on the file system to store the appropriate relay log information.

NOTE *It is important to review the grant privileges for all users. With these new tables, access to SELECT from the mysql schema would enable viewing the replication user password, which is stored in plain text.*

By default, these new tables exist in the mysql schema for MySQL 5.6; however, they contain no information:

```
slave> SELECT * FROM mysql.slave_master_info;
Empty set (0.00 sec)
slave> SELECT * FROM mysql.slave_relay_log_info;
Empty set (0.00 sec)
```

The following configuration is enabled on a slave to demonstrate the information available:

```
[mysqld]
master-info-repository=TABLE
relay-log-info-repository=TABLE

slave> SELECT * FROM mysql.slave_master_info\G
*************************** 1. row ***************************
             Master_id: 3
       Number_of_lines: 23
       Master_log_name: alpha-bin.000003
        Master_log_pos: 187
                  Host: alpha
             User_name: repl
         User_password: *clear_password_text*
                  Port: 3306
         Connect_retry: 60
           Enabled_ssl: 0
                Ssl_ca:
            Ssl_capath:
              Ssl_cert:
            Ssl_cipher:
               Ssl_key:
 Ssl_verify_server_cert: 0
             Heartbeat: 1800
                  Bind:
     Ignored_server_ids: 0
                  Uuid: ba7ac732-b707-11e1-a1b3-0800275824dc
           Retry_count: 86400
               Ssl_crl:
           Ssl_crlpath:
  Enabled_auto_position: 1
```

```
mysql> SELECT * FROM mysql.slave_relay_log_info\G
*************************** 1. row ***************************
          Master_id: 3
    Number_of_lines: 6
     Relay_log_name: ./gamma-relay-bin.000006
      Relay_log_pos: 346
    Master_log_name: alpha-bin.000002
     Master_log_pos: 391
          Sql_delay: 0
Number_of_workers: 0
1 row in set (0.00 sec)
```

The default storage engine for the two new tables defined with `slave_master_info` and `slave_relay_log_info` is MyISAM. It is important to note that you will need to change the engine of these tables to InnoDB in order for replication to be crash safe. It is recommended you stop MySQL replication during this process. For example:

```
slave> STOP SLAVE;
slave> ALTER TABLE mysql.slave_master_info ENGINE = InnoDB;
slave> ALTER TABLE mysql.slave_relay_log_info ENGINE = InnoDB;
slave> START SLAVE;
```

NOTE   *MySQL will not operate if you attempt to change the storage engine from MyISAM for any other `mysql` schema tables.*

Keep in mind that you can use other storage engines for these tables; however, the same transactional engine should be used so replication information can be added to transactions and committed with the corresponding transaction. More information can be found at http://dev.mysql.com/doc/refman/5.6/en/slave-logs.html.

Delayed Replication

Time delayed replication has been used through the history of MySQL replication for disaster recovery purposes and testing application behavior while a slave is lagging. Making a slave host in a MySQL topology lag behind by a certain amount of time can help avoid catastrophic operational errors introduced on the master, for example, a TRUNCATE TABLE. In the event a TRUNCATE TABLE command was issued on the master host, an administrator would be able to skip the physical statement and then promote the delayed slave to master. This new feature is implemented with the CHANGE MASTER TO statement and the MASTER_DELAY attribute:

● **MASTER_DELAY**   This attribute specifies how much time in seconds the SQL_THREAD will pause execution of events on the slave host. The default value is zero (0), or no lag, with an upper bound of 68 years, or $2^{31} - 1$.

A time delay can be set on any slave server and acts independently of other replication streams. An administrator could set a time delay during the initial CHANGE MASTER TO statement or after replication has started with the following commands:

```
slave> STOP SLAVE;
slave> CHANGE MASTER TO MASTER_DELAY = 10;
slave> START SLAVE;
```

You can observe time delay in action with the SHOW SLAVE STATUS\G command on the slave. For example:

```
slave> SHOW SLAVE STATUS\G
*********************** 1. row ***********************
              Slave_IO_State: Waiting for master to send event
                 Master_Host: master.example.com
...
                   SQL_Delay: 10
         SQL_Remaining_Delay: 6
      Slave_SQL_Running_State: Waiting until MASTER_DELAY seconds after
 master executed event
...
```

The SQL_Delay column shows the desired lag time in seconds; in this example, we want ten seconds of delay. The SQL_Remaining_Delay indicates how many seconds the slave needs to wait until new events are applied to the slave. The Slave_SQL_Running_State corresponds to the Slave_IO_State and displays the same information shown with SHOW FULL PROCESSLIST:

```
slave> SHOW FULL PROCESSLIST\G
*********************** 1. row ***********************
     Id: 10
   User: system user
   Host:
     db: NULL
Command: Connect
   Time: 1414
  State: Waiting for master to send event
   Info: NULL
*********************** 2. row ***********************
     Id: 11
   User: system user
   Host:
     db: NULL
```

```
Command: Connect
   Time: 10
  State: Waiting until MASTER_DELAY seconds after master executed event
   Info: NULL
*********************** 3. row ************************
     Id: 12
   User: root
   Host: localhost
     db: NULL
Command: Query
   Time: 0
  State: init
   Info: SHOW FULL PROCESSLIST
```

More information can be found at http://dev.mysql.com/doc/refman/5.6/en/replication-delayed.html.

Checksums for Replicated Data

Prior to version 5.6 an administrator would have to use SSL replication as a workaround to implement checksums. With the implementation of CRC32 checksums, you can be assured that data being replicated to a slave has the same integrity as that applied to the master. If data corruption occurs an error will be returned and slave replication is stopped. Checksum information is recorded in the master binary log and the slave relay logs and can be activated on a per server basis.

To enable checksums with the master binary log, the following setting is needed:

- **binlog_checksum**   When this option is set to CRC32 the master will write a checksum for each event into the binary log. binlog_ checksum is a dynamic global variable with the default value of NONE. Changing this option to CRC32 will rotate the binary log, as checksums are always written to an entire binary log file. If the default is set for this option, the server will verify that only complete events are written to the binary log by writing and checking the event length.

Enabling binlog_checksum does not force verification of the checksums created. There are two system variables, one for the master host and the other for slave host(s) to enforce the verification of CRC32 checksums. On the master host:

- **master_verify_checksum**   This variable is disabled by default. When this variable is set to one (1) or ON, the master host will examine checksums when reading from the binary log.

On the slave host:

- `slave_sql_verify_checksum`   This option is also disabled by default. When slave_verify_checksum is enabled with a value of one (1) or ON, the slave host will examine and verify checksums when reading the relay log.

When enabled, the binary log provides the following information:

```
$ mysqlbinlog binary-logs.000008
#111129 22:29:25 server id 1  end_log_pos 584974 CRC32 0x3e864aba
Query thread_id=19 exec_time=0 error_code=0
SET TIMESTAMP=1322605765/*!*/;
INSERT INTO ...
/*!*/;
# at 584974
#111129 22:29:25 server id 1  end_log_pos 585005 CRC32 0x1376938a
Xid = 24943
COMMIT/*!*/;
DELIMITER ;
# End of log file
ROLLBACK /* added by mysqlbinlog */;
/*!50003 SET COMPLETION_TYPE=@OLD_COMPLETION_TYPE*/;
```

The following details are recorded in the slave relay log for comparison:

```
$ mysqlbinlog mysqld-relay-bin.000007
#111129 22:29:25 server id 1  end_log_pos 584974 CRC32 0x3e864aba
Query thread_id=19 exec_time=0 error_code=0
SET TIMESTAMP=1322605765/*!*/;
INSERT INTO ...
# at 585133
#111129 22:29:25 server id 1  end_log_pos 585005 CRC32 0x1376938a
Xid = 24943
COMMIT/*!*/;
DELIMITER ;
# End of log file
ROLLBACK /* added by mysqlbinlog */;
/*!50003 SET COMPLETION_TYPE=@OLD_COMPLETION_TYPE*/;
```

More information can be found at http://dev.mysql.com/doc/refman/5.6/en/replication-options-binary-log.html#option_mysqld_binlog-checksum.

New Performance Improvements for Replication

Two new performance related additions in MySQL 5.6 for replication are multi-threaded slaves and row image control within row-based replication (RBR).

Multi-Threaded Slaves

Parallel transaction execution on a slave host provides better scalability in replication, especially on multicore systems, but there is a catch.

The SQL thread acts as a coordinator for what are referred to as ˚slave worker threads, which work on a per database schema level and can be enabled and tuned with the `slave_parallel_workers` system variable. To utilize multi-threaded slaves, your data will need to be partitioned into multiple database schemas. This allows worker threads on the slave to process transactions on a given database without blocking when updates are processed on others. You also need to ensure there are no foreign key dependencies across schemas and there are no cross schema *DML* queries (i.e., INSERT INTO **db1**.t1 SELECT * FROM **db2**.t2).

When `slave_parallel_workers` is set to a non-zero value on the slave, host transactions will not necessarily be applied on the slave in the same order as they were recorded in the master host binary log. This can lead to recovery complexity along with interpreting relay log information. This variable is defined in the `my.cnf` configuration file. A MySQL instance restart is necessary for these configuration settings to take effect:

```
[mysqld]
slave_parallel_workers=3
relay_log_info_repository=TABLE
```

With the implementation of `slave_parallel_workers` a new table has been added to the `mysql` database, `slave_worker_info`. Along with the new crash-safe tables you should also convert the `slave_worker_info` table to InnoDB:

```
master> ALTER TABLE mysql.slave_worker_info ENGINE=InnoDB;
```

Parallel threads will only work when both master and slave hosts are MySQL version 5.6 or higher. If you attach a version 5.6 slave to a version 5.5 master, replication will slow down exponentially when the multi-threaded configuration is enabled on the slave.

When running a test on multiple schemas using the example procedure to test replication found in the appendix, you can observe the following information:

```
slave> SELECT * FROM mysql.slave_worker_info\G
*************************** 1. row ***************************
               Master_id: 3
               Worker_id: 0
```

```
           Relay_log_name:
            Relay_log_pos: 0
          Master_log_name:
           Master_log_pos: 0
  Checkpoint_relay_log_name:
   Checkpoint_relay_log_pos: 0
 Checkpoint_master_log_name:
  Checkpoint_master_log_pos: 0
          Checkpoint_seqno: 0
     Checkpoint_group_size: 64
   Checkpoint_group_bitmap:
*************************** 2. row ***************************
                Master_id: 3
                Worker_id: 1
           Relay_log_name:
            Relay_log_pos: 0
          Master_log_name:
           Master_log_pos: 0
  Checkpoint_relay_log_name:
   Checkpoint_relay_log_pos: 0
 Checkpoint_master_log_name:
  Checkpoint_master_log_pos: 0
          Checkpoint_seqno: 0
     Checkpoint_group_size: 64
   Checkpoint_group_bitmap:
*************************** 3. row ***************************
                Master_id: 3
                Worker_id: 2
           Relay_log_name: ./gamma-relay-bin.000009
            Relay_log_pos: 13641
          Master_log_name: alpha-bin.000003
           Master_log_pos: 21209
  Checkpoint_relay_log_name: ./gamma-relay-bin.000009
   Checkpoint_relay_log_pos: 13329
 Checkpoint_master_log_name: alpha-bin.000003
  Checkpoint_master_log_pos: 20897
          Checkpoint_seqno: 0
     Checkpoint_group_size: 64
   Checkpoint_group_bitmap:
3 rows in set (0.00 sec)
```

More information can be found at http://dev.mysql.com/doc/refman/5.6/en/replication-options-slave.html#option_mysqld_slave-parallel-workers.

Row-Based Replication – Row Image Control

Row-based replication (RBR), when compared to statement-based replication (SBR), has traditionally taken up more space in the binary log. This is due to the default behavior of RBR where all column values are sent to the slave where a write occurs instead of just sending the values in the row where the write occurs. With row image control it is now possible to save system and network resources by toggling the behavior of row-based replication. Detailed next are examples of all three settings for the new system variable, `binlog_row_image`.

First we need to create a table, in the following example, called `test_rbr_image`:

```
master> use book3
master> CREATE TABLE test_rbr_image (
    ->    id INT UNSIGNED NOT NULL,
    ->    col1 INT DEFAULT NULL,
    ->    var2 CHAR(3) DEFAULT NULL,
    ->    comment TEXT NULL
) ENGINE=InnoDB DEFAULT CHARSET=utf8;
```

When the `binlog_row_image` system variable is set to full (the default), all columns will be logged to the binary log after a write event. With the INSERT statement, we are adding a row to the table but only adding values to three (3) columns to the row:

```
master> SET SESSION binlog_format = ROW;
master> SHOW MASTER STATUS\G
*********************** 1. row ***********************
            File: mysql-bin.000002
        Position: 11783
    Binlog_Do_DB:
 Binlog_Ignore_DB:
Executed_Gtid_Set:
master> INSERT INTO test_rbr_image (id, col1, var2)
    -> VALUES(1, 2, '3');
```

Now we can see what this event looks like in the binary log using the `mysqlbinlog` client utility and the values from the output of SHOW MASTER STATUS:

```
$ mysqlbinlog --base64-output=DECODE-ROWS \
  --verbose --start-position=11783 mysql-bin.000002
# at 11783
...
# at 11912
#120613 17:11:10 server id 1  end_log_pos 11912
Table_map: `book3`.`test_rbr_image` mapped to number 73
#120613 17:11:10 server id 1  end_log_pos 11952
```

```
Write_rows: table id 73 flags: STMT_END_F
### INSERT INTO book3.test_rbr_image
### SET
###    @1=1
###    @2=2
###    @3='3'
###    @4=NULL
...
```

Although we only added three column values to the row, all four of the column values end up in the binary log. The value for the fourth column in the row (in bold), in this case column comment, is set to NULL even though we did not reference the column in the INSERT statement.

When binlog_row_image is set to minimal, only the changed columns are added to the binary log. The following is an example SQL statement with this format:

```
master> SET SESSION binlog_row_image=minimal;
master> SHOW MASTER STATUS\G
*********************** 1. row ***********************
            File: mysql-bin.000002
        Position: 12169
...
master> INSERT INTO test_rbr_image(id) VALUES(4);
```

Let's take a look inside the binary log using the mysqlbinlog client utility:

```
$ mysqlbinlog --base64-output=DECODE-ROWS --verbose  \
   --start-position=12169 mysql-bin.000002
...
# at 12298
#120613 17:22:43 server id 1  end_log_pos 12298
Table_map: `book3`.`test_rbr_image` mapped to number 73
#120613 17:22:43 server id 1  end_log_pos 12332
Write_rows: table id 73 flags: STMT_END_F
### INSERT INTO book3.test_rbr_image
### SET
###    @1=4
# at 12332
```

You can see there is only one (1) column specified in the binary log for this event. It is relatively easy to see that with this new behavior less disk space and network bandwidth will be used during replication.

The last setting for `binlog_row_image` is `noblob`. In this case all non-text or blob columns are omitted from the binary log unless those columns are being added or changed. For example:

```
master> SET SESSION binlog_row_image=noblob;
master> SHOW MASTER STATUS\G
*************************** 1. row ***************************
            File: mysql-bin.000002
        Position: 12359
...
master> INSERT INTO test_rbr_image(id,var2) VALUES(5,'abc');
$ mysqlbinlog --base64-output=DECODE-ROWS --verbose  \
  --start-position=12359 mysql-bin.000002
# at 12488
#120613 17:44:48 server id 1  end_log_pos 12488
Table_map: `book3`.`test_rbr_image` mapped to number 73
#120613 17:44:48 server id 1  end_log_pos 12526
Write_rows: table id 73 flags: STMT_END_F
### INSERT INTO book3.test_rbr_image
### SET
###   @1=5
###   @2=NULL
###   @3='abc'
```

It is also important to mention that when using `minimal` or `noblob` for `binlog_row_image` the tables from the master host to the slave(s) need to have the same columns in the same order with the same data type and identical primary keys.

More information can be found at http://dev.mysql.com/doc/refman/5.6/en/replication-options-binary-log.html#sysvar_binlog_row_image.

New Replication Management Features

The MySQL server and client utilities have always been easy to use, and now there are two additions that make administration more robust. Binary log backups through the `mysqlbinlog` client utility and Universally Unique Identifiers (UUID) are now available in MySQL 5.6.

Remote Binary Log Backup

When running point in time recovery it is necessary to save the master binary logs. This is generally implemented by copying binary logs to a shared storage device or another server. The `mysqlbinlog` client utility now has this functionality built in, making it easier to copy binary logs to different servers and locations.

There are several new options for `mysqlbinlog` that are used to back up binary logs to a second server:

- **`--raw`** This option ensures that the copied binary log will be in the same format as the original and not in text format.

- **`--read-from-remote-server`** | **`-R`** This option tells `mysqlbinlog` to connect to a server and request the binary log(s) from the host.

- **`--read-from-remote-master=type`** This option reads the binary logs. The value of `BINLOG-DUMP-NON-GTIDS` is equivalent to `--read-from-remote-server`. The other valid value is `BINLOG-DUMP_GTIDS`.

- **`--to-last-log`** Will gather all binary logs starting with the binary log specified to the last binary log on the server.

- **`--stop-never`** Will run `mysqlbinlog` in a daemon mode and stay connected to the server after reaching the end of the last log. If `--stop-never` is specified, it is not necessary to add the `--to-last-log` option, as this is implied with `--stop-never`.

- **`--results-file`** When added in conjunction with `--raw` the value of this option will be added as a prefix name to the output files.

In the following examples we will be using the nine (9) binary logs specified here:

```
master> SHOW BINARY LOGS;
+--------------------+-----------+
| Log_name           | File_size |
+--------------------+-----------+
| binary-logs.000001 |     60286 |
| binary-logs.000002 |    909656 |
| binary-logs.000003 | 124878902 |
| binary-logs.000004 |  52616276 |
| binary-logs.000005 |    158611 |
| binary-logs.000006 | 700233141 |
| binary-logs.000007 |  18865438 |
| binary-logs.000008 | 342192894 |
| binary-logs.000009 |      1364 |
+--------------------+-----------+
```

To make a static backup of all the binary logs, you can use the following command:

```
$ mysqlbinlog -usomeuser --host=master.example.com \
--port=3306 --raw --read-from-remote-server \
--to-last-log binary-logs.000001
```

On the host where the `mysqlbinlog` command was executed we can now see the binary logs on the file system:

```
$ ls -l |awk '{print $9 "   |   " $5}'
binary-logs.000001  |    60286
binary-logs.000002  |    909656
binary-logs.000003  |    124878902
binary-logs.000004  |    52616276
binary-logs.000005  |    158611
binary-logs.000006  |    700233141
binary-logs.000007  |    18865438
binary-logs.000008  |    342192894
binary-logs.000009  |    1364
```

To run `mysqlbinlog` in daemon mode and keep a live running backup of all binary logs, you can use the following command:

```
$ mysqlbinlog -uroot --host=master.example.com --port=3306 \
--raw --read-from-remote-server \
--stop-never binary-logs.000001
```

The binary backups will continue to be recorded while `mysqlbinlog` is running with the `--stop-never` option. After some write operations on the master host you can see that the byte value of `binary-logs.000009` has changed to `585352` from its previous value of `1364` on the backup server:

```
$ ls -l |awk '{print $9 "   |   " $5}'
binary-logs.000007  |    18865438
binary-logs.000008  |    342192894
binary-logs.000009  |    585352
```

Binary logs will continue to be recorded up until `mysqlbinlog` is stopped or the master server is shut down. Appropriate system monitoring should be in place if this daemon operation is implemented to ensure this does not stop unexpectedly.

For more information visit http://dev.mysql.com/doc/refman/5.6/en/mysqlbinlog.html.

Universally Unique Identifier (UUID)

The UUID is now added to every server running MySQL version 5.6 and above. This addition allows easier tracking and auto discovery for remote monitoring and inventory systems. The new system variable server_uuid is accessible with a SELECT statement and, if replication is turned on, through the SHOW SLAVE STATUS command. For example:

```
master> SELECT @@GLOBAL.server_uuid;
+----------------------------------------+
| @@GLOBAL.server_uuid                   |
+----------------------------------------+
| cae53eb6-1aa8-11e1-a608-00238b979631   |
+----------------------------------------+
```

This information is stored in the auto.cnf file found in the data directory:

```
$ cat auto.cnf
[auto]
server-uuid= cae53eb6-1aa8-11e1-a608-00238b979631
```

Viewing the master host UUID on the slave host:

```
slave> SHOW SLAVE STATUS\G
*********************** 1. row ***********************
               Slave_IO_State: Waiting for master to send event
                  Master_Host: master.example.com
                  Master_User: repl
                  Master_Port: 3306
...
             Master_Server_Id: 1
                  Master_UUID: cae53eb6-1aa8-11e1-a608-00238b979631
...
```

For more information see http://dev.mysql.com/doc/refman/5.6/en/replication-options.html#sysvar_server_uuid.

Global Transaction Identifier (GTID)

GTIDs make it easier to keep track of replication between a master and slave and with other topologies, including cascading and circular replication. Building a mechanism in house to keep track of replication, run failovers, and promote slaves is no longer necessary with the new GTID utilities that accompany this new feature.

Global transaction identifiers are composed of the original master host UUID and a sequence that is automatically generated for every event written to the binary log. This means that every transaction written to the binary log has a unique GTID assigned to it, making it very easy to track and compare the progress of replicated events on every slave host in a replication topology. To enable GTID usage you need all four of the following configuration variables in the my.cnf file:

```
[mysqld]
log-bin
log-slave-updates
gtid-mode=ON
disable-gtid-unsafe-statements
```

There are several limitations to GTID usage. GTID will not work when:

- Using nontransactional statements, i.e., MyISAM tables, including for example running the mysql_secure_installation command

- CREATE TABLE ... SELECT

- Temporary tables within transactions

This means that you will not be able to use GTID unless you are using InnoDB specifically. Using GTID-based replication is different from using traditional replication. When gtid_mode is active on all master and slave servers you will be able to use MASTER_AUTO_POSITION in the CHANGE MASTER TO statement. MASTER_AUTO_POSITION is new in MySQL 5.6.5 and utilizes the GTID on the master to synchronize slave servers within a replication topology. If you do choose to use MASTER_AUTO_POSITION, you will no longer be able to specify MASTER_LOG_FILE and MASTER_LOG_POS in the CHANGE MASTER TO statement. Here is an example of MASTER_AUTO_POSITION usage:

```
slave> CHANGE MASTER TO
    ->    MASTER_HOST='master.example.com',
    ->    MASTER_USER='repl',
    ->    MASTER_PASSWORD='somepassword,
    ->    MASTER_PORT=3306,
    ->    MASTER_AUTO_POSITION = 1;
Query OK, 0 rows affected, 2 warnings (0.24 sec)
```

There are two warnings that have been added in version 5.6 when running a CHANGE MASTER TO statement. The following is the output of SHOW WARNINGS after the CHANGE MASTER TO statement has been issued:

```
slave> SHOW WARNINGS\G
*********************** 1. row ************************
  Level: Note
   Code: 1756
Message: Sending passwords in plain text without SSL/TLS is extremely
 insecure.
*********************** 2. row ************************
  Level: Note
   Code: 1757
Message: Storing MySQL user name or password information in the master.info
 repository is not secure and is therefore not recommended. Please see the
 MySQL Manual for more about this issue and possible alternatives.
```

NOTE   *The output specifies MySQL best practices for securing replication and storing passwords.*

We can now start GTID-based replication on the slave host and view the corresponding replication thread connection on the master host:

```
slave> START SLAVE;

master> SHOW PROCESSLIST\G
*********************** 1. row ************************
      Id: 3
    User: repl
    Host: master.example.com:40709
      db: NULL
Command: Binlog Dump GTID
    Time: 65
   State: Master has sent all binlog to slave; waiting
for binlog to be updated
    Info: NULL
```

NOTE   *You can see the* Command *column value now indicates that we are using GTID for replication.*

In the event you would like to move back to non-GTID replication you will need to disable MASTER_AUTO_POSITION and then run the correct CHANGE MASTER TO statement. The following example running GTID-based replication will show the error condition and correct syntax to switch back to non-GTID replication:

```
slave> STOP SLAVE;
slave> SHOW SLAVE STATUS\G
              Slave_IO_State:
                  Master_Host: master.example.com
                  Master_User: repl
```

```
                Master_Port: 3306
              Connect_Retry: 10
            Master_Log_File: binary-logs.000010
          Read_Master_Log_Pos: 191
             Relay_Log_File: mysqld-relay-bin.000003
              Relay_Log_Pos: 365
      Relay_Master_Log_File: binary-logs.000010
           Slave_IO_Running: No
          Slave_SQL_Running: No
            Replicate_Do_DB:
        Replicate_Ignore_DB:
         Replicate_Do_Table:
     Replicate_Ignore_Table:
    Replicate_Wild_Do_Table:
 Replicate_Wild_Ignore_Table:
                 Last_Errno: 0
                 Last_Error:
               Skip_Counter: 0
        Exec_Master_Log_Pos: 191
            Relay_Log_Space: 784
            Until_Condition: None
             Until_Log_File:
              Until_Log_Pos: 0
          Master_SSL_Allowed: No
         Master_SSL_CA_File:
         Master_SSL_CA_Path:
            Master_SSL_Cert:
          Master_SSL_Cipher:
             Master_SSL_Key:
      Seconds_Behind_Master: NULL
Master_SSL_Verify_Server_Cert: No
              Last_IO_Errno: 0
              Last_IO_Error:
             Last_SQL_Errno: 0
             Last_SQL_Error:
   Replicate_Ignore_Server_Ids:
            Master_Server_Id: 1
                Master_UUID:
f52e965a-b18d-11e1-bdfe-00238b979631
            Master_Info_File: /local/mysql/slave/master.info
                  SQL_Delay: 0
        SQL_Remaining_Delay: NULL
     Slave_SQL_Running_State:
          Master_Retry_Count: 86400
                Master_Bind:
     Last_IO_Error_Timestamp:
    Last_SQL_Error_Timestamp:
             Master_SSL_Crl:
         Master_SSL_Crlpath:
          Retrieved_Gtid_Set:
           Executed_Gtid_Set:
8A94F357-AAB4-11DF-86AB-C80AA429562:1-9,
F52E965A-B18D-11E1-BDFE-00238B979631:1-155
```

```
slave> CHANGE MASTER TO
    ->    MASTER_HOST='master.example.com',
    ->    MASTER_USER='repl',
    ->    MASTER_PASSWORD='somepassword',
    ->    MASTER_PORT=3306,
    ->    MASTER_LOG_FILE='binary-logs.000010',
    ->    MASTER_LOG_POS=191,
    ->    MASTER_CONNECT_RETRY=10;
ERROR 1775 (HY000): Parameters MASTER_LOG_FILE, MASTER_LOG_POS,
RELAY_LOG_FILE and RELAY_LOG_POS cannot be set when MASTER_AUTO_POSITION
is active.
```

As you can see there is an error when you just issue a CHANGE MAS-TER TO statement. We will now set MASTER_AUTO_POSITION to 0 and re-run the CHANGE MASTER TO statement:

```
slave> CHANGE MASTER TO MASTER_AUTO_POSITION = 0;
slave> CHANGE MASTER TO
    ->    MASTER_HOST='master.example.com',
    ->    MASTER_USER='repl',
    ->    MASTER_PASSWORD='somepassword',
    ->    MASTER_PORT=3306,
    ->    MASTER_LOG_FILE='binary-logs.000010',
    ->    MASTER_LOG_POS=191,
    ->    MASTER_CONNECT_RETRY=10;
 slave> START SLAVE;
```

We are now replicating with non-GTID replication.

More information on GTID configuration setting can be found at http://dev.mysql.com/doc/refman/5.6/en/replication-options-gtids.html.

There are two new utilities, which help monitor and, if needed, promote or fail over to another server in your replication environment. These utilities are discussed in Chapter 5.

Binary Log Group Commit

The most recent version of MySQL 5.6.6 (2012-08-07) includes a feature to improve performance of binary log writing. By grouping several writes together in a high volume environment, throughput can be greatly improved. This feature is very important when ensuring maximum durability via the sync_binlog=1 setting. No additional configuration is necessary as this is enabled by default. This feature introduces the configuration variables bin-log_order_commits, binlog_max_flush_queue_time, and innodb_flush_log_at_timeout to provide additional compatibility and fine-tuning option.

More information including a detailed technical description can be found at http://mysqlmusings.blogspot.in/2012/06/binary-log-group-commit-in-mysql-56.html.

Initial work on improving group commit was first included with MariaDB, a fully compatible version of MySQL. This work by Monty Program AB was provided as part of the MySQL open source license for Oracle or any other organization to implement or modify. More information on this work is available at http://kristiannielsen.livejournal.com/12254.html.

Balancing Read and Write Load

With the introduction of a MySQL topology using replication, your application may require modification to support read operations and write operations with different connection parameters. Fortunately, several of the MySQL connectors provide this functionality natively to minimize the requirements for application modifications.

Connector/J for Java has enabled the splitting of read and write SQL statements for many years. Recent improvements in Connector/J 5.1.12 and 5.1.13 have further improved these load balancing features to include failover support. More information is available at http://dev.mysql.com/doc/refman/5.0/en/connector-j-usagenotes-j2ee-concepts-managing-load-balanced-connections.html and http://dev.mysql.com/doc/refman/5.0/en/connector-j-usagenotes-j2ee-concepts-load-balancing-failover.html.

The PHP native driver (mysqlnd) also provides appropriate connection management for reads and writes. Refer to http://dev.mysql.com/doc/refman/5.5/en/apis-php-book.mysqlnd-ms.html and http://blog.ulf-wendel.de/2012/peclmysqlnd_ms-14-a-failover-standby-using-weightedprioritized-load-balancing/ for more information. This driver is the default in PHP 5.4 and higher. You can also find information in the PHP reference manual at http://php.net/manual/en/mysqlnd-ms.rwsplit.php.

MySQL proxy was another product to consider for load balancing. Available from http://dev.mysql.com/downloads/mysql-proxy/, this product has stalled in development in recent years and future work is undetermined. An example for load balancing and splitting connections with MySQL proxy can be found at http://agiletesting.blogspot.com/2009/04/mysql-load-balancing-and-read-write.html.

Additional products can be used to manage load balancing read connections to a pool of slaves. The primary concern is the necessary management and monitoring of replication lag, and the proactive removal of slave servers to ensure data is consistent.

Conclusion

This chapter has covered many new features of MySQL replication in 5.5 and 5.6. For any large MySQL environment using replication with a previous version, these are significant reasons to consider upgrading and benefiting from performance, data integrity, network optimizations, and improved failover capabilities when replication is an important component of your MySQL topology.

Examples and links in this chapter are available for download from http://EffectiveMySQL.com/book/replication-techniques.

4

Using Multi-Master Replication

MySQL replication can be used for many benefits, including supporting scalability and higher availability. By default, MySQL replication does not support an environment that manages failover situations, or writing concurrently to multiple servers in a replication topology, without additional configuration and management.

In this chapter we will discuss:

- Configuring MySQL replication to support failover
- Demonstrating the manual steps for failover and failback
- More advanced replication topologies

MySQL Replication Failover Capabilities

A common way to set up a highly available (HA) MySQL environment is to use a multi-master topology with two servers. Multi-master, also known as a MySQL pair, is configured with two servers, and both servers can act as a master and slave in replication terms. In this situation this is an active/passive master configuration that is a common MySQL deployment approach. A true active/active master/master MySQL configuration is when both servers are supporting write activity at the same time. This type of setup is not typically recommended, given the number of data and scalability problems you may encounter. Writing to both servers does not actually increase throughput but only adds a level of redundancy. This configuration makes failure situations more complex in order to support the same amount of writes on one server when the volume is supported with two servers under normal conditions.

A better practice is to set up a multi-master environment with two servers, where writes are supported on one server at a time and the other server is acting as a standby that can support read load.

Active/Passive Multi-Master Replication

Multi-master replication is when each server replicates to the other, so server A would replicate to server B and server B would replicate to server A. An active/passive or active/standby configuration is a safe approach to run a multi-master environment to support higher availability. This means that one server, the active server, will support all write activity along with reads and the other server, the passive server, only supports read activity if necessary. The passive or standby server in this case will be ready and available if the active server should fail or a planned failover occurs. Figure 4-1 shows a normal master and slave topology with a single replication stream.

Figure 4-1   *MySQL master/slave replication*

Figure 4-2 shows an improved multi-master topology with two replication streams.

Required Multi-Master Configuration Settings

A multi-master topology is relatively easy to set up. In addition to the configuration variables needed for standard replication (server-id and log-bin) there is one more mandatory configuration variable when setting up multi-master replication:

```
# my.cnf
[mysqld]
log-slave-updates
```

Used in conjunction with log-bin, this option enables a slave host to write activity from the SQL slave thread to its own binary log.

Optional Multi-Master Configuration Settings

It is highly recommended to set the passive server to read only. It is a requirement of the failover steps to ensure that read-only is set to FALSE at the appropriate time to enable future writes.

```
# my.cnf
[mysqld]
read-only
```

This causes the host to only accept write activity from the I/O thread or from users that have the SUPER privilege granted.

Figure 4-2   *MySQL master/master replication*

TIP   *A system monitoring alert check for identifying any users with SUPER privilege other than a predefined list will provide protection in the future.*

Other Configuration Variables to Consider

There are other options that you may need to consider when setting up multi-master replication and you plan to write to both servers simultaneously. The following settings are not required in an active/passive setup; however, if you plan to write to both hosts simultaneously you will need to set these.

NOTE   *The following variables protect against duplication of auto-increment fields only. Duplicates can still occur on the server if you write the same data to both masters and update the same row(s). In this case, MySQL may silently overwrite records, leading to invalid or missing data. You can also encounter key clashes when UNIQUE keys are present.*

- `auto_increment_increment`   Controls the interval between successive column values.
- `auto_increment_offset`   Determines the starting point of the AUTO_INCREMENT column.
- `slave_exec_mode`   If `slave_exec_mode` is IDEMPOTENT, which is generally only used for multi-master replication and the MySQL Cluster NDB storage engine, a failure to apply changes when using row-based replication (RBR) because the original row cannot be found does not trigger an error, causing replication to fail.

CAUTION   *Setting `slave_exec_mode` to IDEMPOTENT can cause data drift between the master and slave.*

NOTE   *If you have set `replicate-do-db` or `replicate-ignore-db`, you will need to ensure these are set the same on both servers.*

Example Configuration

The following outlines the recommended configuration file options for a MySQL pair or MySQL active/passive master setup. For this chapter we will use the VirtualBox environment that is defined in the appendix with the servers running MySQL 5.5. These server names are `alpha` and `beta`.

Active Server (alpha)
On the master server, the following configuration is defined:

```
[mysqld]
server-id = 51
log-bin = mysql-bin
relay-log = relay-log
read_only = FALSE
log-slave-updates
skip-slave-start
```

Passive/Standby Server (beta)
On the failover server, the following configuration is defined:

```
[mysqld]
server-id = 52
log-bin = mysql-bin
relay-log = relay-log
read_only = TRUE
log-slave-updates
```

NOTE   The slave replication that is operating on the master is disabled on initial server startup. This is important for certain specific error situations with multiple replication streams for a failed failover or unexpected server restart. This does require an additional management check and execution step when MySQL is initiated on both servers. An alternative view is to disable slave startup on both servers. This ensures the configuration files are more consistent between both servers, and then ensures a human verification step is necessary before starting replication.

CAUTION   These configuration settings are defined to demonstrate the setup and manual failover of an active/passive environment. The use of appropriate additional configuration to maintain durability is important for any production system.

Replication Setup

The key to this setup and failover is the configuration of replication between both servers. Replication only travels one way, from the master to the slave. When setting up multi-master there are two replication streams to set up. Replication runs from the active server to the passive server, where the passive server is the active server's slave. Replication also runs from the passive server to the active server, where the active server acts as a slave to the passive server. This means that SHOW MASTER STATUS and SHOW SLAVE STATUS work on both servers.

Obtain Master Status on Active Server

Replication requires the master log file and position available from SHOW MASTER STATUS. This can be obtained from both servers:

```
alpha> SHOW MASTER STATUS\G
*********************** 1. row ***********************
            File: mysql-bin.000001
        Position: 107
    Binlog_Do_DB:
Binlog_Ignore_DB:
beta> SHOW MASTER STATUS\G
*********************** 1. row ***********************
            File: mysql-bin.000001
        Position: 107
    Binlog_Do_DB:
Binlog_Ignore_DB:
```

Create Replication User

In order for a slave server to use replication, an appropriate user has to be configured on each server:

```
alpha> GRANT REPLICATION SLAVE ON *.* TO repl@beta IDENTIFIED BY 'repl';
beta>  GRANT REPLICATION SLAVE ON *.* TO repl@alpha IDENTIFIED BY 'repl';
```

TIP   It is recommended that when using GRANT with IDENTIFIED BY you first determine the hash of the password and use this value directly rather than a clear text password. The syntax shown here is for readability purposes and is not secure.

Configure First Replication Stream

The active and passive server can now be connected for replication with the CHANGE MASTER TO command:

```
beta> CHANGE MASTER TO
    -> MASTER_HOST='alpha', MASTER_PORT=3306,
    -> MASTER_USER='repl', MASTER_PASSWORD='repl',
    -> MASTER_LOG_FILE='mysql-bin.000001', MASTER_LOG_POS=107,
    -> MASTER_CONNECT_RETRY=10;
beta> START SLAVE;
beta> SHOW SLAVE STATUS\G
```

```
*************************** 1. row ***************************
Slave_IO_State: Waiting for master to send event
            Master_Host: alpha
            Master_User: repl
            Master_Port: 3306
          Connect_Retry: 10
        Master_Log_File: mysql-bin.000001
    Read_Master_Log_Pos: 364
         Relay_Log_File: relay-log.000002
          Relay_Log_Pos: 510
  Relay_Master_Log_File: mysql-bin.000001
       Slave_IO_Running: Yes
      Slave_SQL_Running: Yes
...
         Master_Server_Id: 51
```

Configure Second Replication Stream

Repeating the same steps on the active server, which also acts as a slave server, configure the second replication stream with CHANGE MASTER TO:

```
alpha> CHANGE MASTER TO
    -> MASTER_HOST='beta', MASTER_PORT=3306,
    -> MASTER_USER='repl', MASTER_PASSWORD='repl',
    -> MASTER_LOG_FILE='mysql-bin.000001', MASTER_LOG_POS=107,
    -> MASTER_CONNECT_RETRY=10;
alpha> START SLAVE;
alpha> SHOW SLAVE STATUS\G
*************************** 1. row ***************************
            Slave_IO_State: Waiting for master to send event
            Master_Host: beta
            Master_User: repl
            Master_Port: 3306
          Connect_Retry: 10
        Master_Log_File: mysql-bin.000001
    Read_Master_Log_Pos: 504
         Relay_Log_File: relay-log.000002
          Relay_Log_Pos: 393
  Relay_Master_Log_File: mysql-bin.000001
       Slave_IO_Running: Yes
      Slave_SQL_Running: Yes
...
         Master_Server_Id: 52
```

Multi-master replication is now up and running.

CAUTION   *With multi-master replication, the SHOW MASTER STATUS and SHOW SLAVE STATUS commands operate on both systems, unlike a traditional setup where SHOW MASTER STATUS displays binary log information, and SHOW SLAVE STATUS displays replication information on the slave.*

Multi-Master Replication Verification

A simple verification step can be used to ensure that both replication streams are working. That is, a *DML* or *DDL* statement on the active master is replicated to the slave, and a *DML* or *DDL* statement on the slave (i.e., the passive master) is replicated to the master. This verification is used to demonstrate and confirm operation.

This verification only works when we use a MySQL user that has been granted the SUPER privilege along with CREATE, DROP, SELECT, INSERT, and DELETE. The SUPER privilege bypasses `read_only` on the slave host and allows DML queries to run on any production system without impact.

CAUTION   *Never use a user with SUPER privilege for application access to your data. When an application requires this privilege to manage objects, for example, triggers in MySQL 5.0, it is recommended that a dedicated DBA user with localhost only privileges is defined and used.*

First Replication Stream Verification

On the active master server:

```
alpha> CREATE SCHEMA IF NOT EXISTS verify_failover;
alpha> USE verify_failover
alpha> CREATE TABLE rpl_test (id SERIAL) ENGINE = InnoDB;
alpha> INSERT INTO rpl_test(id) VALUES(1),(2),(3);
alpha> SELECT * FROM rpl_test;
+----+
| id |
+----+
|  1 |
|  2 |
|  3 |
+----+
3 rows in set (0.01 sec)
```

On the passive master server:

```
beta> USE verify_failover
beta> SELECT * FROM rpl_test;
+----+
| id |
+----+
|  1 |
|  2 |
|  3 |
+----+
3 rows in set (0.01 sec)
```

Second Replication Stream Verification

On the passive master server:

```
beta> USE verify_failover
beta> DELETE FROM rpl_test WHERE id=2;
beta> INSERT INTO rpl_test(id) VALUES (11),(22);
beta> SELECT * FROM rpl_test;
+----+
| id |
+----+
|  1 |
|  3 |
| 11 |
| 22 |
+----+
4 rows in set (0.00 sec)
```

On the active master server:

```
alpha> USE verify_failover
alpha> SELECT * FROM rpl_test;
+----+
| id |
+----+
|  1 |
|  3 |
| 11 |
| 22 |
+----+
4 rows in set (0.00 sec)
alpha> DROP SCHEMA verify_failover;
```

And a final verification on the passive master server, which should result in the error provided:

```
beta> USE verify_failover
ERROR 1049 (42000): Unknown database 'verify_failover'
```

Application Usage and Verification

The final setup step is to define an application user for normal access and for any further testing during failover:

```
alpha> CREATE SCHEMA book3;
alpha> CREATE USER app@'192.168.1.%' IDENTIFIED BY 'sakila';
alpha> GRANT INSERT,UPDATE,DELETE,SELECT ON book3.* TO app@'192.168.1.%';
alpha> USE book3
alpha> CREATE TABLE verify (id SERIAL) ENGINE = InnoDB;
```

Manual Failover Process

In this section we will step through the manual slave promotion process. This example is intended to highlight the complexities of automating this process. In summary:

- Restrict write access to active master
- Verify no write access
- Ensure MySQL replication is up to date
- Enable write access on failover master
- Support application needs

Restrict Write Access

Stop application access to the active master server but keep MySQL running. You accomplish this by first setting read_only to TRUE and optionally changing or dropping application user access or setting an appropriate firewall rule with iptables.

In this case, set the active master read_only variable to TRUE. This operation requires a user with the SUPER privilege.

```
alpha> SET GLOBAL read_only = TRUE;
```

At this time you should also modify the default configuration of MySQL on the server to match the new read-only status. This is necessary to define the startup state if MySQL is restarted at a future time. If the active master also has skip-slave-start defined and this is not specified also on the failover master, this should also be removed to reflect the startup state of the passive master.

Verify No Write Access

Verify the active master is read only with a user that does not have the SUPER privilege. It is recommended that you do not run any SQL that would damage your current data:

```
$ mysql -uapp -psakila -halpha book3
alpha> INSERT INTO verify VALUES(NULL);
ERROR 1290 (HY000): The MySQL server is running with the --read-only option
 so it cannot execute this statement
```

Ensure Replication Is Up to Date

A verification of the master and slave status is necessary to ensure the slave that will be promoted to the active master has replication running and has completed all transactions.

On the current active master, obtain the current master replication position:

```
alpha> SHOW MASTER STATUS\G
*************************** 1. row ***************************
            File: mysql-bin.000003
        Position: 26312
    Binlog_Do_DB:
Binlog_Ignore_DB:
```

On the failover slave, confirm the position matches the master:

```
beta> SHOW SLAVE STATUS\G
*************************** 1. row ***************************
...
             Master_Log_File: mysql-bin.000003
...
            Slave_IO_Running: Yes
           Slave_SQL_Running: Yes
...
         Exec_Master_Log_Pos: 26312
...
            Master_Server_Id: 51
```

CAUTION   *This step relies on the requirement that no additional data changes are occurring on the master. The read-only status can be easily overridden by any user that has the SUPER privilege. This is another primary reason why an application user should never have this privilege.*

Enable Write Access on New Master

At this time, the current master is defined as read-only and replication is confirmed as operational. A sanity check is shown to indicate the new failover master is not currently supporting writes:

```
$ mysql -uapp -psakila -hbeta book3
beta> INSERT INTO verify VALUES(NULL);
ERROR 1290 (HY000): The MySQL server is running with the --read-only option
 so it cannot execute this statement
```

CAUTION   *If the new failover master fails the read-only check, failover may still continue. However, this is an indication that data inconsistency is possible. Having an appropriate check of data consistency via checksums is an important monitoring step in a multi-master environment.*

Using a user with the SUPER privilege, the slave that is now the new active master is enabled to accept writes:

```
beta> SET GLOBAL read_only = FALSE;
$ mysql -uapp -psakila -hbeta book3
```

A final sanity check with an application user with appropriate privileges can be performed, i.e., the earlier check that failed due to the read-only state:

```
beta> INSERT INTO verify VALUES(NULL);
Query OK, 1 row affected (0.01 sec)
```

Additional steps, for example, enabling suitable application user permissions that are disabled by default, or removing a firewall restriction, may also be needed depending on what additional steps are required in the environment.

TIP   *Additional care has to be taken when adding and removing MySQL user privileges, as the replication of the* mysql *schema would cause this to be replicated also. Certain commands may need to be excluded from binary logging.*

Verifying Resumed Operations

A final check should be performed with transaction throughput on the new active master to ensure the second replication stream is operating as expected. A SHOW PROCESSLIST will confirm statements are being executed on the new active master. It is important that the SHOW MASTER STATUS and SHOW SLAVE STATUS is performed on the correct servers, i.e., the inverse of what was performed before commencing the manual failover:

```
beta> SHOW MASTER STATUS\G
*************************** 1. row ***************************
            File: mysql-bin.000001
        Position: 33426
    Binlog_Do_DB:
Binlog_Ignore_DB:

alpha > SHOW SLAVE STATUS\G
*************************** 1. row ***************************
               Slave_IO_State: Waiting for master to send event
                  Master_Host: beta
```

```
            Master_User: repl
            Master_Port: 3306
          Connect_Retry: 10
        Master_Log_File: mysql-bin.000001
    Read_Master_Log_Pos: 33426
         Relay_Log_File: relay-log.000002
          Relay_Log_Pos: 1044
  Relay_Master_Log_File: mysql-bin.000001
       Slave_IO_Running: Yes
      Slave_SQL_Running: Yes
...

      Exec_Master_Log_Pos: 33426
...

        Master_Server_Id: 52
1 row in set (0.00 sec)
```

CAUTION   *The location of the* `Read_Master_Log_Pos` *column in the SHOW SLAVE STATUS output should not be mistaken for the need to verify the* `Exec_Master_Log_Pos` *that occurs later in the output.*

NOTE   *It is very easy to be confused when running SHOW MASTER STATUS and SHOW SLAVE STATUS on the wrong servers in a MySQL pair configuration. Both servers act as a master and a slave in a replication sense.*

Manage Application Access

In these examples, there is a clear manual understanding of which server is the active master and which server becomes the new active master. In an application situation, that must be pre-determined or managed in addition to the steps just highlighted to minimize application downtime. A common approach is to use a virtual IP (VIP) address that may optionally resolve to a common *DNS* name. The application configuration always communicates with the VIP or common name rather than the physical IP address of the active master server. The failover approach then manages the changing of the VIP to point to the correct server that is acting as an active master. For example, add a VIP address to an existing physical network adapter on the master:

```
alpha$ sudo ifconfig eth1:0 192.168.1.101 up
alpha$ ifconfig
...
eth1      Link encap:Ethernet  HWaddr 08:00:27:d4:5f:91
          inet addr:192.168.1.51  Bcast:192.168.1.255  Mask:255.255.255.0
          inet6 addr: fe80::a00:27ff:fed4:5f91/64 Scope:Link
          UP BROADCAST RUNNING MULTICAST  MTU:1500  Metric:1
          RX packets:370474 errors:0 dropped:0 overruns:0 frame:0
```

```
          TX packets:1184045 errors:0 dropped:0 overruns:0 carrier:0
          collisions:0 txqueuelen:1000
          RX bytes:31804703 (31.8 MB)  TX bytes:1671393644 (1.6 GB)

eth1:0    Link encap:Ethernet  HWaddr 08:00:27:d4:5f:91
          inet addr:192.168.1.101  Bcast:192.168.1.255  Mask:255.255.255.0
          UP BROADCAST RUNNING MULTICAST  MTU:1500  Metric:1
...
```

In addition, this should be added to the `/etc/network/interfaces` file, or applicable file for your operating system, to preserve this state when the system is restarted.

The application is modified to always connect to this IP address or a DNS entry. The use of an IP address for database connections removes additional DNS translation overhead and possible DNS server lookup failures. For this example the new host information is defined on all servers in the test environment:

```
#/etc/hosts
192.168.1.101 master
```

When performing a failover, the removal of the IP address from the master should be performed when the server is set to read-only:

```
alpha$ sudo ifconfig eth1:0 down
```

When read-only access is removed on the failover master, the IP address should then be enabled on the new active master:

```
beta$ sudo ifconfig eth1:0 192.168.1.101 up
beta$ ifconfig
```

The application will operate with this VIP because the application user privileges were defined for a wildcard host, i.e., 192.168.1.%

A further complication with this network mapping is you may need to have a network admin run an Address Resolution Protocol (ARP) cache clear to ensure the passive slave's Media Access Control (MAC) address will be assigned to the VIP. ARP is primarily used to connect the OSI Model Network Layer (Layer 3) to the Data Link Layer (Layer 2). For most networks this refers to IP and MAC mapping. The `arp` and `arping` commands can be used in identification and notification steps. This link provides a good introduction to these commands: http://homepage.smc.edu/morgan_david/cs75/labs/arp-and-arping.htm.

Review

The manual slave promotion process has a lot of steps and is prone to human error. Floating IP addresses or VIPs add a level of complexity in that a network administrator will need to be involved, plus a MySQL administrator may not have access to run the IP removal and addition to the servers, possibly needing a system administrator to run those commands.

Certain cloud infrastructures may not be able to assign a second IP address that can float from server to server. Until very recently, it was not possible to have a second IP address with Amazon Web Services (AWS). This was announced on July 6, 2012 (see http://aws.typepad.com/aws/2012/07/multiple-ip-addresses-for-ec2-instances-in-a-virtual-private-cloud.html). This requires a different approach to steps 6, 7, and 8 earlier, which may include changing a connection string in your application and restarting your web server.

Real World Usage Complications

While these steps hint at a plausible solution, the reality is there are many additional situations where this process has potential flaws or additional complications. In a fully controlled situation, these initial steps do provide a viable solution. Some of the complexities that have to be considered include

- Management or administrative processes that are executed on the master, for example, batch processes. These should be stopped before a controlled failover. These processes may require additional configuration if they are designed to run on the local master server.

- The unavailability of the actual master server does not enable a controlled failover. There is no guarantee MySQL replication is up to date, and the managed state of changing the master read-only at runtime and configuration is not possible. If a VIP is in use, this is not actively removed. This situation can result in a split-brain where both masters could receive data. This is a disaster situation that can cause data corruption.

- The use of persistent connections, for example, Connector/J, can add additional complexities to connection management. Additional testing and error validation are necessary to ensure the application supports the physical change of the underlying server that is servicing requests with the VIP. It is recommended that a flush of persistent connection pool on application servers is performed to minimize complexities during the failover.

- Long running queries on the master may result in additional complications. While the setting of read-only will address new writes, including within a transaction, any long running queries should be monitored before completing a failover.

- In an uncontrolled failover situation the write consistency, especially of slave information, may cause replication issues. Additional configuration settings may be necessary to ensure file synchronization of important replication information; however, this has a performance impact for all transactions. The specific issue of file consistency of replication slave information has been addressed with crash-consistent slaves available in MySQL 5.6.

- A management server or arbitrator can be used to manage split-brain or other network unavailability situations. When the MySQL pair is initiated, each server asks an arbitrator (i.e., a third party) who is the master rather than starting with a default state.

- Unless continuously checksummed, there is no absolute confirmation that data on both servers is synchronized.

Additional Slave Servers

While this initial example used two MySQL servers, it is possible to have additional replication slaves in the MySQL topology. The use of a MySQL pair, i.e., two servers to support writes and additional slaves to support reads, can easily be supported with the described multi-master replication environment. These additional servers can be managed with:

- Replication slaves connected with the active master.

- Replication slaves moved from the active master to the new master before the failover occurs.

In the example, by adding a third server using the virtual environment defined in the appendix, these steps can be demonstrated.

Slave Server Setup (gamma)

On a new slave server, the following configuration is defined:

```
[mysqld]
server-id = 53
relay-log = relay-log
read_only=TRUE
```

The setup of the slave repeats the same steps for the initial replication streams. First create an appropriate replication user:

```
alpha> GRANT REPLICATION SLAVE ON *.* TO repl@gamma
IDENTIFIED BY 'repl';
```

Initiate replication on the new slave:

```
gamma> CHANGE MASTER TO
    -> MASTER_HOST='alpha', MASTER_PORT=3306,
    -> MASTER_USER='repl', MASTER_PASSWORD='repl',
    -> MASTER_LOG_FILE='mysql-bin.000001', MASTER_LOG_POS=107,
    -> MASTER_CONNECT_RETRY=10;
gamma> START SLAVE;
gamma> DO SLEEP(2);
gamma> SHOW SLAVE STATUS\G
```

The MySQL topology now has three MySQL servers, a master server (alpha), a failover master (beta), and an additional slave (gamma). Figure 4-3 shows the servers and the replication streams currently configured. This figure includes an indication that additional slave servers can be added in the same fashion.

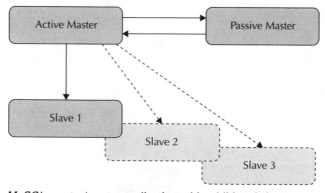

Figure 4-3 *MySQL master/master replication with additional slaves*

It is also possible to split slaves between both the active and passive master and not move slaves during the failover. This has the added benefit that in an uncontrolled failure half the slaves are always in operation. This also has the added risk that with certain replication failure situations, half the slaves are out of date.

Slave Server Management

As described in the introduction, the key to using additional slaves effectively is for the slaves to connect to the active master. In a failover situation the slave should be moved to the new master prior to failover. This involves the following steps:

1. Ensure slave is operating and up to date.

2. Obtain a consistent view of both replication streams on the failover server.

Ensure Slave Operation

```
gamma> SHOW SLAVE STATUS\G
*************************** 1. row ***************************
               Slave_IO_State: Waiting for master to send event
                  Master_Host: alpha
                  Master_User: repl
                  Master_Port: 3306
                Connect_Retry: 10
              Master_Log_File: mysql-bin.000003
...

             Slave_IO_Running: Yes
            Slave_SQL_Running: Yes
...

          Exec_Master_Log_Pos: 26661
...

        Seconds_Behind_Master: 0
...

             Master_Server_Id: 51

gamma> STOP SLAVE SQL_THREAD;
```

Prior to stopping the SQL thread, ensure the slave is running (`Slave_IO_Running` and `Slave_SQL_Running`) and slave is up to date (`Seconds_Behind_Master`) and confirm the current master (`Master_Host`).

Determine Failover Position   On the master you are failing over to (i.e., the current passive master and not the host described in the SHOW SLAVE

STATUS output), obtain a consistent snapshot of the slave replication stream and the master replication stream on the instance. For example:

```
beta> STOP SLAVE SQL_THREAD;
beta> SHOW SLAVE STATUS\G
beta> SHOW MASTER STATUS\G
beta> START SLAVE SQL_THREAD;
```

With the SHOW SLAVE STATUS output you have the `Master_Log_File` and the `Exec_Master_Log_Pos`. For example:

```
beta> SHOW SLAVE STATUS\G
...
            Master_Log_File: mysql-bin.000003
...
          Slave_IO_Running: Yes
         Slave_SQL_Running: No
...
       Exec_Master_Log_Pos: 26661
...
```

This is used to construct the SQL statement.

```
START SLAVE UNTIL
  MASTER_LOG_FILE='mysql-bin.000003', MASTER_LOG_POS=26661;
```

With the SHOW MASTER STATUS OUTPUT you have to use the new `File` and `Position`. For example:

```
beta> SHOW MASTER STATUS\G
*************************** 1. row ***************************
            File: mysql-bin.000001
        Position: 33566
    Binlog_Do_DB:
Binlog_Ignore_DB:
```

You can use this to create the following SQL statement:

```
CHANGE MASTER TO
  MASTER_LOG_FILE='mysql-bin.000001', MASTER_LOG_POS=33566;
```

Unfortunately, this is insufficient access to information to obtain the connection details of the new master. There is no easy way to obtain this information in one step. Some information can be obtained and inferred from the SHOW SLAVE STATUS, for example, the `Master_User` and `Master_Port`, providing these are consistent across your topology. Also required are the host and the password. The host can be obtained with the following SQL statement in MySQL 5.1 or better:

```
beta> SELECT variable_value AS host_name
   -> FROM information_schema.global_variables
```

```
   -> WHERE variable_name='hostname';
+-----------+
| host_name |
+-----------+
| beta      |
+-----------+
```

This still leaves the required replication user password. There are two options, either use a known value for the password (i.e., you hardcode this in your subsequent SQL statement), or find all the information and the password by using the second replication stream on the current master in the `master.info` file found in the MySQL data directory:

```
$ cd  /path/to/datadir
$ head -7 master.info | tail -4
beta
repl
repl
3306
```

In plain text you now have all the new master connection details from the existing replication stream that is the slave on the new failover master. This information is used to construct the full SQL statement necessary:

```
CHANGE MASTER TO
  MASTER_HOST='beta', MASTER_USER='repl', MASTER_PASSWORD='repl',
  MASTER_LOG_FILE='mysql-bin.000001', MASTER_LOG_POS=33566;
```

NOTE   *In MySQL 5.6 when using crash-safe slaves, the information from the*
      `master.info` *file is available in the* `mysql.slave_master_info` *table.*

Perform Slave Failover   We now execute on the attached slave that is being moved the following SQL to align the replication stream with the recorded failover position:

```
gamma> START SLAVE UNTIL
    -> MASTER_LOG_FILE='mysql-bin.000003', MASTER_LOG_POS=26661;
gamma> DO SLEEP(1);
gamma> SHOW SLAVE STATUS\G
*************************** 1. row ***************************
...
             Master_Log_File: mysql-bin.000003
...
              Slave_IO_Running: Yes
             Slave_SQL_Running: No
...
        Exec_Master_Log_Pos: 26661
            Until_Condition: Master
```

```
       Until_Log_File: mysql-bin.000003
        Until_Log_Pos: 26661
...
```

A confirmation should be performed to ensure the slave is at the correct location by comparing the `Master_Log_File` + `Exec_Master_Log_Pos` and `Until_Log_File` + `Until_Log_Pos` values.

The final step is to reset the slave and point to the current master position of the failover master:

```
gamma> STOP SLAVE;
gamma> RESET SLAVE;
gamma> CHANGE MASTER TO
    -> MASTER_HOST='beta', MASTER_USER='repl', MASTER_PASSWORD='repl',
    -> MASTER_LOG_FILE=' mysql-bin.000001', MASTER_LOG_POS=33566;
gamma> START SLAVE;
gamma> DO SLEEP(1);
gamma> SHOW SLAVE STATUS\G

*************************** 1. row ***************************
            Slave_IO_State: Waiting for master to send event
               Master_Host: beta
               Master_User: repl
               Master_Port: 3306
             Connect_Retry: 10
...
         Slave_IO_Running: Yes
        Slave_SQL_Running: Yes
...
         Master_Server_Id: 52
1 row in set (0.00 sec)
```

These steps need to be repeated for each attached slave. In an environment when you have a larger number of slaves, the chaining of the slaves via a relay server (aka just another slave) enables you to move just one slave (i.e., the relay slave) to achieve the same result. Figure 4-4 shows an example replication topology between the servers for this situation.

TIP   When using a large number of slaves with a relay slave, the use of the BLACKHOLE storage engine on the relay slave can improve replication performance. This minimizes the writes of the actual data, as the BLACKHOLE engine simply discards the data. What is necessary is the binary log on the relay that is used for replication with all attached slaves.

CAUTION   You should only use the BLACKHOLE storage engine with the technique described above when `binlog-format` is set to STATEMENT.

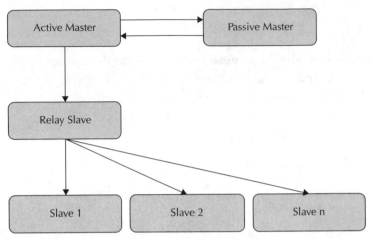

Figure 4-4   *MySQL master/master replication with relay slave*

Read and Write Load Balancing

The implementation of an active/passive multi-master environment generally uses a virtual IP (VIP) to support the management of writes. In an
active/active configuration, the application will need to make the decision
of which master to write to, and balancing these writes may be an important consideration to manage load. The use of additional slave servers for
read scalability also requires the application to support splitting reads and
writes, and also balancing reads between a pool of read slaves if applicable.
Chapter 3 described several techniques for managing these requirements.

Circular Replication

A MySQL pair is the use of two MySQL instances in a multi-master replication configuration. While the recommendation is to use an active/passive
implementation, the same approach is used for an active/active implementation. As previously mentioned, additional configuration settings, for
example, when using auto increment columns, is critical. MySQL replication
does not support collision detection, so depending on the complexity of the
application using the active/active environment, additional tricks are needed
to minimize conditions that may cause replication to break.

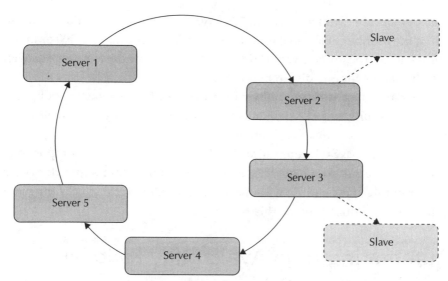

Figure 4-5 *MySQL master/master circular replication*

MySQL can support more than two servers via a circular replication configuration. Again, while not recommended this is indeed possible. Figure 4-5 shows how replication may be configured in this situation.

NOTE A more complex MySQL replication topology is not due to the configuration and effective use. The complexity and significant difficulties are in managing an environment after the result of some replication failure, which can then cause cascading replication failures or data corruption that can be extremely difficult to plan for and even correct. The need to consider a more complex topology for a more highly available replication environment indicates the importance of the system, and the need for high uptime should be carefully weighted with the increased risk of the inherent dangers that can occur.

Other Replication Topologies

There are many other types of MySQL replication topologies in addition to the simple, multi-master, and circular replication approaches that have been described. A tree or hierarchical architecture can produce a fan-out environment to support massive read scalability. MySQL replication can work remarkably well with 100 to 200 MySQL slaves attached to a master. When the number of slaves continues to increase, for example, 300 or more, a multi-level tree architecture is definitely needed for performance as well as redundancy for any disaster situation.

Other approaches include a hybrid circular and multi-master configuration, and complex systems that include sharding and using several different topologies all with one environment.

The current MySQL replication implementation does not support one significant type of topology. That is a slave instance that supports writes from multiple masters. We will discuss this in Chapter 6 with a Tungsten Replicator that does provide this feature.

Automating High Availability Failovers

From these steps you can determine there are many moving parts to a successful multi-master replication environment, and there is complexity in ensuring all operations are performed and verified as expected.

The following open source utilities exist in the MySQL ecosystem for automating failover architectures:

- MHA for MySQL: Master High Availability Manager and tools for MySQL was created by Yoshinori Matsunobu and is a viable way to automate master failover and slave promotion.

- MMM or Multi-Master Replication Manager for MySQL is another tool that monitors and automates management and failover of multi-master MySQL clusters.

- Flipper is another legacy tool that supports managing a simple MySQL pair configuration.

More information about these tools is available in Chapter 5.

Starting with MySQL 5.6, many of these steps and additional utilities can be simplified or eliminated with the introduction of features including UUID, GTID, and crash-safe slaves that were discussed in Chapter 3. In Chapter 5 several utilities leveraging these new features are also discussed.

Conclusion

Running multi-master topologies with native MySQL replication has been around for a long time. Multi-master replication is not complex to configure; however, it is complex to manage and support for all production situations and possible disaster recovery needs. Successful implementations using multi-master replication generally involve designing the application to be aware of, and cater for, the inherent limitations and risks.

Examples and links in this chapter are available for download from http://EffectiveMySQL.com/book/replication-techniques.

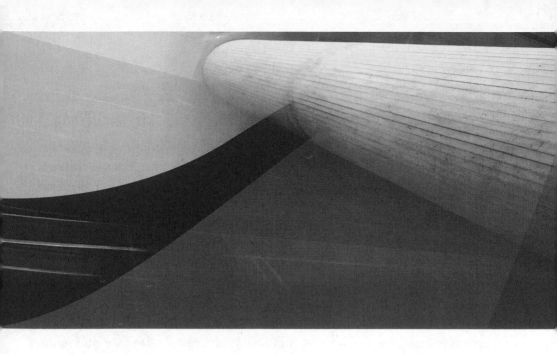

5

MySQL Replication Tools

The MySQL ecosystem includes many different tools that can be used to support, manage, and monitor MySQL replication. These tools have been developed to enhance the default MySQL installation. Over time MySQL has incorporated some of these community features and tools.

In this chapter we discuss:

- Various available toolkits, including Openark Kit, Percona Toolkit, Maatkit, and MySQL Workbench Utilities

- Replication prefetch options

- MySQL failover managers, including MySQL MHA, MMM, and Flipper

Various MySQL Toolkits

Several individuals and companies have created a number of tools and combined them into various toolkits. The most common toolkits and the relevant MySQL replication utilities are included. Each of the examples in the following toolkits relies on the configuration of a suitable MySQL topology. The MySQL Sandbox and/or the VirtualBox setup that is defined in the appendix is used.

Openark Kit

Created and maintained by the 2009 MySQL community member of the year and Oracle ACE Shlomi Noach (http://code.openark.org), Openark provides a number of common utilities to administer, diagnose, and audit MySQL databases. The following are the related MySQL replication utilities.

This software is written in Python and is available under the open source *BSD* license. More information can be found at http://code.openark.org/forge/openark-kit.

Installation

The following steps install Openark and the necessary dependencies on an Ubuntu/Debian server:

```
$ cd /tmp
$ wget http://openarkkit.googlecode.com/files/openark-kit-180-1.deb
$ sudo apt-get install python-mysqldb
$ sudo dpkg -i openark-kit-*.deb
$ rm -f openark-kit-*.deb
$ oak-get-slave-lag -help
```

The following steps install Openark and the necessary dependencies on a Red Hat/CentOS/Oracle Linux server:

```
$ cd /tmp
$ wget http://openarkkit.googlecode.com/files/openark-kit-180-1.noarch.rpm
$ sudo yum install MySQL-python
$ sudo rpm -i openark-kit-*.noarch.rpm
$ rm -f openark-kit-*.noarch.rpm
$ oak-get-slave-lag -help
```

Refer to http://code.google.com/p/openarkkit/downloads/list for details of the most current version and software for other operating systems.

oak-get-slave-lag

The `oak-get-slave-lag` utility provides a convenience script of capturing the `Seconds_Behind_Master` information from SHOW SLAVE STATUS. This also supports an acceptable amount before providing an error. The following examples use a MySQL Sandbox environment as defined in the appendix:

```
$ cd $HOME/sandboxes/rsandbox_5_5_24
$ oak-get-slave-lag --defaults-file=node1/my.sandbox.cnf
0
```

In an error situation when replication lag exceeds a given number of seconds specified:

```
$ oak-get-slave-lag --defaults-file=node1/my.sandbox.cnf -e 5
-- ERROR: 8
```

When replication is not running:

```
$ ./s1 -e "STOP SLAVE"
$ oak-get-slave-lag --defaults-file=node1/my.sandbox.cnf
None
$ ./s1 -e "START SLAVE
```

References

Code: http://openarkkit.googlecode.com/svn/trunk/openarkkit/doc/html/oak-get-slave-lag.html.

oak-show-replication-status

This command provides a convenient report of the MySQL topology for a given master. This will automatically detect and check all slaves for the specified master. This will not report slaves in a nested topology. For example:

```
$ cd $HOME/sandboxes/rsandbox_5_5_24
$ oak-show-replication-status --defaults-file=master/my.sandbox.cnf
-- master log: mysql-bin.000003
-- Slave host Slave port   Master_Log_File       Seconds_Behind_Master
Status
-- ERROR: Cannot SHOW SLAVE STATUS on SBslave1:21380
-- ERROR: Cannot SHOW SLAVE STATUS on SBslave2:21381
```

In this situation you can see errors. This is due to the underlying process of using SHOW SLAVE HOSTS, which requires the `--report-host` option to be defined on slaves. By adding `SBslave1` and `SBslave2` to your machine hosts file, a correct output is provided to demonstrate the utility:

```
$ oak-show-replication-status --defaults-file=master/my.sandbox.cnf
-- master log: mysql-bin.000001
-- Slave host Slave port   Master_Log_File      Seconds_Behind_Master      Status
-- SBslave1            21380  mysql-bin.000001            0               Good
-- SBslave2            21381  mysql-bin.000001            0               Good
```

CAUTION   *There is no validation in MySQL for the* `--report-host` *value as shown with using MySQL Sandbox. If this is not an actual server name, this utility will not produce the results you may be expecting.*

When using the virtual environment as defined in the appendix:

```
$ oak-show-replication-status -uroot -ppasswd -Halpha
-- master log: alpha-bin.000007
-- Slave host  Slave port  Master_Log_File   Seconds_Behind_Master      Status
-- beta               3306 alpha-bin.000007            0               Good
```

`oak-show-replication-status` does not support nested master/slave topologies as demonstrated in the later MySQL Workbench Utilities example.

References

Code: http://openarkkit.googlecode.com/svn/trunk/openarkkit/doc/html/oak-show-replication-status.html.

oak-purge-master-logs

The master binary logs require monitoring and management to ensure available disk space exists on the master server for normal database operations. The `expire_logs_days` configuration option and the PURGE MASTER LOGS command can be used to maintain a healthy amount of files. While `expire_logs_days` will only delete binary logs older than the specific amount when a new binary log is created, PURGE MASTER LOGS can remove files by name or to a certain date and time. In addition the `oak-purge-master-logs` command can perform removal of binary logs for an applicable retention policy with the number of available files. For example:

```
$ cd $HOME/sandboxes/rsandbox_5_5_24
$ oak-purge-master-logs --retain-logs=3 --print-only \
   --defaults-file=master/my.sandbox.cnf
PURGE MASTER LOGS TO 'mysql-bin.000005'
```

This syntax will provide what can be run manually. To confirm the correct information you can review the existing binary logs in place with:

```
$ ls -l master/data/mysql-bin*
-rw-rw---- 1 uid gid6309531 May 21 22:10 master/data/mysql-bin.000001
-rw-rw---- 1 uid gid    5327 Jun  7 09:26 master/data/mysql-bin.000002
-rw-rw---- 1 uid gid    2981 Jun 12 18:42 master/data/mysql-bin.000003
-rw-rw---- 1 uid gid     126 Jun 12 18:50 master/data/mysql-bin.000004
-rw-rw---- 1 uid gid    6354 Jun 14 12:18 master/data/mysql-bin.000005
-rw-rw---- 1 uid gid   27650 Jun 14 13:32 master/data/mysql-bin.000006
-rw-rw---- 1 uid gid     107 Jun 14 13:32 master/data/mysql-bin.000007
-rw-rw---- 1 uid gid     133 Jun 14 13:32 master/data/mysql-bin.index

$ oak-purge-master-logs --retain-logs=3 \
  --defaults-file=master/my.sandbox.cnf
$ ls -l master/data/mysql-bin*
-rw-rw---- 1 uid gid    6354 Jun 14 12:18 master/data/mysql-bin.000005
-rw-rw---- 1 uid gid   27650 Jun 14 13:32 master/data/mysql-bin.000006
-rw-rw---- 1 uid gid     107 Jun 14 13:32 master/data/mysql-bin.000007
-rw-rw---- 1 uid gid     133 Jun 14 13:32 master/data/mysql-bin.index
```

This utility can also ensure that binary logs are maintained for any slaves that may be out of date.

CAUTION   *It is important you keep the current binary logs from the last static backup available. This should be part of your standard backup and recovery process. If your system writes a large number of files per day, for example, 100 files, removing files by a constant number without an adequate backup may delete important binary logs for a disaster recovery from the previous static backup or an older static backup. These are important business considerations to review in addition to the technical needs.*

The *Effective MySQL: Backup and Recovery* book (McGraw-Hill, 2012) provides extensive details on how to manage the MySQL binary logs, including how to make copies, and how to monitor and verify copied files.

References
Code: http://openarkkit.googlecode.com/svn/trunk/openarkkit/doc/html/oak-purge-master-logs.html.

Percona Toolkit

The Percona toolkit, by the product name owners, provides various utilities including the following commands relevant to MySQL replication. This software is available under the GPL v2 license and can be obtained from http://www.percona.com/software/percona-toolkit/.

Installation

The following instructions install Percona Toolkit on an Ubuntu/Debian distribution:

```
$ wget http://www.percona.com/redir/downloads/percona-toolkit/2.1.1/
percona-toolkit_2.1.1_all.deb
$ sudo apt-get install libterm-readkey-perl
$ sudo dpkg -i percona-toolkit_2.1.1_all.deb
$ pt-slave-find -help
```

The following instructions install Percona Toolkit on a Red Hat/CentOS/ Oracle Linux distribution:

```
$ wget http://www.percona.com/redir/downloads/percona-toolkit/2.1.1/
percona-toolkit-2.1.1-1.noarch.rpm
$ sudo yum install perl-TermReadKey
$ sudo yum install perl-DBD-MySQL
$ sudo rpm -i percona-toolkit-2.1.1-1.noarch.rpm
$ pt-slave-find -help
```

Refer to http://www.percona.com/downloads/percona-toolkit/LATEST/ for the most current version and software for other operating systems and distributions.

pt-table-checksum

One feature that is essential for managing and ensuring replication data consistency is appropriate table checksum verification. The Percona Toolkit provides the pt-table-checksum command, which replaces the Maatkit mk-table-checksum tool. The following example shows a test table that is missing a row on the slave using the MySQL Sandbox environment that is defined in the appendix:

CAUTION   *This utility is disk intensive for large databases as by default this reads the entire table for the specified schemas and tables.*

```
$ cd $HOME/sandboxes/rsandbox_5_5_24
$ ./m
master> CREATE SCHEMA IF NOT EXISTS book3;
master> USE book3
master> CREATE TABLE difference_test (id INT NOT NULL);
master> INSERT INTO difference_test VALUES (1),(2),(3);
$ ./s1
slave> USE book3
slave> DELETE FROM difference_test LIMIT 1;
```

Running the `pt-table-checksum` command:

```
$ pt-table-checksum --databases=book3 --defaults-file=master/my.sandbox.cnf \
  --replicate book3.checksum
TS                ERRORS  DIFFS    ROWS  CHUNKS SKIPPED    TIME TABLE
06-14T15:57:31       0      0        3      1        0   0.031 book3.difference_test
06-14T15:57:31       0      0        1      1        0   0.028 book3.no_tbl_on_slave
06-14T15:57:32       0      0  1048576      7        0   1.148 book3.numbers
06-14T15:57:32       0      0        2      1        0   0.030 book3.rbr_test
06-14T15:57:32       0      0        4      1        0   0.027 book3.uniq_test
```

Full details of the checksums between the master and slave tables can be found in the `book3.checksum` table. The following SQL will provide a difference recorded in this table if any exists:

```
$ ./s1
slave> SELECT db, tbl, SUM(this_cnt) AS total_rows,
   -> COUNT(*) AS chunks
   -> FROM book3.checksum
   -> WHERE (  master_cnt <> this_cnt  OR
   -> master_crc <> this_crc  OR
   -> ISNULL(master_crc) <> ISNULL(this_crc))
   -> GROUP BY db, tbl;
+-------+-----------------+------------+--------+
| db    | tbl             | total_rows | chunks |
+-------+-----------------+------------+--------+
| book3 | difference_test |          2 |      1 |
+-------+-----------------+------------+--------+
1 row in set (0.00 sec)
```

For comparison, the second slave shows no differences:

```
$ ./s2
slave>  SELECT ...
Empty set (0.01 sec)
```

If there are missing schema objects in your slave schema, this command will break replication. For example:

```
$ ./s1
slave> SHOW SLAVE STATUS\G
*************************** 1. row ***************************
...
          Slave_IO_Running: Yes
         Slave_SQL_Running: No
...
                Last_Errno: 1146
                Last_Error: 'Table 'book3.no_tbl_on_slave' doesn't exist'
on query. Default database:'book3'.Query: 'REPLACE INTO `book3`.`checksum` (db,
 tbl, chunk, chunk_index, lower_boundary, upper_boundary, this_cnt, this_crc)
```

```
SELECT 'book3', 'no_tbl_on_slave', '1', NULL, NULL, NULL, COUNT(*) AS cnt,
COALESCE(LOWER(CONV(BIT_XOR(CAST(CRC32(`id`) AS UNSIGNED)), 10, 16)), 0) AS crc
 FROM `book3`.`no_tbl_on_slave` /*checksum table*/'
...
```

The following utility describes how to identify the actual row differences.

References

Documentation: http://www.percona.com/doc/percona-toolkit/pt-table-checksum.html.

pt-table-sync

This tool attempts to identify data changes and synchronize these via re-applying commands on the MySQL master. **This tool does change data and comes with a recommendation that you backup your data before use.** You can also run the tool in print-only mode to see what operations would be run. This is generally used in conjunction with an identified data drift from the output of pt-table-checksum.

Demonstrating how to identify the difference of the slave data as described with the pt-table-checksum command:

```
# This is needed for the full connection string required for this utility
$ cat node1/my.sandbox.cnf
$ pt-table-sync --print --sync-to-master --databases=book3 h=localhost,P=21380,
u=msandbox,p=msandbox,S=/tmp/mysql_sandbox21380.sock
REPLACE INTO `book3`.`checksum`(`db`, `tbl`, `chunk`, `chunk_time`,
`chunk_index`, `lower_boundary`, `upper_boundary`, `this_crc`, `this_cnt`,
`master_crc`, `master_cnt`, `ts`) VALUES ('book3', 'difference_test', '1',
'0.008657', NULL, NULL, NULL, 'f4dbdf21', '3', 'f4dbdf21', '3', '2012-06-14
15:57:31');
REPLACE INTO `book3`.`difference_test`(`id`) VALUES ('1')
  /*percona-toolkit src_db:book3 src_tbl:difference_test ... */;
Table book3.no_tbl_on_slave does not exist on P=21380,S=/tmp/mysql_sandbox21380.
sock,h=localhost,p=...,u=msandbox
while doing book3.no_tbl_on_slave on localhost
```

As you can see from the output, more information was provided than expected. This utility does identify the data drift in the difference_table and provides a suitable REPLACE command that, if run on the master, would provide for consistent data in this table. What is also shown are modifications to synchronize the actual checksum table that you do not want to be modified. The utility also highlights a difference of a missing table.

CAUTION   While this tool can be used to identify physical data differences, it is recommended that all SQL statements are carefully verified before execution to ensure no data loss.

References

Documentation: http://www.percona.com/doc/percona-toolkit/pt-table-sync.html.

pt-heartbeat

This utility attempts to monitor replication delay by monitoring actual replicated information. This is performed in two parts, the `--update` command, and the `--check` or `--monitor` command:

```
$ cd $HOME/sandboxes/rsandbox_5_5_24
$ pt-heartbeat --defaults-file=master/my.sandbox.cnf \
  --create-table --database=book3 --table=heartbeat --update &
```

You can review what is actually being created with:

```
$ ./m
master> SELECT * FROM book3.heartbeat\G
*************************** 1. row ***************************
                   ts: 2012-05-21T17:19:20.001820
            server_id: 1
                 file: mysql-bin.000001
             position: 231760
relay_master_log_file: NULL
  exec_master_log_pos: NULL
1 row in set (0.00 sec)

master> SELECT * FROM book3.heartbeat\G
*************************** 1. row ***************************
                   ts: 2012-05-21T17:19:21.001820
            server_id: 1
                 file: mysql-bin.000001
             position: 232097
relay_master_log_file: NULL
  exec_master_log_pos: NULL
1 row in set (0.00 sec)
```

Replication is monitored with:

```
$ pt-heartbeat --defaults-file=master/my.sandbox.cnf \
  --database=book3 --master-server-id 1 --check

0.00
```

or

```
$ pt-heartbeat --defaults-file=master/my.sandbox.cnf \
  --database=book3 --master-server-id 1 --monitor
0.00s [  0.00s,  0.00s,  0.00s ]
0.00s [  0.00s,  0.00s,  0.00s ]
0.00s [  0.00s,  0.00s,  0.00s ]
0.00s [  0.00s,  0.00s,  0.00s ]
0.00s [  0.00s,  0.00s,  0.00s ]
```

References

Documentation: http://www.percona.com/doc/percona-toolkit/pt-heart-beat.html.

pt-slave-delay

This utility allows a MySQL slave to have a certain delay behind the MySQL master. In some environments this feature can offer access to data that may be modified or deleted accidently on a master. This is not a replacement for a backup if data is deleted; however, it can provide a more convenient view of the data in question.

```
$ cd $HOME/sandboxes/rsandbox_5_5_24
$ pt-slave-delay --delay 1m --interval 15s --defaults-file=node2/my.sandbox.cnf
17:03:16 slave running 0 seconds behind
17:03:16 STOP SLAVE until 17:04:16 at master position mysql-bin.000001/2081
17:03:31 slave stopped at master position mysql-bin.000001/2081
17:03:46 slave stopped at master position mysql-bin.000001/2081
17:04:01 slave stopped at master position mysql-bin.000001/2081
17:04:16 no new binlog events
17:04:31 slave stopped at master position mysql-bin.000001/8063
17:04:46 slave stopped at master position mysql-bin.000001/18465
17:05:01 slave stopped at master position mysql-bin.000001/23666
17:05:16 slave stopped at master position mysql-bin.000001/23666
17:05:31 START SLAVE until master 17:04:31 mysql-bin.000001/8063
```

NOTE   MySQL 5.6 provides delayed replication as a core feature using the CHANGE MASTER TO MASTER_DELAY command. See http://dev.mysql .com/doc/refman/5.6/en/replication-delayed.html for more details.

References

Documentation: http://www.percona.com/doc/percona-toolkit/pt-slave-delay.html.

pt-slave-find

This utility will connect to a MySQL master and print the replication topology and additional summary information. This also finds nested master/slaves in a MySQL topology. For example, using the virtual environment from the appendix:

```
$ pt-slave-find u=root,p=passwd --host=alpha
alpha
Version        5.6.5-m8-log
Server ID      51
Uptime         33:42 (started 2012-06-25T14:55:39)
Replication    Is not a slave, has 1 slaves connected, is not read_only
Filters
```

```
Binary logging  STATEMENT
Slave status
Slave mode      STRICT
Auto-increment  increment 1, offset 1
InnoDB version  1.2.5
+- beta
   Version         5.6.5-m8-log
   Server ID       52
   Uptime          14:30 (started 2012-06-25T15:14:51)
   Replication     Is a slave, has 1 slaves connected, is not read_only
   Filters
   Binary logging  STATEMENT
   Slave status    0 seconds behind, running, no errors
   Slave mode      STRICT
   Auto-increment  increment 1, offset 1
   InnoDB version  1.2.5
   +- gamma
      Version         5.6.5-m8
      Server ID       53
      Uptime          12:29 (started 2012-06-25T15:16:52)
      Replication     Is a slave, has 0 slaves connected, is not read_only
      Filters
      Binary logging  STATEMENT
      Slave status    0 seconds behind, running, no errors
      Slave mode      STRICT
      Auto-increment  increment 1, offset 1
      InnoDB version  1.2.5
```

When used in MySQL Sandbox, the output is not as expected for a master server with two connected slaves:

```
$ cd $HOME/sandboxes/rsandbox_5_5_24
$ pt-slave-find --defaults-file=master/my.sandbox.cnf --host localhost \
  --report-format summary
localhost
Version         5.5.24-log
Server ID       1
Uptime          22:45 (started 16:33:12)
Replication     Is not a slave, has 2 slaves connected,
                is not read_only
Filters
Binary logging  STATEMENT
Slave status
Slave mode      STRICT
Auto-increment  increment 1, offset 1
InnoDB version  1.1.8
```

This was logged as a bug with Percona Toolkit; see https://bugs.launch-pad.net/percona-toolkit/+bug/1002512.

CAUTION   *Do not always rely on the output of third-party utilities. The software may have bugs, be incomplete, or operate differently in a test environment, as demonstrated here with multiple MySQL instances on a single server. Adequate testing is always advisable.*

References
Documentation: http://www.percona.com/doc/percona-toolkit/2.1/pt-slave-find.html.

Maatkit
The predecessor to Percona Toolkit, Maatkit is no longer developed or maintained and has a number of commands that have not been incorporated. It is unclear if this is due to the tools' limitations or stability. Some Maatkit tools are specifically deprecated by the authors as incomplete tools and are no longer recommended for use.

MySQL Workbench Utilities

The MySQL Workbench is a graphical user interface (GUI) for designing and managing your MySQL database objects. In addition to a fully functional entity relationship (ER) visual modeling tool, a migration tool from other RDBMS products, and a tool to reverse engineer MySQL schemas, MySQL Workbench also includes a number of command line utilities. These utilities are written in Python and are available under a GNU GPL v2 license. More information can be found at https://launchpad.net/mysql-utilities.

NOTE   MySQL version 5.6 is a Development Milestone Release (DMR). This clearly means this is not production-ready software, and is subject to change. These MySQL Workbench utilities are also works in progress. Some utilities are more mature than others, and in some situations the functionality is not complete. While it would be ideal to demonstrate the full functionality of all tools, the release of this book is not aligned with the unknown future release date of MySQL 5.6.

CAUTION   Consider the MySQL Workbench Utilities as development software. Every attempt has been made in this chapter to show the likely use; however, this is subject to change. Examples provided at the time of publication do show reported errors that will change in the future.

Installation
The MySQL Workbench Utilities are included with MySQL Workbench. This can be downloaded from http://www.mysql.com/downloads/workbench/. In addition the MySQL Workbench Utilities are individually

available on Launchpad; however, there is no single download file available at the time of this publication. This requires the use of Bazaar version control software to obtain these files. Refer to http://bazaar.canonical.com/ for download instructions for your operating system. The following commands will install these utilities on a VirtualBox virtual server, as defined in the appendix:

```
$ cd /tmp
$ sudo apt-get install -y bzr
$ bzr branch lp:mysql-utilities
$ cd mysql-utilities
$ sudo python setup.py install
$ mysqlrplshow --version
MySQL Utilities mysqlrplshow version 1.0.6-preview
Copyright (c) 2012, Oracle and/or its affiliates. All
rights reserved.
```

The following list shows all of the utilities that are currently available at the time of publication. In addition to the following utilities that are discussed, additional commands support database management for importing, exporting, and comparison schemas and data.

```
$ ls -l /usr/local/bin/mysql*
-rwxrwxr-x 1 uid gid 6415 Jun 14 17:29 /usr/local/bin/mysqldbcompare
-rwxrwxr-x 1 uid gid 7257 Jun 14 17:29 /usr/local/bin/mysqldbcopy
-rwxrwxr-x 1 uid gid 8474 Jun 14 17:29 /usr/local/bin/mysqldbexport
-rwxrwxr-x 1 uid gid 6581 Jun 14 17:29 /usr/local/bin/mysqldbimport
-rwxrwxr-x 1 uid gid 5516 Jun 14 17:29 /usr/local/bin/mysqldiff
-rwxrwxr-x 1 uid gid 5818 Jun 14 17:29 /usr/local/bin/mysqldiskusage
-rwxrwxr-x 1 uid gid 6992 Jun 14 17:29 /usr/local/bin/mysqlfailover
-rwxrwxr-x 1 uid gid 5098 Jun 14 17:29 /usr/local/bin/mysqlindexcheck
-rwxrwxr-x 1 uid gid 3979 Jun 14 17:29 /usr/local/bin/mysqlmetagrep
-rwxrwxr-x 1 uid gid 3821 Jun 14 17:29 /usr/local/bin/mysqlprocgrep
-rwxrwxr-x 1 uid gid 5133 Jun 14 17:29 /usr/local/bin/mysqlreplicate
-rwxrwxr-x 1 uid gid 7640 Jun 14 17:29 /usr/local/bin/mysqlrpladmin
-rwxrwxr-x 1 uid gid 4294 Jun 14 17:29 /usr/local/bin/mysqlrplcheck
-rwxrwxr-x 1 uid gid 4708 Jun 14 17:29 /usr/local/bin/mysqlrplshow
-rwxrwxr-x 1 uid gid 4954 Jun 14 17:29 /usr/local/bin/mysqlserverclone
-rwxrwxr-x 1 uid gid 4119 Jun 14 17:29 /usr/local/bin/mysqlserverinfo
-rwxrwxr-x 1 uid gid 5391 Jun 14 17:29 /usr/local/bin/mysqluserclone
```

These utilities also require the MySQL Python/Connector to operate. More information can be found at https://launchpad.net/myconnpy.

```
$ cd /tmp
$ wget https://launchpad.net/myconnpy/0.3/0.3.2/+download/
```

```
    mysql-connector-python-0.3.2-devel.tar.gz
$ tar xvfz mysql-connector-python-0.3.2-devel.tar.gz
$ cd mysql-connector-python-0.3.2-devel/
$ sudo python setup.py install
```

Documentation

Documentation for the MySQL Utilities can be found at http://dev.mysql .com/doc/workbench/en/mysql-utilities.html. Additional documentation is included with the utilities; however, this must be generated from the source using Sphinx. The following steps will install Linux man pages for the MySQL Utilities:

```
$ cd /tmp/mysql-utilities
$ sudo apt-get install python-setuptools
$ sudo easy_install -U Sphinx
$ sudo python setup.py build_sphinx -b man
$ sudo python setup.py build_man
$ sudo cp build/sphinx/man/* /usr/local/man/man1
$ man mysqlreplicate
```

Refer to http://sphinx.pocoo.org/ for additional instructions regarding installing and configuring Sphinx.

`mysqlreplicate`

The following command will set up the necessary user permissions and settings for replication between two servers. These MySQL servers must have the following minimum configuration already defined in order to complete the replication configuration. Using the virtual environment as defined in the appendix:

Server 1:

```
[mysqld]
server-id=51
log-bin
```

Server 2:

```
[mysqld]
server-id=52
```

This command will perform the necessary steps to have a master/slave replication environment:

```
$ mysqlreplicate --master=root:passwd@alpha \
                 --slave=root:passwd@beta \
                 --rpl-user=repl:repl --pedantic
# master on alpha: ... connected.
# slave on beta: ... connected.
# Checking for binary logging on master...
# Setting up replication...
# ...done.
```

This can be verified with SHOW SLAVE STATUS:

```
$ mysql -uroot -ppasswd -hbeta -e "SHOW SLAVE STATUS\G"
*************************** 1. row ***************************
               Slave_IO_State: Waiting for master to send event
                  Master_Host: alpha
                  Master_User: repl
                  Master_Port: 3306
                Connect_Retry: 60
              Master_Log_File: alpha-bin.000002
          Read_Master_Log_Pos: 147
               Relay_Log_File: beta-relay-bin.000005
                Relay_Log_Pos: 349
        Relay_Master_Log_File: alpha-bin.000002
             Slave_IO_Running: Yes
            Slave_SQL_Running: Yes
...
```

If the necessary MySQL configuration is not in place, you will receive errors, including:

```
$ mysqlreplicate --master=root:passwd@alpha \
                 --slave=root:passwd@beta \
                 --rpl-user=repl:repl \--pedantic
# master on alpha: ... connected.
# slave on beta: ... connected.
ERROR: Slave server_id is set to 0.
```

This utility can be run remotely. This does not have to be executed on the master or slave host that is specified. The use of --pedantic verifies the list of storage engines are consistent between the master and slave. You can also use this utility to reinitialize a MySQL slave and retrieve necessary binary log information from a given master. This will be demonstrated later.

A second nested master/slave relationship can be created in the same MySQL topology with:

```
$ mysqlreplicate --master=root:passwd@beta \
                 --slave=root:passwd@gamma \
                 --rpl-user=repl:repl --pedantic
```

mysqlrplshow

This utility shows the replication topology of your MySQL instances. Using the MySQL Sandbox example configuration:

```
$ cd $HOME/sandboxes/rsandbox_5_5_24
$ mysqlrplshow --master=msandbox:msandbox@localhost:21379
# master on localhost: ... connected.
# Finding slaves for master: localhost:21379
# Replication Topology Graph
localhost:21379 (MASTER)
    |
    +--- SBslave1:21380 - (SLAVE)
    |
    +--- SBslave2:21381 - (SLAVE)
```

NOTE   *The output uses the* --report-host *information on the slave to present a name. This is not a required parameter in MySQL. If not defined, the output will report an unknown host.*

Using the previously configured replication setup on the virtual server environment that was defined with the `mysqlreplicate` command:

```
$ mysqlrplshow --master=root:passwd@alpha --recurse
...
# Replication Topology Graph
alpha:3306 (MASTER)
    |
    +--- beta:3306 - (SLAVE + MASTER)
        |
        +--- gamma:3306 - (SLAVE)
```

This utility can be run remotely. This does not have to be executed on the master host that is specified. This utility is capable of traversing a full topology using the `--recurse` option as shown, providing the top level master is specified. All slaves must define the optional `report-host` with a value that matches the physical hostname. This option will also identify circular topologies.

mysqlrplcheck

This utility performs a sanity check on the MySQL configuration between a master and a slave:

```
$ mysqlrplcheck --master=root:passwd@alpha --slave=root:passwd@beta
# master on alpha: ... connected.
# slave on beta: ... connected.
Test Description                                                  Status
------------------------------------------------------------------------
```

```
Checking for binary logging on master                          [pass]
Are there binlog exceptions?                                   [pass]
Replication user exists?                                       [pass]
Checking server_id values                                      [pass]
Checking server_uuid values                                    [pass]
Is slave connected to master?                                  [pass]
Check master information file                                  [WARN]
Cannot read master information file from a remote machine.
Checking InnoDB compatibility                                  [pass]
Checking storage engines compatibility                         [pass]
Checking lower_case_table_names settings                       [pass]
Checking slave delay (seconds behind master)                   [pass]
# ...done.
```

The warning message is because the utility has no present capability to connect physically to the slave server. When using `master-info-rep =TABLE` in the master and slave configuration, the following occurs.

```
...
Is slave connected to master?                                  [pass]
Check master information file                                  [pass]
Checking InnoDB compatibility                                  [pass]
...
```

There is currently a reported issue regarding replication usernames and host wildcards, as shown when using MySQL Sandbox:

```
$ cd $HOME/sandboxes/rsandbox_5_5_24
$ mysqlrplcheck --master=msandbox:msandbox@localhost:21379  \
                --slave=msandbox:msandbox@localhost:21380
# master on localhost: ... connected.
# slave on localhost: ... connected.
Test Description                                              Status
----------------------------------------------------------------------
...

Replication user exists?                                       [FAIL]
The replication user rsandbox@127.0.0.1 was not found on the master.
```

Contrary to the reported FAIL message, a replication user does exist using a wildcard hostname within MySQL Sandbox:

```
$ ./m
master> SELECT host,user,password FROM mysql.user;
+-----------+-------------+------------------------------------------+
| host      | user        | password                                 |
+-----------+-------------+------------------------------------------+
...
| 127.%     | rsandbox    | *B07EB15A2E7BD9620DAE47B194D5B9DBA14377AD |
+-----------+-------------+------------------------------------------+
```

This example shows both the strengths and weaknesses of any open source utilities. If there was an error in MySQL replication, the running of this command regularly (e.g., daily) is a good management monitoring approach. However, when the tool reports a problem that is not actually a problem (due to a software bug), this can complicate the benefits of a monitoring approach.

CAUTION *This is an example where software may have bugs, be incomplete, or operate differently in a test environment as demonstrated here. Adequate testing is always advisable.*

`mysqlrpladmin`

The `mysqlrpladmin` utility provides a number of commands for managing a MySQL topology. These commands currently include

- **start**   Start replication on all slaves specified.
- **stop**   Stop replication on all slaves specified.
- **reset**   Stop and reset replication on all slaves specified.
- **health**   Display the replication health of the defined master and slave topology.
- **gtid**   Verify the status of global transaction identifier (GTID) variables to ensure these are correctly configured for the defined masters and slaves. This command also displays UUID information for all specified servers.
- **elect**   Perform a best slave election and report which slave to use for switchover.
- **switchover**   Perform a slave promotion of an elected slave to master and reconfigure the existing master as a slave.
- **failover**   Conduct a failover from an unavailable master to the best available slave.

Prerequisite Configuration

When using the elect, switchover, or failover commands you will have to enable the following settings in all of the servers' `my.cnf` files to support GTID:

```
[mysqld]
log-bin
log-slave-updates
disable-gtid-unsafe-statements
gtid-mode=ON
```

If you fail to include the `log-slave-updates` option on the master, or `log-bin` and `log-slave-updates` on slaves, the following error will be found in the MySQL error log:

```
120614 18:51:42 [ERROR] --gtid-mode=ON or UPGRADE_STEP_1 or UPGRADE_STEP_2
 requires --log-bin and --log-slave-updates
```

Refer to Chapter 3 for more information about the GTID configuration settings.

If GTID is not correctly configured on all hosts, you will run into the following replication error when running SHOW SLAVE STATUS\G:

```
slave> SHOW SLAVE STATUS\G
...
Last_IO_Errno: 1593
Last_IO_Error: The slave IO thread stops because the master has
GTID_MODE OFF and this server has GTID_MODE ON
```

health command

The following example shows the health of a master/slave configuration:

```
$ mysqlrpladmin --master=root:passwd@alpha --slave=root:passwd@beta health
# Checking privileges.
# Replication Topology Health:
+---------+-------+---------+--------+------------+---------+
| host    | port  | role    | state  | gtid_mode  | health  |
+---------+-------+---------+--------+------------+---------+
| alpha   | 3306  | MASTER  | UP     | OFF        | OK      |
| beta    | 3306  | SLAVE   | UP     | OFF        | OK      |
+---------+-------+---------+--------+------------+---------+
# ...done.
```

NOTE　*You must specify all the slave servers you wish to check. This utility does not discover what slaves exist in the replication topology.*

If there are any issues with the slaves operating correctly you will find output similar to the following:

```
$ cd $HOME/sandboxes/rsandbox_5_5_24
$ mysqlrpladmin --master=msandbox:msandbox@localhost:21379 \
                --slaves=msandbox:msandbox@localhost:21380, \
                      msandbox:msandbox@localhost:21381 health
# Checking privileges.
# Replication Topology Health:
+-------------+-------+---------+--------+------------+---------------------------+
| host        | port  | role    | state  | gtid_mode  | health                    |
+-------------+-------+---------+--------+------------+---------------------------+
| localhost   | 21379 | MASTER  | UP     | NO         | OK                        |
| localhost   | 21380 | SLAVE   | WARN   |            | Cannot connect to slave.  |
```

```
| localhost  | 21381 | SLAVE   | WARN  |             | Cannot connect to slave. |
+------------+-------+---------+-------+-------------+--------------------------+
# ...done.
```

When using the `health` command for this utility, this can be run remotely.

The following example shows two slaves connected in a MySQL environment using a GTID setup. This example shows an error situation when one slave is not correctly configured:

```
$ mysqlrpladmin --master=root:passwd@alpha \
                --slave=root:passwd@beta,root:passwd@gamma health
# Checking privileges.
# Replication Topology Health:
+--------+-------+---------+--------+-----------+---------------+
| host   | port  | role    | state  | gtid_mode | health        |
+--------+-------+---------+--------+-----------+---------------+
| alpha  | 3306  | MASTER  | UP     | ON        | OK            |
| beta   | 3306  | SLAVE   | UP     | ON        | OK            |
| gamma  | 3306  | SLAVE   | UP     | OFF       | Not connected |
+--------+-------+---------+--------+-----------+---------------+
# ...done.
```

NOTE *For the global transaction identifier (GTID) to work correctly in a MySQL topology all servers must be configured accordingly.*

Alternatively, if GTID is correctly configured but one or more of the slave threads is not running, the following will be reported. With this grid display output it is important to review all columns for different error conditions:

```
# Checking privileges.
#
# Replication Topology Health:
+--------+-------+---------+--------+-----------+---------+
| host   | port  | role    | state  | gtid_mode | health  |
+--------+-------+---------+--------+-----------+---------+
| alpha  | 3306  | MASTER  | UP     | ON        | OK      |
| beta   | 3306  | SLAVE   | UP     | ON        | OK      |
| gamma  | 3306  | SLAVE   | UP     | ON        | ERROR   |
+--------+-------+---------+--------+-----------+---------+
```

The utility will also provide feedback on any slave lag. For example:

```
+-------+------+--------+-------+------+-------------------------------------------
| host  | port | role   | state | gtid | health
+-------+------+--------+-------+------+-------------------------------------------
| alpha | 3306 | MASTER | UP    | ON   | OK
| beta  | 3306 | SLAVE  | UP    | ON   | Slave has 1 transactions behind master
| gamma | 3306 | SLAVE  | WARN  |      | Cannot connect to slave.
+-------+------+--------+-------+------+-------------------------------------------
```

gtid Command

The enabling of GTID with `gtid_mode=ON`, `log-slave-updates` and `disable-gtid-unsafe-statements` configuration settings will support the most impressive feature of these utilities, that is, the ability for a master switchover or failover to a slave. You can confirm the GTID configuration for the full MySQL topology is valid with:

```
alpha$ mysqlrpladmin --master=root:passwd@alpha --slave=root:passwd@beta gtid
#
# UUIDS for all servers:
+--------+-------+---------+---------------------------------------+
| host   | port  | role    | uuid                                  |
+--------+-------+---------+---------------------------------------+
| alpha  | 3306  | MASTER  | ba7ac732-b707-11e1-a1b3-0800275824dc  |
| beta   | 3306  | SLAVE   | 0941e912-b709-11e1-a1bc-0800278bd7a3  |
+--------+-------+---------+---------------------------------------+
#
# Transactions executed on the server:
+--------+-------+---------+-----------------------------------------+
| host   | port  | role    | gtid                                    |
+--------+-------+---------+-----------------------------------------+
| alpha  | 3306  | MASTER  | BA7AC732-B707-11E1-A1B3-0800275824DC:1  |
| beta   | 3306  | SLAVE   | 0941E912-B709-11E1-A1BC-0800278BD7A3:1-4|
| beta   | 3306  | SLAVE   | BA7AC732-B707-11E1-A1B3-0800275824DC:1  |
+--------+-------+---------+-----------------------------------------+
# ...done.
```

Refer to Chapter 3 for the details of what MySQL configuration variables are necessary for correct GTID configuration and usage. If GTID has not been configured correctly in your MySQL topology, the following types of error messages can be presented:

```
alpha$ mysqlrpladmin --master=root:passwd@alpha \
                     --slave=root:passwd@beta gtid
# Checking privileges.
# WARNING: GTIDs are not supported on this topology.
# ...done.

alpha$ mysqlrpladmin --master=root:passwd@alpha \
                     --slave=root:passwd@beta,root:passwd@gamma gtid
# Checking privileges.
# UUIDS for all servers:
+--------+-------+---------+---------------------------------------+
| host   | port  | role    | uuid                                  |
+--------+-------+---------+---------------------------------------+
| alpha  | 3306  | MASTER  | ba7ac732-b707-11e1-a1b3-0800275824dc  |
| beta   | 3306  | SLAVE   | 0941e912-b709-11e1-a1bc-0800278bd7a3  |
| gamma  | 3306  | SLAVE   | e6193aa0-b714-11e1-a209-080027530628  |
+--------+-------+---------+---------------------------------------+
# ERROR retrieving GTID information: Global Transaction IDs are not enabled.
# ...done.
```

This command will not operate correctly when run remotely. The following information was obtained when the command was run on the master (i.e., `alpha`) server.

reset Command

This command will reset replication for the specified instance. Following the correction of the required MySQL configuration on the second slave to support GTID, and restarting the MySQL instance, we can use a combination of these utilities described to correctly configure and confirm replication in our MySQL topology. For example, to reset replication on a MySQL slave:

```
$ mysqlrpladmin --slave=root:passwd@gamma reset
# Checking privileges.
# Performing STOP on all slaves.
#   Executing stop on slave gamma:3306 Ok
# Performing RESET on all slaves.
#   Executing reset on slave gamma:3306 Ok
# ...done.
```

To reconfigure the MySQL server as a slave with the MySQL topology:

```
$ mysqlreplicate --master=root:passwd@alpha   \
                 --slave=root:passwd@gamma     \
                 --rpl-user=repl:repl --pedantic
# master on alpha: ... connected.
# slave on gamma: ... connected.
# Checking for binary logging on master...
# Setting up replication...
# ...done.
```

To confirm that the slave is now correctly configured and operating in the MySQL topology:

```
$ mysqlrpladmin --master=root:passwd@alpha    \
                --slave=root:passwd@beta,root:passwd@gamma health
# Checking privileges.
#
# Replication Topology Health:
+--------+-------+---------+--------+------------+---------+
| host   | port  | role    | state  | gtid_mode  | health  |
+--------+-------+---------+--------+------------+---------+
| alpha  | 3306  | MASTER  | UP     | ON         | OK      |
| beta   | 3306  | SLAVE   | UP     | ON         | OK      |
| gamma  | 3306  | SLAVE   | UP     | ON         | OK      |
+--------+-------+---------+--------+------------+---------+
# ...done.
```

TIP   *These new MySQL 5.6 Utilities can help in providing easy command line configuration and management of your MySQL topology, eliminating the legacy approach that required more administration management. It is recommended that you understand how to leverage* mysqladmin, *and the various commands that provide replication-specific information, with the* mysql *client to learn how these tools actually work for verification.*

elect Command

This command will provide information about which slave is the best to promote to a master. In order to support switchover and failover with these utilities the following MySQL 5.6 prerequisites are necessary. You should also ensure that your hardware environment is the same for high volume environments to ensure a slave can support future master load.

- GTID is correctly configured and operating with the master and all slaves in the MySQL topology.

- All slaves are correctly configured as crash-safe slaves.

You can confirm how a switchover would operate by verifying what slave would be elected:

```
$ mysqlrpladmin -vv --master=root:passwd@alpha \
   --slave=root:passwd@beta,root:passwd@gamma elect
# Checking privileges.
# Electing candidate slave from known slaves.
# Checking eligibility of slave beta:3306 for candidate.
#   Slave connected to master ... Ok
#   GTID_MODE=ON ... Ok
#   Logging filters agree ... Ok
#   Replication user exists ... Ok
# Best slave found is located on beta:3306.

# ...done.
```

switchover Command

When the MySQL topology can determine a new slave can be elected, it is now possible to perform a controlled switchover from the master to a different slave in the MySQL replication topology. This will also reconfigure the current master as a slave.

```
$  mysqlrpladmin -vv --master=root:passwd@alpha \
   --new-master=root:passwd@beta --demote-master switchover
```

```
# Checking privileges.
# Performing switchover from master at alpha:3306 to slave at beta:3306.
# Checking candidate slave prerequisites.
# GTID_MODE=ON is set for all servers.
# Checking eligibility of slave beta:3306 for candidate.
#   Slave connected to master ... Ok
#   GTID_MODE=ON ... Ok
#   Logging filters agree ... Ok
#   Replication user exists ... Ok
# Creating replication user if it does not exist.
# Blocking writes on master.
# LOCK STRING: FLUSH TABLES WITH READ LOCK
# Waiting for slaves to catch up to old master.
# Stopping slaves.
# Performing STOP on all slaves.
# UNLOCK STRING: UNLOCK TABLES
# Demoting old master to be a slave to the new master.
# Switching slaves to new master.
# Executing CHANGE MASTER on alpha:3306.
# CHANGE MASTER TO MASTER_HOST = 'beta', MASTER_USER = 'repl',
MASTER_PASSWORD = 'repl', MASTER_PORT = 3306, MASTER_AUTO_POSITION=1
# Starting all slaves.
# Performing START on all slaves.
# Checking slaves for errors.
# Switchover complete.
# Attempting to contact beta ... Success
#
# Replication Topology Health:
+------+------+--------+-------+-----+--------+--------------+------
| host | port | role   | state | gtid| health | version      | ...
+------+------+--------+-------+-----+--------+--------------+------
| beta | 3306 | MASTER | UP    | ON  | OK     | 5.6.5-m8-log | beta-
| alpha| 3306 | SLAVE  | UP    | ON  | OK     | 5.6.5-m8-log | alpha
+------+------+--------+-------+-----+--------+--------------+------
# ...done.
```

You should verify the health of the new replication topology appropriately defining the new master and slave hosts.

```
$ mysqlrpladmin --master=root:passwd@beta \
               --slave=root:passwd@alpha,root:passwd@gamma health
# Checking privileges.
#
# Replication Topology Health:
+--------+------+---------+--------+-----------+------------------------
| host   | port | role    | state  | gtid_mode | health
+--------+------+---------+--------+-----------+------------------------
| beta   | 3306 | MASTER  | UP     | ON        | OK
| alpha  | 3306 | SLAVE   | UP     | ON        | OK
| gamma  | 3306 | SLAVE   | WARN   |           | Slave is not connected
+--------+------+---------+--------+-----------+------------------------
# ...done.
```

As you can see, in this switchover example, the second slave was not correctly assigned to the new master. Under normal execution this would occur. This is demonstrated to show an error message.

failover Command

Finally, the failover command can be used when the master is no longer accessible and a suitable slave is elected to become the master:

```
$ mysqlrpladmin -vv --slave=root:passwd@beta,root:passwd@gamma failover
# Checking privileges.
# Performing failover.
# Checking eligibility of slave beta:3306 for candidate.
#    GTID_MODE=ON ... Ok
#    Replication user exists ... Ok
# Candidate slave beta:3306 will become the new master.
# Preparing candidate for failover.
# LOCK STRING: FLUSH TABLES WITH READ LOCK
# Connecting candidate to gamma:3306 as a master to retrieve unprocessed GTIDs.
# Change master command for beta:3306
# CHANGE MASTER TO MASTER_HOST = 'gamma', MASTER_USER = 'repl',
MASTER_PASSWORD = 'repl', MASTER_PORT = 3306, MASTER_AUTO_POSITION=1
# UNLOCK STRING: UNLOCK TABLES
# Waiting for candidate to catch up to slave gamma:3306.
# Slave beta:3306:
# QUERY = SELECT SQL_THREAD_WAIT_AFTER_GTIDS(
'0C50EA14-E74E-11E1-9C7E-0800275824DC:1-5', 3)
# Return Code = 0
# Slave beta:3306:
# QUERY = SELECT SQL_THREAD_WAIT_AFTER_GTIDS(
'11603F93-E74E-11E1-9C7E-0800273BF04E:1-6', 3)
# Return Code = None
# Creating replication user if it does not exist.
# Stopping slaves.
# Performing STOP on all slaves.
#    Executing stop on slave beta:3306 Ok
#    Executing stop on slave gamma:3306 Ok
# Switching slaves to new master.
# Change master command for beta:3306
# CHANGE MASTER TO MASTER_HOST = 'beta', MASTER_USER = 'repl',
MASTER_PASSWORD = 'repl', MASTER_PORT = 3306, MASTER_AUTO_POSITION=1
# Change master command for gamma:3306
# CHANGE MASTER TO MASTER_HOST = 'beta', MASTER_USER = 'repl',
MASTER_PASSWORD = 'repl', MASTER_PORT = 3306, MASTER_AUTO_POSITION=1
# Starting slaves.
# Performing START on all slaves.
#    Executing start on slave gamma:3306 Ok
# Checking slaves for errors.
# gamma:3306 status: Ok
# Failover complete.
# Attempting to contact beta ... Success
# Attempting to contact gamma ... Success
#
```

mysqlfailover

This script provides continuous replication monitoring and enables auto-matic failover to a designated or most up-to-date slave in the event of an unplanned outage on the master for MySQL 5.6. Promotion policies are configurable, but the default policy is to promote the most current slave in the topology based on the global transaction identifier (GTID) that was discussed in detail in Chapter 3. Think of `mysqlfailover` as a daemon that will automatically fail over your environment in the event of a master failure.

The `mysqlfailover` utility will report as follows in this case:

```
$ mysqlfailover --master=root:passwd@alpha:3306 \
  --slaves=root:passwd@beta:3306,root:passwd@gamma:3306 \
  --failover-mode=auto
MySQL Replication Failover Utility
Failover Mode = auto      Next Interval = Wed Aug 15 23:50:44 2012
Master Information
------------------
Binary Log File   Position  Binlog_Do_DB  Binlog_Ignore_DB
alpha-bin.000004  187
Replication Health Status
+---------+-------+---------+--------+------------+---------+
| host    | port  | role    | state  | gtid_mode  | health  |
+---------+-------+---------+--------+------------+---------+
| alpha   | 3306  | MASTER  | UP     | ON         | OK      |
| beta    | 3306  | SLAVE   | UP     | ON         | OK      |
| gamma   | 3306  | SLAVE   | UP     | ON         | OK      |
+---------+-------+---------+--------+------------+---------+
Q-quit R-refresh H-health G-GTID Lists U-UUIDs
```

When using the `mysqlfailover` utility a new table is added only to the master host in the `mysql` schema called `failover_console`. This table contains information about the master host:

```
master> SHOW CREATE TABLE mysql.failover_console\G
*********************** 1. row ***********************
       Table: failover_console
Create Table: CREATE TABLE `failover_console` (
  `host` char(30) DEFAULT NULL,
  `port` char(10) DEFAULT NULL
) ENGINE=InnoDB DEFAULT CHARSET=utf8

master> SELECT * FROM mysql.failover_console\G
*********************** 1. row ***********************
host: alpha
port: 3306
```

Simulating Master Failure

When the `mysqld` process and the `mysqld_safe` angel process are killed on the master, the `mysqlfailover` script will perform the failover to a suitable slave within a few seconds. The following information is shown during this step:

```
Failover starting in 'auto' mode...
# Candidate slave beta:3306 will become the new master.
# Preparing candidate for failover.
# Creating replication user if it does not exist.
# Stopping slaves.
# Performing STOP on all slaves.
# Switching slaves to new master.
# Starting slaves.
# Performing START on all slaves.
# Checking slaves for errors.
# Failover complete.
Failover console will restart in 5 seconds.

MySQL Replication Failover Utility
Failover Mode = auto     Next Interval = Thu Aug 16 00:20:18 2012
Master Information
------------------
Binary Log File  Position  Binlog_Do_DB  Binlog_Ignore_DB
beta-bin.000003  6985
Transactions executed on the servers:
+--------+-------+--------+--------+------------+--------+
| host   | port  | role   | state  | gtid_mode  | health |
+--------+-------+--------+--------+------------+--------+
| beta   | 3306  | MASTER | UP     | ON         | OK     |
| gamma  | 3306  | SLAVE  | UP     | ON         | OK     |
+--------+-------+--------+--------+------------+--------+
```

You can then reset and include the original master in the topology with the following commands:

CAUTION   *The following commands show the syntax to reset a MySQL instance as a slave. This is for demonstration purposes. In a production situation, you will need to implement an appropriate recovery of your dataset from a backup.*

```
$ mysqlrpladmin --slave=root:passwd@alpha reset
$ mysqlreplicate --master=root:passwd@beta \
  --slave=root:passwd@alpha --rpl-user=repl:repl --pedantic
# master on beta: ... connected.
# slave on alpha: ... connected.
# Checking for binary logging on master...
# Setting up replication...
# ...done.
$ mysqlrpladmin --master=root:passwd@beta \
              --slave=root:passwd@alpha,root:passwd@gamma health
```

```
# Checking privileges.
#
# Replication Topology Health:
+--------+-------+---------+--------+-----------+-----------+
| host   | port  | role    | state  | gtid_mode | health    |
+--------+-------+---------+--------+-----------+-----------+
| beta   | 3306  | MASTER  | UP     | ON        | OK        |
| alpha  | 3306  | SLAVE   | UP     | ON        | OK        |
| gamma  | 3306  | SLAVE   | UP     | ON        | OK        |
+--------+-------+---------+--------+-----------+-----------+
# ...done.
```

Replication Failover Managers

MySQL replication easily enables a read scalable architecture by supporting multiple slaves. This provides a straightforward approach for replacing
a failed MySQL slave for high availability. It does not, by default, provide
high availability for the primary master database that performs all writes.
It is possible to define a MySQL replication configuration where failover,
and possibly failback, is possible, thus enabling high availability on the
MySQL master.

Prior to MySQL 5.6, with the introduction of new features including
GTID and crash-safe slaves, a more complicated approach was necessary.
In a controlled situation it is possible with a correct configuration to manu-
ally perform a failover with these steps:

- Ensure appropriate MySQL configuration to support failover and
  failback operations.

- Move slaves from the primary master to the failover master with
  appropriate replication checks.

- Stop write access to the primary master and set the MySQL instance
  to read only on the running server and in the server configuration file.

- Confirm the failover master has received and performed all
  replication events.

- Disable read-only access on the MySQL failover master.

- Update the default startup state of the original MySQL master and
  failover master.

- Redirect application and batch write operations to the failover master. There is no single way to manage this step. This depends on the application technology in use. A general approach is via a virtual IP (VIP).

The setup of a MySQL pair and the regular use of performing a controlled failover and failback is an excellent way to be prepared for what steps are necessary in a true failover situation for your disaster recovery (DR) strategy. This is a popular approach for managing software upgrades, database modifications, and application upgrades. The configuration of a MySQL pair is discussed in detail in Chapter 4 on multi-master replication. In a failure situation, however, there are several edge cases that can cause potential data loss and corruption in different disaster scenarios. A number of tools are available in the MySQL ecosystem to help in the management and automation of failover.

MySQL MHA

Created by MySQL expert and Oracle ACE Director Yoshinori Matsunobu (http://yoshinorimatsunobu.blogspot.com/), the MySQL-MHA: MySQL Master High Availability manager and tools (MySQL MHA) provide a wrapper to support the management of a MySQL replication and failover environment. This is one of the newer tools available and is being actively developed and used. This tool is written in Perl.

A primary objective of MHA is automating master failover and slave promotion within short (usually 10 to 30 seconds) downtime, without suffering from replication consistency problems, without spending money for lots of new servers, without performance penalty, without complexity (easy to install), and without changing existing deployments.

Node Software Installation

On each MySQL master and slave server and management server, the installation of the MHA node software is necessary. You should always check for the most current version to download at http://code.google.com/p/mysql-master-ha/.

Ubuntu/Debian

```
$ sudo apt-get install libdbd-mysql-perl
$ cd /tmp
$ wget http://mysql-master-ha.googlecode.com/files/
  mha4mysql-node_0.53_all.deb
$ sudo dpkg -i mha4mysql-node_*.deb
$ rm -f i mha4mysql-node_*.deb
```

RHEL/CentOS/OL

```
$ sudo yum install perl-DBD-MySQL
$ cd /tmp
$ wget https://mysql-master-ha.googlecode.com/files/
  mha4mysql-node-0.53-0.noarch.rpm
$ sudo rpm -ivh mha4mysql-node-*.noarch.rpm
$ rm -f i mha4mysql-node_*.noarch.rpm
```

Source Code

Refer to http://code.google.com/p/mysql-master-ha/wiki/Installation for instructions on installing MySQL MHA from the source code.

Manager Software Installation

MHA is a management process and should be operated on a separate management server that is not part of the MySQL master/slave topology. The installation of the MHA manager software is performed with the following.

Ubuntu/Debian

```
$ sudo apt-get install -y libdbd-mysql-perl libconfig-tiny-perl \
  liblog-dispatch-perl libparallel-forkmanager-perl
$ cd /tmp
$ wget http://mysql-master-ha.googlecode.com/files/
  mha4mysql-manager_0.53_all.deb
$ sudo dpkg -i mha4mysql-manager_*_all.deb
$ rm -f mha4mysql-manager_*_all.deb
```

RHEL/CentOS/OL

```
$ sudo yum install perl-Config-Tiny1 perl-Log-Dispatch perl-Parallel-ForkManager
$ cd /tmp
$ wget https://mysql-master-ha.googlecode.com/files/
  mha4mysql-manager-0.53-0.noarch.rpm
$ sudo rpm -ivh mha4mysql-manager-*.noarch.rpm
$ rm -f mha4mysql-manager-*.noarch.rpm
```

References

MHA is an open source project available under the GPL v2 license. More information can be found at the following links:

- **Code** http://code.google.com/p/mysql-master-ha/
- **Blog** http://yoshinorimatsunobu.blogspot.com/2011/07/announcing-mysql-mha-mysql-master-high.html

Usage with Virtual Environment

In this example we will use the three virtual servers that are defined in the instructions in the appendix. The alpha server is the MySQL master, the beta server is the failover master, and the gamma server will be used for a management server. In this example we will use MySQL version 5.5.

Configuration Setup MHA requires a number of configuration settings regarding the definition of the MySQL topology and the *SSH* and MySQL communication between the servers. On the management server the following is required:

```
$ cd $HOME
$ mkdir -p mha/etc
$ echo "[server default]
# mysql user and password
user=root
password=passwd
ssh_user=user
# working directory on the manager
manager_workdir=/home/user/mha/log
# working directory on MySQL servers
remote_workdir=/home/user/mha/log
master_binlog_dir=/home/user/mysql/data
[server1]
hostname=alpha
[server2]
hostname=beta" > $HOME/mha/etc/mha.cnf
$ sudo touch /etc/masterha_default.cnf
```

SSH Access

MHA uses SSH for server communication between databases. This will require you to set up SSH keyed authentication to enable automated commands. The following MHA command will check and confirm access between the management server and all MySQL nodes:

```
$ masterha_check_ssh --conf=$HOME/mha/etc/mha.cnf
[info] Reading default configurations from /etc/masterha_default.cnf..
[info] Reading application default configurations from
/home/user/mha/etc/mha.cnf..
[info] Reading server configurations from /home/user/mha/etc/mha.cnf..
[info] Starting SSH connection tests..
[debug]  Connecting via SSH from user@alpha(192.168.1.51:22) to
 user@beta(192.168.1.52:22)..
[debug]    ok.
[debug]  Connecting via SSH from user@beta(192.168.1.52:22) to
 user@alpha(192.168.1.51:22)..
[debug]    ok.
[info] All SSH connection tests passed successfully.
```

MySQL Configuration Optimizations

The default slave configurations as defined in the appendix will produce the following warning when running masterha_check_repl:

```
[warning]  relay_log_purge=0 is not set on slave
beta(192.168.1.52:3306).
```

This can be corrected with the following additional MySQL configuration and restarting the MySQL instances on all servers:

```
# $HOME/mysql/etc/my.cnf
[mysqld]
relay_log_purge=0
```

The manager requires mysqlbinlog in the PATH on each server to run successfully via SSH. While the mysqldump command may be in the PATH on the management server, and also on the MySQL instances when you connect manually, you may experience the following error:

```
[info]   Connecting to user@192.168.1.52(beta:22)..
Can't exec "mysqlbinlog": No such file or directory at
/usr/share/perl5/MHA/BinlogManager.pm line 99.
mysqlbinlog version not found!
 at /usr/bin/apply_diff_relay_logs line 463
```

The SSH command used here is a non-interactive shell, and while the /etc/profile.d/mysql.sh script is executed for interactive shell usage, it is not for non-interactive usage (i.e., if you manually ssh to a server, the MYSQL_HOME environment variable is defined and $MYSQL_HOME/bin is added to your PATH).

The solution is to add to the start of the $HOME/.bashrc file a reference to source this file specifically:

```
[ -s /etc/profile.d/mysql.sh ] && . /etc/profile.d/mysql.sh
```

Adding to the end of the file will not work with the virtual environments configured, as Ubuntu uses this line in the user $HOME/.bashrc file to stop reading the file in non-interactive mode:

```
# If not running interactively, don't do anything
[ -z "$PS1" ] && return
```

By default design, the slave replication stream on the active master server is not running. The masterha_check_repl will correctly report this with:

```
[warning] SQL Thread is stopped(no error) on alpha(192.168.1.51:3306)
```

This can be solved by starting the slave replication stream on the active master:

```
alpha> SLAVE START;
```

MHA Replication Check

When the MHA node and manager software are installed and configured you can confirm your MySQL topology meets the needs of MHA with:

```
$ masterha_check_repl --conf=$HOME/mha/etc/mha.cnf
[info] Reading default configurations from /etc/masterha_default.cnf..
[info] Reading application default configurations from
 /home/user/mha/etc/mha.cnf..
[info] Reading server configurations from /home/user/mha/etc/mha.cnf..
[info] MHA::MasterMonitor version 0.53.
[info] Multi-master configuration is detected. Current primary(writable)
 master is alpha(192.168.1.51:3306)
[info] Master configurations are as below:
Master alpha(192.168.1.51:3306), replicating from beta(192.168.1.52:3306)
Master beta(192.168.1.52:3306), replicating from alpha(192.168.1.51:3306),
read-only
[info] Dead Servers:
[info] Alive Servers:
[info]    alpha(192.168.1.51:3306)
[info]    beta(192.168.1.52:3306)
[info] Alive Slaves:
[info]    beta(192.168.1.52:3306)  Version=5.5.24-log (oldest major version
 between slaves) log-bin:enabled
[info]      Replicating from alpha(192.168.1.51:3306)
[info] Current Alive Master: alpha(192.168.1.51:3306)
[info] Checking slave configurations..
[info] Checking replication filtering settings..
```

```
[info]   binlog_do_db= , binlog_ignore_db=
[info]   Replication filtering check ok.
[info] Starting SSH connection tests..
[info] All SSH connection tests passed successfully.
[info] Checking MHA Node version..
[info]   Version check ok.
[info] Checking SSH publickey authentication settings on the current master..
[info] HealthCheck: SSH to alpha is reachable.
[info] Master MHA Node version is 0.53.
[info] Checking recovery script configurations on the current master..
[info]   Executing command: save_binary_logs --command=test --start_pos=4
--binlog_dir=/home/user/mysql/data
--output_file=/home/user/mha/log/save_binary_logs_test
--manager_version=0.53 --start_file=mysql-bin.000005
[info]   Connecting to user@alpha(alpha)..
  Creating /home/user/mha/log if not exists..    ok.
  Checking output directory is accessible or not..
   ok.
  Binlog found at /home/user/mysql/data, up to mysql-bin.000005
[info] Master setting check done.
[info] Checking SSH publickey authentication and checking recovery
script configurations on all alive slave servers..
[info]   Executing command : apply_diff_relay_logs --command=test
--slave_user=root --slave_host=beta --slave_ip=192.168.1.52
--slave_port=3306 --workdir=/home/user/mha/log --target_version=5.5.24-log
--manager_version=0.53 --relay_log_info=/home/user/mysql/data/relay-log.info
--relay_dir=/home/user/mysql/data/   --slave_pass=xxx
[info]   Connecting to user@192.168.1.52(beta:22)..
Creating directory /home/user/mha/log.. done.
  Checking slave recovery environment settings..
    Opening /home/user/mysql/data/relay-log.info ... ok.
    Relay log found at /home/user/mysql/data, up to relay-log.000012
    Temporary relay log file is /home/user/mysql/data/relay-log.000012
    Testing mysql connection and privileges.. done.
    Testing mysqlbinlog output.. done.
    Cleaning up test file(s).. done.
[info] Slaves settings check done.
[info]
alpha (current master)
 +--beta
[info] Checking replication health on beta..
[info]   ok.
[warning] master_ip_failover_script is not defined.
[warning] shutdown_script is not defined.
[info] Got exit code 0 (Not master dead).
MySQL Replication Health is OK.
$ echo $?
0
```

If MySQL is not running you will find errors similar to:

```
[error][/usr/share/perl5/MHA/ServerManager.pm, ln188] There is no alive server.
We can't do failover
```

```
[error][/usr/share/perl5/MHA/MasterMonitor.pm, ln383] Error happened on checking
configurations.  at /usr/share/perl5/MHA/MasterMonitor.pm line 298
[error][/usr/share/perl5/MHA/MasterMonitor.pm, ln478] Error happened on
 monitoring servers.
[info] Got exit code 1 (Not master dead).
MySQL Replication Health is NOT OK!
$ echo $?
1
```

Running the MHA Manager

After successfully configuring SSH and MySQL access for MHA and confirming the replication environment is suitable to be managed by MHA, you can start the MHA manager with:

```
$ masterha_manager --conf=$HOME/mha/etc/mha.cnf
...
[info] Slaves settings check done.
[info]
alpha (current master)
 +--beta
[warning] master_ip_failover_script is not defined.
[warning] shutdown_script is not defined.
[info] Set master ping interval 3 seconds.
[warning] secondary_check_script is not defined. It is highly recommended
setting it to check master reachability from two or more routes.
[info] Starting ping health check on alpha(192.168.1.51:3306)..
[info] Ping(SELECT) succeeded, waiting until MySQL doesn't respond..
```

This command is run in the foreground in this situation and will not return access to the session until completed. For production operation, this command should be wrapped to create an applicable daemon process and monitored accordingly. The warnings described will be discussed at a later time.

In a new terminal session you can verify the operation of the manager that was just started. This command should be added to applicable system and MySQL monitoring to detect any issues or failure with the manager.

```
$ masterha_check_status --conf=$HOME/mha/etc/mha.cnf
mha (pid:16387) is running(0:PING_OK), master:alpha
$ echo $?
0
```

If the MHA manager is not running, the following will occur:

```
$ masterha_check_status --conf=$HOME/mha/etc/mha.cnf
mha is stopped(2:NOT_RUNNING).
$ echo $?
2
```

Stopping the MHA Manager

The running MHA manager can be terminated with:

```
$ masterha_stop --conf=$HOME/mha/etc/mha.cnf
Stopped mha successfully.
```

MySQL MHA Operation

The power of using MySQL MHA is to handle the situation of an uncontrolled failover (i.e., the loss of the MySQL master). MHA can also be used to perform a controlled failover. This can be very helpful in managing software releases and database maintenance windows.

MHA Controlled Failover

You can simulate a controlled failover with the following command on the management server:

```
$ masterha_master_switch --conf=$HOME/mha/etc/mha.cnf \
  --master_state=alive --new_master_host=beta --orig_master_is_new_slave \
   --interactive=0
[info] MHA::MasterRotate version 0.53.
[info] Starting online master switch..
[info] * Phase 1: Configuration Check Phase..
[info] Reading default configurations from /etc/masterha_default.cnf..
[info] Reading application default configurations from
/home/user/mha/etc/mha.cnf..
[info] Reading server configurations from /home/user/mha/etc/mha.cnf..
[info] Multi-master configuration is detected. Current primary(writable)
master is alpha(192.168.1.51:3306)
[info] Master configurations are as below:
Master alpha(192.168.1.51:3306), replicating from beta(192.168.1.52:3306)
Master beta(192.168.1.52:3306), replicating from alpha(192.168.1.51:3306),
read-only
[info] Current Alive Master: alpha(192.168.1.51:3306)
[info] Alive Slaves:
[info]    beta(192.168.1.52:3306)  Version=5.5.24-log (oldest major version
between slaves) log-bin:enabled
[info]      Replicating from alpha(192.168.1.51:3306)
[info] Executing FLUSH NO_WRITE_TO_BINLOG TABLES. This may take long time..
[info]   ok.
[info] Checking MHA is not monitoring or doing failover..
[info] Checking replication health on beta..
[info]   ok.
[info] beta can be new master.
[info]
From:
alpha (current master)
 +--beta
```

```
To:
beta (new master)
 +--alpha
[info] Checking whether beta(192.168.1.52:3306) is ok for the new master..
[info]   ok.
[info] ** Phase 1: Configuration Check Phase completed.
[info]
[info] * Phase 2: Rejecting updates Phase..
[info]
[warning] master_ip_online_change_script is not defined.
Skipping disabling writes on the current master.
[info] Locking all tables on the orig master to reject updates
from everybody (including root):
[info] Executing FLUSH TABLES WITH READ LOCK..
[info]   ok.
[info] Orig master binlog:pos is mysql-bin.000002:107.
[info]   Waiting to execute all relay logs on beta(192.168.1.52:3306)..
[info]   master_pos_wait(mysql-bin.000002:107) completed on
beta(192.168.1.52:3306). Executed 0 events.
[info]    done.
[info] Getting new master's binlog name and position..
[info]   mysql-bin.000002:107
[info]   All other slaves should start replication from here.
Statement should be: CHANGE MASTER TO MASTER_HOST='beta or 192.168.1.52',
MASTER_PORT=3306, MASTER_LOG_FILE='mysql-bin.000002', MASTER_LOG_POS=107,
MASTER_USER='repl', MASTER_PASSWORD='xxx';
[info] Setting read_only=0 on beta(192.168.1.52:3306)..
[info]   ok.
[info] * Switching slaves in parallel..
[info] Unlocking all tables on the orig master:
[info] Executing UNLOCK TABLES..
[info]   ok.
[info] Starting orig master as a new slave..
[info]   Resetting slave alpha(192.168.1.51:3306) and starting replication
from the new master beta(192.168.1.52:3306)..
[info]   Executed CHANGE MASTER.
[info]   Slave started.
[info] All new slave servers switched successfully.
[info] * Phase 5: New master cleanup phase..
[info]   beta: Resetting slave info succeeded.
[info] Switching master to beta(192.168.1.52:3306) completed successfully.
```

This command also has an interactive mode. This can be used with
`--interactive=1`.

MHA Automated Failover

In the defined virtual environment from the appendix that is being used,
we can test MHA by stopping MySQL on the master:

```
alpha$ mysqladmin shutdown
```

The following output from the MySQL MHA Manager session occurs within a few seconds:

```
[warning] Got error on MySQL select ping: 2006 (MySQL server has gone away)
[info] Executing SSH check script: save_binary_logs --command=test --start_pos=
4 --binlog_dir=/home/user/mysql/data --output_file=/home/user/mha/log/
save_binary_logs_test --manager_version=0.53 --binlog_prefix=mysql-bin
   Creating /home/user/mha/log if not exists..      ok.
   Checking output directory is accessible or not..
   ok.
   Binlog found at /home/user/mysql/data, up to mysql-bin.000005
[info] HealthCheck: SSH to alpha is reachable.
[warning] Got error on MySQL connect: 2003 (Can't connect to MySQL server on
'192.168.1.51' (111))
[warning] Connection failed 1 time(s)..
[warning] Got error on MySQL connect: 2003 (Can't connect to MySQL server on
'192.168.1.51' (111))
[warning] Connection failed 2 time(s)..
[warning] Got error on MySQL connect: 2003 (Can't connect to MySQL server on
'192.168.1.51' (111))
[warning] Connection failed 3 time(s)..
[warning] Master is not reachable from health checker!
[warning] Master alpha(192.168.1.51:3306) is not reachable!
[warning] SSH is reachable.
[info] Connecting to a master server failed. Reading configuration file /etc/
masterha_default.cnf and /home/user/mha/etc/mha.cnf again, and trying to connect
to all servers to check server status..
[info] Reading default configurations from /etc/masterha_default.cnf..
[info] Reading application default configurations from /home/user/mha/etc/mha.
cnf..
[info] Reading server configurations from /home/user/mha/etc/mha.cnf..
[info] Dead Servers:
[info]    alpha(192.168.1.51:3306)
[info] Alive Servers:
[info]    beta(192.168.1.52:3306)
[info] Alive Slaves:
[info]    beta(192.168.1.52:3306)  Version=5.5.24-log (oldest major version
between slaves) log-bin:enabled
[info]       Replicating from alpha(192.168.1.51:3306)
[info] Checking slave configurations..
[info] Checking replication filtering settings..
[info]  Replication filtering check ok.
[info] Master is down!
[info] Terminating monitoring script.
[info] Got exit code 20 (Master dead).
[info] Reading default configurations from /etc/masterha_default.cnf..
[info] Reading application default configurations from /home/user/mha/etc/mha.
cnf..
[info] Reading server configurations from /home/user/mha/etc/mha.cnf..
[info] MHA::MasterFailover version 0.53.
[info] Starting master failover.
[info]
[info] * Phase 1: Configuration Check Phase..
```

```
[info]
[info] Dead Servers:
[info]    alpha(192.168.1.51:3306)
[info] Checking master reachability via mysql(double check)..
[info]   ok.
[info] Alive Servers:
[info]    beta(192.168.1.52:3306)
[info] Alive Slaves:
[info]    beta(192.168.1.52:3306)  Version=5.5.24-log (oldest major version
between slaves) log-bin:enabled
[info]        Replicating from alpha(192.168.1.51:3306)
[info] ** Phase 1: Configuration Check Phase completed.
[info]
[info] * Phase 2: Dead Master Shutdown Phase..
[info]
[info] Forcing shutdown so that applications never connect to the current master
[warning] master_ip_failover_script is not set. Skipping invalidating dead
master ip address.
[warning] shutdown_script is not set. Skipping explicit shutting down of the
dead master.
[info] * Phase 2: Dead Master Shutdown Phase completed.
[info]
[info] * Phase 3: Master Recovery Phase..
[info]
[info] * Phase 3.1: Getting Latest Slaves Phase..
[info]
[info] The latest binary log file/position on all slaves is mysql-bin.000005:107
[info] Latest slaves (Slaves that received relay log files to the latest):
[info]    beta(192.168.1.52:3306)  Version=5.5.24-log (oldest major version
between slaves) log-bin:enabled
[info]        Replicating from alpha(192.168.1.51:3306)
[info] The oldest binary log file/position on all slaves is mysql-bin.000005:107
[info] Oldest slaves:
[info]    beta(192.168.1.52:3306)  Version=5.5.24-log (oldest major version
between slaves) log-bin:enabled
[info]        Replicating from alpha(192.168.1.51:3306)
[info]
[info] * Phase 3.2: Saving Dead Master's Binlog Phase..
[info]
[info] Fetching dead master's binary logs..
[info] Executing command on the dead master alpha(192.168.1.51:3306): save_
binary_logs --command=save --start_file=mysql-bin.000005  --start_pos=107
--binlog_dir=/home/user/mysql/data --output_file=/home/user/mha/log/
saved_master_binlog_from_alpha_3306_20120617202902.binlog --handle_raw_binlog=1
--disable_log_bin=0 --manager_version=0.53
  Creating /home/user/mha/log if not exists..    ok.
 Concat binary/relay logs from mysql-bin.000005 pos 107 to mysql-bin.000005 EOF
into /home/user/mha/log/saved_master_binlog_from_alpha_3306_20120617202902.
binlog ..
  Dumping binlog format description event, from position 0 to 107.. ok.
  Dumping effective binlog data from /home/user/mysql/data/mysql-bin.000005
position 107 to tail(126).. ok.
 Concat succeeded.
saved_master_binlog_from_alpha_3306_20120617202902.binlog
```

```
100%  126     0.1KB/s   00:00
[info] scp from user@192.168.1.51:/home/user/mha/log/saved_master_binlog_from_
alpha_3306_
20120617202902.binlog to local:/home/user/mha/log/saved_master_binlog_from_
alpha_3306_20120617202902.binlog succeeded.
[info] HealthCheck: SSH to beta is reachable.
[info]
[info] * Phase 3.3: Determining New Master Phase..
[info]
[info] Finding the latest slave that has all relay logs for recovering other
slaves..
[info] All slaves received relay logs to the same position. No need to resync
each other.
[info] Searching new master from slaves..
[info]  Candidate masters from the configuration file:
[info]  Non-candidate masters:
[info] New master is beta(192.168.1.52:3306)
[info] Starting master failover..
[info]
From:
alpha (current master)
 +--beta

To:
beta (new master)
[info]
[info] * Phase 3.3: New Master Diff Log Generation Phase..
[info]
[info]  This server has all relay logs. No need to generate diff files from
the latest slave.
[info] Sending binlog..
saved_master_binlog_from_alpha_3306_20120617202902.binlog
100%  126     0.1KB/s   00:00
[info] scp from local:/home/user/mha/log/saved_master_binlog_from_al-
pha_3306_20120617202902.
binlog to user@beta:/home/user/mha/log/saved_master_binlog_from_alpha_
3306_20120617202902.binlog succeeded.
[info]
[info] * Phase 3.4: Master Log Apply Phase..
[info]
[info] *NOTICE: If any error happens from this phase, manual recovery is needed.
[info] Starting recovery on beta(192.168.1.52:3306)..
[info]  Generating diffs succeeded.
[info] Waiting until all relay logs are applied.
[info]  done.
[info] Getting slave status..
[info] This slave(beta)'s Exec_Master_Log_Pos equals to Read_Master_Log_Pos(
mysql-bin.000005:107). No need to recover from Exec_Master_Log_Pos.
[info] Connecting to the target slave host beta, running recover script..
[info] Executing command: apply_diff_relay_logs --command=apply --slave_user=
root --slave_host=beta --slave_ip=192.168.1.52  --slave_port=3306 --apply_files
=/home/user/mha/log/saved_master_binlog_from_alpha_3306_20120617202902.binlog
--workdir=/home/user/mha/log --target_version=5.5.24-log
--timestamp=20120617202902 --handle_raw_binlog=1 --disable_log_bin=0
```

```
--manager_version=0.53 --slave_pass=xxx
[info]
Applying differential binary/relay log files /home/user/mha/log/saved_master_
binlog_from_alpha_3306_20120617202902.binlog
on beta:3306. This may take long time...
Applying log files succeeded.
[info]  All relay logs were successfully applied.
[info] Getting new master's binlog name and position..
[info]  mysql-bin.000003:107
[info]  All other slaves should start replication from here. Statement should
be: CHANGE MASTER TO MASTER_HOST='beta or 192.168.1.52', MASTER_PORT=3306,
MASTER_LOG_FILE='mysql-bin.000003', MASTER_LOG_POS=107, MASTER_USER='repl',
MASTER_PASSWORD='xxx';

[warning] master_ip_failover_script is not set. Skipping taking over new
master ip address.
[info] Setting read_only=0 on beta(192.168.1.52:3306)..
[info]   ok.
[info] ** Finished master recovery successfully.
[info] * Phase 3: Master Recovery Phase completed.
[info]
[info] * Phase 4: Slaves Recovery Phase..
[info]
[info] * Phase 4.1: Starting Parallel Slave Diff Log Generation Phase..
[info]
[info] Generating relay diff files from the latest slave succeeded.
[info]
[info] * Phase 4.2: Starting Parallel Slave Log Apply Phase..
[info]
[info] All new slave servers recovered successfully.
[info]
[info] * Phase 5: New master cleanup phase..
[info]
[info] Resetting slave info on the new master..
[info]   beta: Resetting slave info succeeded.
[info] Master failover to beta(192.168.1.52:3306) completed successfully.
[info]

----- Failover Report -----
mha: MySQL Master failover alpha to beta succeeded
Master alpha is down!
Check MHA Manager logs at gamma for details.
Started automated(non-interactive) failover.
The latest slave beta(192.168.1.52:3306) has all relay logs for recovery.
Selected beta as a new master.
beta: OK: Applying all logs succeeded.
Generating relay diff files from the latest slave succeeded.
beta: Resetting slave info succeeded.
Master failover to beta(192.168.1.52:3306) completed successfully.
```

As you can see in this first simple example, MySQL MHA successfully detected a loss of communication with the master, and after performing necessary checks and validations has successfully failed over to the slave server.

Additional MHA Configuration Settings

There are several additional configuration options and scripts that can further improve the high availability with MHA. These include the master_ip_failover_script, shutdown_script, and secondary_check_script options, which are indicated as warnings in the previous output.

- **master_ip_failover_script**   In common high availability (HA) environments, in many cases people allocate one virtual IP address on a master. If the master crashes, HA software moves the virtual IP address to the standby server.

A sample script is located under (MHA Manager package)/samples/scripts/master_ip_failover. Sample scripts are included in the MHA Manager tarball and GitHub branch.

MHA Manager calls master_ip_failover_script three times. The first time is before entering the master monitor (for script validity checking), the second time is just before calling shutdown_script, and the third time is after applying all relay logs to the new master.

- **shutdown_script**   You may want to force a shutdown of the master MySQL instance so that it never restarts the instance. This is known as node fencing. This is important to avoid split-brain. A sample script is located at (MHA Manager package)/samples/scripts/power_manager. Sample scripts are included in MHA Manager tarball and GitHub branch.

- **secondary_check_script**   In general, it is highly recommended to have two or more network routes to check MySQL master server availability. By default, MHA Manager checks only using a single route from the manager to the master. This is not recommended in a highly available production environment. MHA can actually have two or more routes for checking network connectivity by calling an external script defined with the secondary_check_script parameter. For example:

```
secondary_check_script = masterha_secondary_check -s remote_1 -s remote_2
```

MMM

The Multi-Master Replication Manager for MySQL (MMM) is a set of scripts that provide management monitoring and failover of a MySQL replication environment.

While this product works in a number of situations, generally just two servers, and is still used with production systems, it is no longer maintained and several important bugs remain unresolved. It is not recommended you use this product. For a good explanation of current issues, see http://mysql-mmm .org/mmm1:development-plans and http://www.xaprb.com/blog/2011/05/04/ whats-wrong-with-mmm/.

More information about MMM can be found at http://mysql-mmm.org/.

Flipper

Another historical product found in MySQL environments for managing MySQL pairs is Flipper. This can still be found in production use. This product is also no longer maintained, and online documentation from the original creator, Proven Scaling, is no longer available. You can find the source code at http://code.google.com/p/flipper/ and more information regarding usage at http://ronaldbradford.com/blog/using-flipper-to-manage-mysql-pairs-2008-12-09/.

Cluster Control

The team from Severalnines provides a wizard approach to create an appropriate MySQL configuration for a highly available MySQL replication environment. This requires the use of the online web form to obtain details of your current configuration to create a suitable configuration, which you can download. No testing of this wizard has been performed by the author. For more details, visit http://www.severalnines.com/replication-configurator/.

Cluster Management

A common approach for using a MySQL pair effectively in a production application environment is to use virtual IPs (VIPs) management for dedicated write and read threads. By using a VIP, application connections can remain defined as a fixed value, while the cluster management determines the host ownership of the VIP address.

For a database like MySQL, connection management is more complex due to several factors, including transactions and persistent connections. An incorrect use of VIP can cause problems like split-brain situations and data corruption. The use of a VIP can be problematic, with persistent connection managers and hanging connections. Depending on the application technology, additional connection management, including killing the connection pool on application servers, may be necessary to minimize risks. This following article gives some great background details related to MySQL: http://scale-out-blog.blogspot.com/2011/01/virtual-ip-addresses-and-their.html.

The Linux High Availability project maintains the building blocks for cluster infrastructure, including the Heartbeat daemon and Cluster Glue. More information can be found at http://linux-ha.org/. Combined with Pacemaker, this Cluster Resource Manager (CRM) helps to provide a suitable solution to be used in conjunction with MySQL replication. More information can be found at http://clusterlabs.org.

Red Hat also provides a high availability cluster manager. See http://www.redhat.com/products/enterprise-linux-add-ons/high-availability/ for more information.

There is some information about clustering MySQL instances using Oracle Clusterware. More details can be found at http://ilmarkerm.blogspot.com/2011/11/clustering-mysql-instances-with-oracle.html.

Providing a highly availability cluster environment combined with a MySQL replication topology is further complicated when the application technology uses persistent connection management (e.g., Java). Any cluster management implementation needs to consider the type of database access and the applicable error detection of a transaction and applicable recovery processes to retry the transaction or report an appropriate error. With persistent connection management technology it is often of benefit to flush the connection pool when changing the underlying host.

Percona Replication Manager (PRM)

By combining Corosync, Pacemaker, a MySQL resource agent and MySQL, the Percona Replication Manager (PRM) provides a cluster management solution with a distributed architecture to reduce a single point of failure (SPOF). The goal of PRM is to provide the following features:

- Reader and writer VIP behaviors similar to MMM.

- If the master fails, a new master is promoted from the slaves; no master to master setup needed. Selection of master is based on, scores published by the slaves, the more up to date slaves have higher scores for promotion.

- Some nodes can be dedicated to be only slaves or less likely to become master.

- A node can be the preferred master.

- If replication on a slave breaks or lags beyond a defined threshold, the reader VIP(s) is removed. MySQL is not restarted.

- If no slaves are OK, all VIPs, readers and writer, will be located on the master.

- During a master switch, connections are killed on the demoted master to avoid replication conflicts.

- All slaves are in read-only mode.

- Simple administrative commands can remove master role from a node.

- Pacemaker stonith devices are supported.

- No logical limits in term of number of nodes.

- Easy to add nodes.

An introduction presentation at http://www.percona.com/files/ presentations/percona-live/dc-2012/PLDC2012-high-availability-with-percona-prm.pdf provides an overview of the PRM product and implementation approach. Detailed instructions for configuration and usage is available from the documentation at https://github.com/jayjanssen/Percona-Pacemaker-Resource-Agents/blob/master/doc/PRM-setup-guide.rst. The outdated article at http://www.mysqlperformanceblog.com/2011/ 11/29/percona-replication-manager-a-solution-for-mysql-high-availability-with-replication-using-pacemaker/ provided the listed features shown and a very detailed description of how PRM is designed to work.

Replication Prefetch

Paul Tuckfield of YouTube presented to the MySQL Community in 2007 the concept of replication slave prefetch. A very simple idea, this improves the performance of the single-threaded slave SQL thread by preloading the necessary data pages by a separate read thread. The ability to predict the future in MySQL replication is possible because the master binary log and the relay log contain all events yet to be applied in the slave replication stream. The following is a code snippet of the work:

```
module(..., package.seeall); required "lusql.mysql"
pattern= {
  ["UPDATE%s+(%w=).*%s(WHERE.*)"] = "SELECT * FROM %1 %2",
  [DELETE%s+FROM%s+(%w+).%s(WHERE.*)"] = SELECT * FROM %1 %2",
}
env = lusql.mysql()
con = env:connect("test", "root", "*****", "localhost", mysql.port)

function before_write(event)
  local line = event.query
  if not line then return end
  for pat,repl in pairs(pattern) do
    local str = string.gsub(line, pat, repl)
    if str then con:execute(str); break; end
  end
end
```

You can preview this code on a page from *MySQL High Availability* (O'Reilly, 2011) at Safari Books online at http://j.mp/EM3-prefetch (no subscription required).

Several articles exist that can provide some input on the various options that have been implemented by different individuals or companies:

- Replication Booster by Yoshinori Matsunobu can be found at https://github.com/yoshinorim/replication-booster-for-mysql. Some more information is at http://yoshinorimatsunobu.blogspot.com/2011/10/making-slave-pre-fetching-work-better.html.

- Domas Mituzas writes about work developments at Facebook at http://dom.as/2011/12/03/replication-prefetching/. The code is available at https://launchpad.net/mysqlatfacebook/tools.

- Anders Karlsson has created a MySQL replication accelerator. Read more at http://karlssonondatabases.blogspot.com/2011/03/want-to-accellerate-mysql-slave-here-is.html. The code is available at http://sourceforge.net/projects/slavereadahead/.

- It is not recommended that `mk-slave-prefetch` be used. This is deprecated as directed by the author of the utility. More information can be found at http://bit.ly/M0raRd.

MySQL Patches and Variants

Patches for MySQL are driven by the necessity of solving a specific problem that the core product may or may not include in the future. These improvements are generally due to the long deployment time of including a feature in the core MySQL product that serves for all general use cases, not just the specific customer case that it was originally developed for.

Patches are provided for the benefit of others, which is great for the community; however, these come at a cost if the needs or specific versions do not match your environment. When these conditions do match, the advantages of the development can be of great benefit. For example, Domas Mituzas wrote about how convenient it was to use the Google Patch for MySQL 4.0.26 because Wikipedia used the exact same point release. Read more at http://dom.as/2007/06/23/mysql-40-google-edition/ and http://dom.as/2010/07/25/mysql-versions-at-wikipedia/.

As you can see by these following company names, large web presences use and extend MySQL for their respective businesses and for the possible benefit of other MySQL users.

Independent Community Users

Several large MySQL users have contributed greatly to the MySQL ecosystem. Some of the patches provided have become core features in more recent versions of MySQL. Led initially by Google as early as 2007, many community provided patches have included improvements around replication. The Google patches for MySQL version 5.0 included global transaction IDs, binary logging event checksums, and semisynchronous replication, now standard features in MySQL 5.6. Facebook is the top organization currently providing MySQL patches to the MySQL community. With several of the top experts in MySQL and InnoDB internals outside of Oracle, Facebook has a continued investment in improving MySQL at scale, specifically in InnoDB multicore usage and replication.

While these patches can provide some exciting benefits, they have been specifically written for the needs of the client in question. They may not be applicable to other workloads and environments, and without a team of specialists that know the internal working code of MySQL may be a high risk to implement.

References
The following are some examples of community contributed works:

- **Google**   http://code.google.com/p/google-mysql-tools/wiki/ Mysql5Patches

- **Facebook**   http://www.facebook.com/MySQLatFacebook and https://launchpad.net/mysqlatfacebook

- **eBay**   http://code.google.com/p/mysql-heap-dynamic-rows/

- **Twitter**   https://github.com/twitter/mysql

Commercial Organizations

The MySQL ecosystem has seen several companies start to provide additional engineering services for supporting new features with MySQL. These provide feature development for a fee, and generally provide a far quicker time to market.

Monty Program
Founded by Michael "Monty" Widenius, one of the original founders of MySQL, Monty Program retains a number of core engineers from the original MySQL AB company. They provide many improvements to the MySQL product and offer these patches for upstream integration in future official MySQL versions. MariaDB is a feature compatible drop-in replacement version of MySQL that also includes many additional storage engines. MariaDB is available under the open source GNU GPL v2 license. More information can be found at http://mariadb.org. For environments that are heavy users of MyISAM, MariaDB provides a number of great performance improvements.

Percona
Percona is the longest established alternative commercial vendor in the MySQL space. They develop and support several MySQL Products, including Percona Server, Percona Cluster (with Galera), XtraDB, XtraBackup, and Percona Toolkit. More information can be found at http://percona.com.

Conclusion

A database administrator should be aware of and use this diverse set of tools to monitor, manage, verify, and improve an existing production MySQL replication environment. Combined with deployment automation and service monitoring as described in Chapter 8, replication can provide powerful benefits in any production environment when configured and operating normally.

Examples and links in this chapter are available for download from http://EffectiveMySQL.com/book/replication-techniques.

6

Extending Replication
for Practical Needs

MySQL replication is essential for any production environment. In the previous chapters we have discussed the use of replication, some of the known limitations, and hinted at some of the ongoing improvements. In many deployments, current MySQL replication provides an adequate approach to improving scalability and availability. Prior to the MySQL 5.6 version there were more complex operations necessary for multi-master replication and high availability management. In addition, some of the features of MySQL replication that are strengths in the flexibility of the replication implementation are also limitations for certain architectures.

The MySQL replication landscape has significantly changed with additional third-party providers. In this chapter we will discuss some of these providers and the features they offer, specifically:

- Supporting synchronous replication

- Active/active multi-master replication supporting bidirectional replication

- Complex topologies, including circular, star, and fan, in support of multiple masters for a given slave

Highly Requested Replication Features

Without a doubt, the ability for synchronous replication ranks as one of the top requests for improvements with native MySQL replication functionality. The asynchronous nature provides several benefits, especially in WAN or network limiting environments; however, this also causes a lack of guaranteed data consistency between all servers, and depending on the needs of the application, that can introduce additional complexity. Many scale-out environments use native replication successfully to support hundreds and thousands of MySQL instances. New features from other providers can add value to these existing environments.

Providing a mixed topology that includes active master/master replication and supporting multiple masters for a given slave is also a common need for ensuring high availability and reducing latency in a global deployment.

Another key feature request is that of automatic sharding and partitioning, especially for cloud-based deployments.

Combining all these features with the need for adequate disaster recovery management and ongoing growth in data storage, throughput, and performance are the key feature areas for using MySQL at scale.

MySQL Cluster

MySQL Cluster, which is a different product than the MySQL database server, provides several of these features natively. Synchronous replication and automatic partitioning are standard features in MySQL Cluster; however, this is a very different product than the MySQL server. The name is appropriate for features, yet deceiving when compared with MySQL.

While this product includes a SQL interface, data access for high through-put environments can be achieved from an Application Programming Interface (API). The strengths and features of MySQL Cluster are not always applicable to an Online Transaction Processing (OLTP) application using traditional MySQL replication. There are also additional limitations, including the database size with available memory. This product is ideal in certain situations and is widely used in the telecommunications and gaming industries. The use, understanding, and benefits of MySQL Cluster are topics for an entire book.

It should be noted that MySQL Cluster mainly differs from a regular MySQL server for the following additional reasons:

- There is currently no referential integrity. Foreign keys are being developed for a future version.

- You can only use the NDB storage engine and are then limited to READ-COMMITTED transaction level.

- While primary key lookups are fast and concurrent access is faster than a regular MySQL server, more complex queries, including table joins and group by operations, are more expensive.

For more information about MySQL Cluster, refer to http://www.mysql.com/products/cluster/.

Galera Cluster for MySQL

Galera Cluster for MySQL provides synchronous replication and multi-master features when using InnoDB. This means a Galera Cluster supports reads and writes to any node, and provides a true multi-master experience with no lag and no loss of transactions.

Galera Cluster is built on a more generic replication API called wsrep (Write Set REPlication). The wsrep API defines an interface between the database server and the replication plugin and is a separate open source project by Codership. MySQL-wsrep is a patch for MySQL to implement the wsrep API in the database server. This patch will enable the MySQL server to use a wsrep provider plugin, for example, Galera. Galera is the wsrep provider including synchronous multi-master replication.

Galera 2.*x* is the currently supported version available with MySQL 5.1 GA and MySQL 5.5 GA. Galera is an open source project available under the GPL v3 license, with integration components available under the GPL v2 license to be compatible with MySQL.

Current Limitations

When comparing Galera with a traditional MySQL server, there are some limitations; however, these are not serious roadblocks to trying and using Galera effectively:

- Only InnoDB tables are supported in replication.
- LOCK and UNLOCK statements, GET_LOCK() and RELEASE_LOCK() functions are not supported.
- Log output to TABLE using `log_output` is not supported. Logging must be to FILE.
- XA (eXtended Architecture) transactions are not currently supported.

References

For more information see:

- **Product Home**   http://www.codership.com/content/using-galera-cluster/
- **Downloads**   http://www.codership.com/downloads/download-mysqlgalera
- **Documentation**   http://www.codership.com/wiki
- Details of wsrep can be found at https://launchpad.net/wsrep

Terminology

When using Galera Cluster, a number of terms are used and referenced in online documentation. These include the following:

- **Galera Cluster**   This refers to the operational nodes that constitute the cluster.
- **Node**   This refers to an individual server instance that is part of a Galera Cluster.
- **Joiner**   This refers to a new node that wishes to join a Galera Cluster.

- **Donor** This refers to a Galera node that is used for synchronizing the Joiner.
- **Group** This is a layer of communication between an individual node and a Galera Cluster.

Installation

Galera provides RedHat/CentOS/Oracle Linux `.rpm` packaging, Ubuntu/Debian `.deb` packaging, and Linux binary `.tar.gz` installation options. The following installation steps will install the binaries on an Ubuntu/Debian Linux system that is defined in the virtual environments from the appendix.

The following steps use specific Galera and MySQL binary versions. Please refer to the downloads link for the most current versions available. For this installation we will be using three servers:

- `alpha` 192.168.1.51
- `beta` 192.168.1.52
- `gamma` 192.168.1.53

Install Galera

The wsrep implementation (i.e., Galera) must be installed first. This is demonstrated on the `alpha` server:

```
$ cd /tmp
$ wget https://launchpad.net/galera/2.x/23.2.1/+download/galera-23.2.1-amd64.deb
$ sudo apt-get install libssl0.9.8
$ sudo dpkg -i galera-*.deb
$ rm -f galera*.deb
```

The following library is installed with the Galera package. This specific file path is required later during configuration:

```
$ ls -l /usr/lib/galera/
total 2104
-rwxr-xr-x 1 root root 2153064 May 18 18:02 libgalera_smm.so
```

The Galera package contains the following files for reference:

```
$ dpkg --contents galera-23.2.1-amd64.deb
drwxr-xr-x root/root          0 2012-05-18 18:02 ./
drwxr-xr-x root/root          0 2012-05-18 18:02 ./etc/
```

```
drwxr-xr-x root/root          0 2012-05-18 18:02 ./etc/init.d/
-rwxr-xr-x root/root       3132 2012-05-18 18:02 ./etc/init.d/garb
drwxr-xr-x root/root          0 2012-05-18 18:02 ./etc/default/
-rw-r--r-- root/root        502 2012-05-18 18:02 ./etc/default/garb
drwxr-xr-x root/root          0 2012-05-18 18:02 ./etc/ld.so.conf.d/
-rw-r--r-- root/root          0 2012-05-18 18:02 ./etc/ld.so.conf.d/galera.conf
drwxr-xr-x root/root          0 2012-05-18 18:02 ./usr/
drwxr-xr-x root/root          0 2012-05-18 18:02 ./usr/share/
drwxr-xr-x root/root          0 2012-05-18 18:02 ./usr/share/doc/
drwxr-xr-x root/root          0 2012-05-18 18:02 ./usr/share/doc/galera/
-rw-r--r-- root/root      35147 2012-05-18 18:02 ./usr/share/doc/galera/COPYING
-rw-r--r-- root/root       5900 2012-05-18 18:02 ./usr/share/doc/galera/
README-MySQL
-rw-r--r-- root/root      21740 2012-05-18 18:02 ./usr/share/doc/galera/README
drwxr-xr-x root/root          0 2012-05-18 18:02 ./usr/lib/
drwxr-xr-x root/root          0 2012-05-18 18:02 ./usr/lib/galera/
-rwxr-xr-x root/root    2153064 2012-05-18 18:02 ./usr/lib/galera/
libgalera_smm.so
drwxr-xr-x root/root          0 2012-05-18 18:02 ./usr/bin/
-rwxr-xr-x root/root    1345448 2012-05-18 18:02 ./usr/bin/garbd
```

Install MySQL 5.5 with wsrep Patch

The patched MySQL version with the wsrep connector from Codership can now be installed with the following commands:

```
$ cd
$ sudo apt-get install libaio1  # MySQL 5.5 dependency
$ wget https://launchpad.net/codership-mysql/5.5/5.5.23-23.6/+download/mysql-
5.5.23_wsrep_23.6-linux-x86_64.tar.gz
$ tar xvfz mysql-5.5.23_wsrep_23.6-linux-x86_64.tar.gz
$ mv mysql-5.5.23_wsrep_23.6-linux-x86_64 mysql
$ cd mysql
```

The installation and verification of MySQL is the same as normal MySQL procedures that are also described in the appendix:

```
$ ./scripts/mysql_install_db
Installing MySQL system tables...
120606 15:02:01 [Note] WSREP: Read nil XID from storage engines,
skipping position init
120606 15:02:01 [Note] WSREP: wsrep_load(): loading provider library 'none'
120606 15:02:05 [Note] WSREP: Service disconnected.
120606 15:02:06 [Note] WSREP: Some threads may fail to exit.
OK
Filling help tables...
120606 15:02:06 [Note] WSREP: Read nil XID from storage engines,
skipping position init
120606 15:02:06 [Note] WSREP: wsrep_load(): loading provider library 'none'
120606 15:02:06 [Note] WSREP: Service disconnected.
120606 15:02:07 [Note] WSREP: Some threads may fail to exit.
OK
...
```

```
$ ./bin/mysqld_safe &
$ tail -20 data/`hostname`.err
$ ./bin/mysql_secure_installation
$ HOSTNAME=`hostname`
$ echo "[client]
user=root
password=passwd
[mysql]
prompt='${HOSTNAME}> '" > $HOME/.my.cnf
$ ./bin/mysql -e "SELECT version()";
+-----------+
| version() |
+-----------+
| 5.5.23    |
+-----------+
```

We can confirm the wsrep deployment by reviewing the new default variables available with:

```
$ bin/mysql -e "SHOW GLOBAL VARIABLES LIKE 'ws%'"
+------------------------------+-------
| Variable_name                | Value
+------------------------------+-------
| wsrep_OSU_method             | TOI
| wsrep_auto_increment_control | ON
| wsrep_causal_reads           | OFF
| wsrep_certify_nonPK          | ON
| wsrep_cluster_address        |
| wsrep_cluster_name           | my_wsrep_cluster
| wsrep_convert_LOCK_to_trx    | OFF
| wsrep_data_home_dir          | /home/user/mysql/data/
| wsrep_dbug_option            |
| wsrep_debug                  | OFF
| wsrep_drupal_282555_workaround | OFF
| wsrep_forced_binlog_format   | NONE
| wsrep_max_ws_rows            | 131072
| wsrep_max_ws_size            | 1073741824
| wsrep_node_address           |
| wsrep_node_incoming_address  | AUTO
| wsrep_node_name              | alpha
| wsrep_notify_cmd             |
| wsrep_on                     | OFF
| wsrep_provider               | none
| wsrep_provider_options       |
| wsrep_recover                | OFF
| wsrep_replicate_myisam       | OFF
| wsrep_retry_autocommit       | 1
| wsrep_slave_threads          | 1
| wsrep_sst_auth               |
| wsrep_sst_donor              |
| wsrep_sst_method             | mysqldump
| wsrep_sst_receive_address    | AUTO
| wsrep_start_position         | 00000000-0000-0000-0000-000000000000:-1
+------------------------------+-------
```

Configuring MySQL with wsrep

MySQL will operate as a normal traditional server by default. Galera usage requires a number of MySQL configuration settings. The following are the minimum recommended settings:

```
$ cd $HOME/mysql
$ mkdir etc
$ echo "[mysqld]
wsrep_provider=/usr/lib/galera/libgalera_smm.so
binlog_format=ROW
default_storage_engine=InnoDB
innodb_autoinc_lock_mode=2
innodb_locks_unsafe_for_binlog=1
# optional
innodb_flush_log_at_trx_commit=0
innodb_doublewrite=0" > etc/my.cnf
```

As you can see, there is no replication-specific configuration necessary. Binary logging is not required, nor is a server ID to use within a Galera Cluster. To define a Galera Cluster you must specify a cluster address. Restarting the MySQL instance with the new configuration and specifying a new empty cluster address with the wsrep_cluster_address configuration parameter enables Galera for this instance:

```
$ ./bin/mysqladmin -uroot shutdown
$ ./bin/mysqld_safe --defaults-file=etc/my.cnf --wsrep_cluster_address=gcomm:// &
```

As you can see from the MySQL error log output, a lot of additional information is now provided:

```
mysqld_safe Starting mysqld daemon with databases from /home/user/mysql/data
InnoDB: The InnoDB memory heap is disabled
InnoDB: Mutexes and rw_locks use GCC atomic builtins
InnoDB: Compressed tables use zlib 1.2.3
InnoDB: Using Linux native AIO
InnoDB: Initializing buffer pool, size = 128.0M
InnoDB: Completed initialization of buffer pool
InnoDB: highest supported file format is Barracuda.
InnoDB: Waiting for the background threads to start
InnoDB: 1.1.8 started; log sequence number 1595843
[Note] Event Scheduler: Loaded 0 events
[Note] WSREP: Read nil XID from storage engines, skipping position init
[Note] WSREP: wsrep_load(): loading provider library
 '/usr/lib/galera/libgalera_smm.so'
[Note] WSREP: wsrep_load(): Galera 23.2.1(r129) by Codership Oy
 <info@codership.com> loaded successfully.
[Warning] WSREP: Could not open saved state file for reading: /home/user/mysql/
data//grastate.dat
```

```
[Note] WSREP: Found saved state: 00000000-0000-0000-0000-000000000000:-1
[Note] WSREP: Preallocating 134219048/134219048 bytes in '/home/user/mysql/
data//galera.cache'...
[Note] WSREP: Passing config to GCS: base_host = 192.168.1.51;
gcache.dir = /home/user/mysql/data/; gcache.keep_pages_size = 0;
gcache.mem_size = 0; gcache.name = /home/user/mysql/data//galera.cache;
gcache.page_size = 128M; gcache.size = 128M; gcs.fc_debug = 0;
gcs.fc_factor = 0.5; gcs.fc_limit = 16; gcs.fc_master_slave = NO; gcs.max_
packet_size = 64500; gcs.max_throttle = 0.25;
gcs.recv_q_hard_limit = 9223372036854775807; gcs.recv_q_soft_limit = 0.25;
gcs.sync_donor = NO; replicator.causal_read_timeout = PT30S; replicator.commit_
order = 3
[Note] WSREP: Assign initial position for certification: -1, protocol version:
-1
[Note] WSREP: Start replication
[Note] WSREP: Setting initial position to 00000000-0000-0000-0000-000000000000:-
1
[Note] WSREP: protonet asio version 0
[Note] WSREP: backend: asio
[Note] WSREP: GMCast version 0
[Note] WSREP: (c3300902-b991-11e1-0800-040d7f7e9e14, 'tcp://0.0.0.0:4567')
 listening at tcp://0.0.0.0:4567
[Note] WSREP: (c3300902-b991-11e1-0800-040d7f7e9e14, 'tcp://0.0.0.0:4567')
 multicast: , ttl: 1
[Note] WSREP: EVS version 0
[Note] WSREP: PC version 0
[Note] WSREP: gcomm: connecting to group 'my_wsrep_cluster', peer ''
[Note] WSREP: view(view_id(PRIM,c3300902-b991-11e1-0800-040d7f7e9e14,1) memb {
      c3300902-b991-11e1-0800-040d7f7e9e14,
} joined {
} left {
} partitioned {
})
[Note] WSREP: gcomm: connected
[Note] WSREP: Changing maximum packet size to 64500, resulting msg size: 32636
[Note] WSREP: Shifting CLOSED -> OPEN (TO: 0)
[Note] WSREP: Opened channel 'my_wsrep_cluster'
[Note] /home/user/mysql/bin/mysqld: ready for connections.
Version: '5.5.23'  socket: '/tmp/mysql.sock'  port: 3306  Source distribution,
wsrep_23.6.r3755
[Note] WSREP: New COMPONENT: primary = yes, bootstrap = no, my_idx = 0,
memb_num = 1
[Note] WSREP: Starting new group from scratch:
c3315364-b991-11e1-0800-59a14f938404
[Note] WSREP: STATE_EXCHANGE: sent state UUID:
c3317547-b991-11e1-0800-4da9e025adff
[Note] WSREP: STATE EXCHANGE: sent state msg:
c3317547-b991-11e1-0800-4da9e025adff
[Note] WSREP: STATE EXCHANGE: got state msg:
c3317547-b991-11e1-0800-4da9e025adff from 0 (alpha)
[Note] WSREP: Quorum results:
      version    = 2,
      component  = PRIMARY,
      conf_id    = 0,
```

```
        members    = 1/1 (joined/total),
        act_id     = 0,
        last_appl. = -1,
        protocols  = 0/4/2 (gcs/repl/appl),
        group UUID = c3315364-b991-11e1-0800-59a14f938404
[Note] WSREP: Flow-control interval: [8, 16]
[Note] WSREP: Restored state OPEN -> JOINED (0)
[Note] WSREP: Member 0 (alpha) synced with group.
[Note] WSREP: Shifting JOINED -> SYNCED (TO: 0)
[Note] WSREP: New cluster view: global state:
c3315364-b991-11e1-0800-59a14f938404:0,
view# 1: Primary, number of nodes: 1, my index: 0, protocol version 2
[Note] WSREP: wsrep_notify_cmd is not defined, skipping notification.
[Note] WSREP: Assign initial position for certification: 0, protocol version: 2
[Note] WSREP: Synchronized with group, ready for connections
[Note] WSREP: wsrep_notify_cmd is not defined, skipping notification.
```

A further confirmation of the `wsrep` process in operation is the use of port 4567 on the server. In a production environment, if there are specific firewall rules for the MySQL port (e.g., 3306), then additional appropriate rules will be necessary for Galera Cluster communication.

```
$ netstat -tulpn | grep -e 4567 -e 3306
tcp    0  0 0.0.0.0:3306   0.0.0.0:*   LISTEN   29329/mysqld
tcp    0  0 0.0.0.0:4567   0.0.0.0:*   LISTEN   29329/mysqld
```

Incorrect MySQL Configuration   Even with a defined `wsrep_cluster_address`, without the `wsrep_provider` argument, MySQL will start without any issues; however, the expected features are not operational, and there is no indication of any problems. The MySQL error log will look like this:

```
$ bin/mysqld_safe --defaults-file=etc/my.cnf  --wsrep_cluster_address=gcomm:// &
$ tail -20 data/`hostname`.err
mysqld_safe Starting mysqld daemon with databases from ...
...
[Note] WSREP: Read nil XID from storage engines, skipping position init
[Note] WSREP: wsrep_load(): loading provider library 'none'
[Note] /home/user/mysql/bin/mysqld: ready for connections.
Version: '5.5.23'  socket: '/tmp/mysql.sock'  port: 3306
Source distribution, wsrep_23.6.r3755
```

State Snapshot Transfer (SST)

While the initial configuration provides a minimum viable single MySQL instance running with Galera, this serves no real purpose and is not sufficient when adding Galera nodes to the cluster. The `wsrep_sst_method` variable is defined to ensure that when a new node is added (i.e., the joiner), this can be initially synchronized with the known cluster (i.e., one node known as the donor).

The diagram at http://www.codership.com/wiki/doku.php?id=state_transfer_protocol provides a great overview of the complexity of performing this initial snapshot and then synchronizing with the cluster.

There are five possible values for the `wsrep_sst_method` configuration variable. These are `rsync`, `rsync_wan`, `xtrabackup`, `mysqldump`, and `skip`. The current default is `mysqldump`; however, this may change in future releases.

The `mysqldump`, `rsync`, and `rsync_wan` options are blocking operations during the data acquisition stage on a joiner node and the donor. The `rsync_wan` option has further optimization for WAN transfers. The `xtrabackup` option provides the most flexibility; however, it requires additional software installation and configuration.

Galera will, by default, use the *IP* address of `eth0` for SST operations. In the example virtual environment being demonstrated, the correct IP is on `eth1`. The IP can be configured on all Galera nodes with the `wsrep_sst_receive_address` variable. For example:

```
#$HOME/mysql/etc/my.cnf  (on alpha)
[mysqld]
wsrep_sst_receive_address=192.168.1.51
```

rsync and rsync_wan   The `rsync` option is the easiest of the options available for SST. When set, and when applicable SSH keys are defined, a new joiner node can be easily synchronized:

```
#$HOME/mysql/etc/my.cnf
[mysqld]
wsrep_sst_method=rsync
```

mysqldump   When using the `mysqldump` method (the current default), the additional `wsrep_sst_auth` option is required on both the joiner and donor nodes. This is a MySQL user account that must exist on all nodes. For example:

```
#$HOME/mysql/etc/my.cnf
[mysqld]
wsrep_sst_method=mysqldump
wsrep_sst_auth=galera:passwd
```

This introduces additional security issues. A new MySQL user is recommended because this requires network-level access (i.e., more than localhost) for the connection from the executed `wsrep_sst_mysqldump` command:

```
mysql> GRANT ALL ON *.* TO galera@'192.168.1.%' IDENTIFIED BY PASSWORD
       '*59C70DA2F3E3A5BDF46B68F5C8B8F25762BCCEF0';
```

This user requires the ability to remove and create the `mysql` schema for the joining node. For security purposes this account could be removed or disabled following use; however, SST may be required at any time if a new node is added or a level of corruption occurs and a resynchronization is necessary. This variable can technically be different between nodes, but would be an unnecessary complexity.

NOTE   While it would appear that `rsync` is a more practical method for SST, `rsync` works on a physical level while `mysqldump` works on a logical level. If the individual nodes have a different MySQL layout and options, for example, the `datadir` or `innodb_log_file_size`, `mysqldump` is necessary.

TIP   Using identical MySQL configuration for all Galera Cluster nodes (aka the KISS principle) will remove unnecessary complexities, especially when trying to diagnose problems.

Adding a Galera Node

In order to add a second server to operate in a Galera Cluster, the installation and configuration is identical. That is, install Galera, install MySQL with `wsrep`, install the MySQL starter database, and configure MySQL, including the definition of the applicable SST method.

The only difference is the instantiation of the `mysqld` process, which requires a connection to one of the other known nodes in the cluster with the `wsrep_cluster_address` configuration option, in this example, the initial server, `alpha`:

```
$ ./bin/mysqld_safe --defaults-file=etc/my.cnf \
  --wsrep_cluster_address=gcomm://alpha &
```

The initial handshake and SST transfer can be seen by viewing the respective error logs on both the joiner node (i.e., `beta`) and the selected donor node (i.e., `alpha`).

SST via `rsync`   On the donor node (e.g., `alpha`), the following error log information confirms a successful SST request:

```
[Note] WSREP: New cluster view: global state: c3315364-b991-11e1-0800-
59a14f938404:4, view# 100: Primary, number of nodes: 2, my index: 0,
protocol version 2
[Note] WSREP: wsrep_notify_cmd is not defined, skipping notification.
[Note] WSREP: Assign initial position for certification: 4, protocol version: 2
[Note] WSREP: Node 1 (beta) requested state transfer from '*any*'.
Selected 0 (alpha)(SYNCED) as donor.
[Note] WSREP: Shifting SYNCED -> DONOR/DESYNCED (TO: 4)
[Note] WSREP: wsrep_notify_cmd is not defined, skipping notification.
[Note] WSREP: Running: 'wsrep_sst_rsync 'donor' '192.168.1.52:4444/rsync_sst'
 'galera:passwd' '/home/user/mysql/data/' '/home/user/mysql/etc/my.cnf'
 'c3315364-b991-11e1-0800-59a14f938404' '4' '0''
[Note] WSREP: sst_donor_thread signaled with 0
[Note] WSREP: Flushing tables for SST...
[Note] WSREP: Provider paused at c3315364-b991-11e1-0800-59a14f938404:4
[Note] WSREP: Tables flushed.
[Note] WSREP: Provider resumed.
[Note] WSREP: 0 (alpha): State transfer to 1 (beta) complete.
[Note] WSREP: Shifting DONOR/DESYNCED -> JOINED (TO: 4)
[Note] WSREP: Member 0 (alpha) synced with group.
[Note] WSREP: Shifting JOINED -> SYNCED (TO: 4)
[Note] WSREP: Synchronized with group, ready for connections
[Note] WSREP: wsrep_notify_cmd is not defined, skipping notification.
[Note] WSREP: 1 (beta): State transfer from 0 (alpha) complete.
[Note] WSREP: Member 1 (beta) synced with group.
```

On the joiner node, you can see the following steps in the MySQL error log:

- A state difference is identified.

- An Incremental State Transfer (IST) is first attempted but not successful due to a fundamental state difference.

- A node is selected to operate in a donor role and a full SST is initiated on that node.

- An InnoDB crash recovery is performed on retrieved state.

- The node is recognized as in sync.

```
[Note] WSREP: Shifting OPEN -> PRIMARY (TO: 4)
[Note] WSREP: State transfer required:
        Group state: c3315364-b991-11e1-0800-59a14f938404:4
        Local state: 00000000-0000-0000-0000-000000000000:-1
[Note] WSREP: New cluster view: global state:
c3315364-b991-11e1-0800-59a14f938404:4,
view# 100: Primary, number of nodes: 2, my index: 1, protocol version 2
[Warning] WSREP: Gap in state sequence. Need state transfer.
```

```
[Note] WSREP: Running: 'wsrep_sst_rsync 'joiner' '192.168.1.52' ''
'/home/user/mysql/data/' '/home/user/mysql/etc/my.cnf' '7285' 2>sst.err'
[Note] WSREP: Prepared SST request: rsync|192.168.1.52:4444/rsync_sst
[Note] WSREP: wsrep_notify_cmd is not defined, skipping notification.
[Note] WSREP: Assign initial position for certification: 4, protocol version: 2
[Warning] WSREP: Failed to prepare for incremental state transfer:
Local state UUID (00000000-0000-0000-0000-000000000000)
does not match group state UUID (c3315364-b991-11e1-0800-59a14f938404): 1
(Operation not permitted)
at galera/src/replicator_str.cpp:prepare_for_IST():439. IST will be unavailable.
[Note] WSREP: Node 1 (beta) requested state transfer from '*any*'.
Selected 0 (alpha)(SYNCED) as donor.
[Note] WSREP: Shifting PRIMARY -> JOINER (TO: 4)
[Note] WSREP: Requesting state transfer: success, donor: 0
[Note] WSREP: 0 (alpha): State transfer to 1 (beta) complete.
[Note] WSREP: Member 0 (alpha) synced with group.
[Note] WSREP: SST complete, seqno: 4
InnoDB: The InnoDB memory heap is disabled
InnoDB: Mutexes and rw_locks use GCC atomic builtins
InnoDB: Compressed tables use zlib 1.2.3
InnoDB: Using Linux native AIO
InnoDB: Initializing buffer pool, size = 128.0M
InnoDB: Completed initialization of buffer pool
InnoDB: highest supported file format is Barracuda.
InnoDB: The log sequence number in ibdata files does not match
InnoDB: the log sequence number in the ib_logfiles!
 InnoDB: Database was not shut down normally!
InnoDB: Starting crash recovery.
InnoDB: Reading tablespace information from the .ibd files...
InnoDB: Restoring possible half-written data pages from the doublewrite
InnoDB: buffer...
InnoDB: Waiting for the background threads to start
InnoDB: 1.1.8 started; log sequence number 1596023
[Note] Event Scheduler: Loaded 0 events
[Note] WSREP: Signalling provider to continue.
[Note] WSREP: Received SST: c3315364-b991-11e1-0800-59a14f938404:4
[Note] WSREP: SST received: c3315364-b991-11e1-0800-59a14f938404:4
[Note] /home/user/mysql/bin/mysqld: ready for connections.
Version: '5.5.23'  socket: '/tmp/mysql.sock'  port: 3306  Source distribution,
 wsrep_23.6.r3755
[Note] WSREP: 1 (beta): State transfer from 0 (alpha) complete.
[Note] WSREP: Shifting JOINER -> JOINED (TO: 4)
[Note] WSREP: Member 1 (beta) synced with group.
[Note] WSREP: Shifting JOINED -> SYNCED (TO: 4)
[Note] WSREP: Synchronized with group, ready for connections
```

Operation Confirmation

Galera provides a number of MySQL status variables to view the running operation of the cluster. Following this initial cluster creation and adding a second node, the values in this example are as shown in the following sections.

alpha **Status**

```
alpha> SHOW GLOBAL STATUS LIKE 'wsrep%';
+---------------------------+-------------------------------------+
| Variable_name             | Value                               |
+---------------------------+-------------------------------------+
| wsrep_local_state_uuid    | 88bdf845-b0a4-11e1-0800-4db1faf4581b |
| wsrep_protocol_version    | 4                                   |
| wsrep_last_committed      | 0                                   |
| wsrep_replicated          | 0                                   |
| wsrep_replicated_bytes    | 0                                   |
| wsrep_received            | 6                                   |
| wsrep_received_bytes      | 376                                 |
| wsrep_local_commits       | 0                                   |
| wsrep_local_cert_failures | 0                                   |
| wsrep_local_bf_aborts     | 0                                   |
| wsrep_local_replays       | 0                                   |
| wsrep_local_send_queue    | 0                                   |
| wsrep_local_send_queue_avg | 0.500000                           |
| wsrep_local_recv_queue    | 0                                   |
| wsrep_local_recv_queue_avg | 0.000000                           |
| wsrep_flow_control_paused | 0.000000                            |
| wsrep_flow_control_sent   | 0                                   |
| wsrep_flow_control_recv   | 0                                   |
| wsrep_cert_deps_distance  | 0.000000                            |
| wsrep_apply_oooe          | 0.000000                            |
| wsrep_apply_oool          | 0.000000                            |
| wsrep_apply_window        | 0.000000                            |
| wsrep_commit_oooe         | 0.000000                            |
| wsrep_commit_oool         | 0.000000                            |
| wsrep_commit_window       | 0.000000                            |
| wsrep_local_state         | 4                                   |
| wsrep_local_state_comment | Synced (6)                          |
| wsrep_cert_index_size     | 0                                   |
| wsrep_causal_reads        | 0                                   |
| wsrep_cluster_conf_id     | 2                                   |
| wsrep_cluster_size        | 2                                   |
| wsrep_cluster_state_uuid  | 88bdf845-b0a4-11e1-0800-4db1faf4581b |
| wsrep_cluster_status      | Primary                             |
| wsrep_connected           | ON                                  |
| wsrep_local_index         | 0                                   |
| wsrep_provider_name       | Galera                              |
| wsrep_provider_vendor     | Codership Oy <info@codership.com>   |
| wsrep_provider_version    | 23.2.1(r129)                        |
| wsrep_ready               | ON                                  |
+---------------------------+-------------------------------------+
39 rows in set (0.00 sec)
```

beta **Status**

```
beta> SHOW GLOBAL STATUS LIKE 'wsrep%';
+---------------------------+-------------------------------------+
| Variable_name             | Value                               |
```

```
+---------------------------+---------------------------------------+
| wsrep_local_state_uuid    | 88bdf845-b0a4-11e1-0800-4db1faf4581b  |
| wsrep_protocol_version    | 4                                     |
| wsrep_last_committed      | 0                                     |
| wsrep_replicated          | 0                                     |
| wsrep_replicated_bytes    | 0                                     |
| wsrep_received            | 3                                     |
| wsrep_received_bytes      | 198                                   |
| wsrep_local_commits       | 0                                     |
| wsrep_local_cert_failures | 0                                     |
| wsrep_local_bf_aborts     | 0                                     |
| wsrep_local_replays       | 0                                     |
| wsrep_local_send_queue    | 0                                     |
| wsrep_local_send_queue_avg| 0.333333                              |
| wsrep_local_recv_queue    | 0                                     |
| wsrep_local_recv_queue_avg| 0.000000                              |
| wsrep_flow_control_paused | 0.000000                              |
| wsrep_flow_control_sent   | 0                                     |
| wsrep_flow_control_recv   | 0                                     |
| wsrep_cert_deps_distance  | 0.000000                              |
| wsrep_apply_oooe          | 0.000000                              |
| wsrep_apply_oool          | 0.000000                              |
| wsrep_apply_window        | 0.000000                              |
| wsrep_commit_oooe         | 0.000000                              |
| wsrep_commit_oool         | 0.000000                              |
| wsrep_commit_window       | 0.000000                              |
| wsrep_local_state         | 4                                     |
| wsrep_local_state_comment | Synced (6)                            |
| wsrep_cert_index_size     | 0                                     |
| wsrep_causal_reads        | 0                                     |
| wsrep_cluster_conf_id     | 2                                     |
| wsrep_cluster_size        | 2                                     |
| wsrep_cluster_state_uuid  | 88bdf845-b0a4-11e1-0800-4db1faf4581b  |
| wsrep_cluster_status      | Primary                               |
| wsrep_connected           | ON                                    |
| wsrep_local_index         | 1                                     |
| wsrep_provider_name       | Galera                                |
| wsrep_provider_vendor     | Codership Oy <info@codership.com>     |
| wsrep_provider_version    | 23.2.1(r129)                          |
| wsrep_ready               | ON                                    |
+---------------------------+---------------------------------------+
```

The Galera Wiki at http://www.codership.com/wiki/doku.php?id= monitoring provides more information on important status variables and their respective values for checking the cluster integrity, node status, replication health, and slow performance bottlenecks.

We can now run a simple test, using the same test steps as described in the appendix, for testing replication. This will create a table and use a simple stored procedure to simulate some load. We can confirm the data is consistent in the table with the following simple test:

```
alpha> PAGER md5sum
alpha> SELECT * FROM numbers ORDER BY id;
bb39b97bfe7e28b8abdbf9b943b0cd3a  -
1048576 rows in set (0.31 sec)
alpha> NOPAGER
beta> PAGER md5sum
beta> SELECT * FROM numbers ORDER BY id;
bb39b97bfe7e28b8abdbf9b943b0cd3a  -
1048576 rows in set (0.40 sec)
beta> NOPAGER
```

In addition we can now see changes in the MySQL Status variables:

```
beta> SHOW GLOBAL STATUS LIKE 'wsrep%';
+------------------------------+------------------------------------+
| Variable_name                | Value                              |
+------------------------------+------------------------------------+
| wsrep_local_state_uuid       | 88bdf845-b0a4-11e1-0800-4db1faf4581b |
| wsrep_protocol_version       | 4                                  |
| wsrep_last_committed         | 47                                 |
| wsrep_replicated             | 0                                  |
| wsrep_replicated_bytes       | 0                                  |
| wsrep_received               | 69                                 |
| wsrep_received_bytes         | 42700075                           |
...
```

Under these normal testing procedures, no addition wsrep information is written to the MySQL error log. In general, after the initial creation and SST-related log messaging in the error log, any later wsrep messages should be considered an error to investigate.

Multi-Master Replication

Galera provides true active multi-master replication by default. There is no additional configuration necessary. We can repeat the same test in a different schema for verification:

```
beta> CREATE SCHEMA IF NOT EXISTS  test2;
beta> USE test2;
beta> SOURCE fill_numbers.sql
```

We can also verify several different status variable changes to indicate the local operations. For example:

```
beta> SHOW GLOBAL STATUS LIKE 'wsrep%';
..
| wsrep_replicated             | 27                                 |
| wsrep_replicated_bytes       | 29514748                           |
| wsrep_received               | 81                                 |
```

```
| wsrep_received_bytes        | 56931329          |
| wsrep_local_commits         | 21                |
..
```

In comparison, the before values were:

```
| wsrep_replicated            | 0                 |
| wsrep_replicated_bytes      | 0                 |
| wsrep_received              | 69                |
| wsrep_received_bytes        | 42700075          |
| wsrep_local_commits         | 0                 |
```

Optimal MySQL Configuration

There are several recommended configuration settings in addition to those that have already been discussed. The full list of recommendations includes

- **wsrep_provider**   This is a path and filename of the Galera library. This is a required parameter.

- **wsrep_cluster_address**   This is a gcomm:// specific address to one node of the cluster. This is a required parameter.

- **wsrep_cluster_name**   This is a name given to the cluster in use.

- **wsrep_sst_method**   This parameter defines the method to perform an initial state snapshot transfer (SST). The current default value when not specified is mysqldump. The recommended setting is rsync or xtrabackup.

- **wsrep_node_address**   This is the IP address of the node. When not specified, this will default to the first retrievable IP address. This may not be ideal for various network configurations that have multiple network connections.

- **wsrep_node_name**   This is the human readable name of the node. This defaults to the hostname if not specified.

- **wsrep_slave_threads**   This specifies the number of parallel slave threads. The recommended value is 4 * cores.

- **wsrep_provider_options**   This option specifies various other options. It is recommended that the gcache_size is set appropriately to maximize throughput.

A default installation shows a large number of possible values for wsrep_provider_options. These currently include

```
mysql> SHOW GLOBAL VARIABLES LIKE 'wsrep_provider_options'\G
base_host = 192.168.1.51;
base_port = 4567;
evs.debug_log_mask = 0x1;
evs.inactive_check_period = PT0.5S;
evs.inactive_timeout = PT15S;
evs.info_log_mask = 0;
evs.install_timeout = PT15S;
evs.join_retrans_period = PT0.3S;
evs.keepalive_period = PT1S;
evs.max_install_timeouts = 1;
evs.send_window = 4;
evs.stats_report_period = PT1M;
evs.suspect_timeout = PT5S;
evs.use_aggregate = true;
evs.user_send_window = 2;
evs.version = 0;
evs.view_forget_timeout = PT5M;
gcache.dir = /home/user/mysql/data/;
gcache.keep_pages_size = 0;
gcache.mem_size = 0;
gcache.name = /home/user/mysql/data//galera.cache;
gcache.page_size = 128M;
gcache.size = 128M;
gcs.fc_debug = 0;
gcs.fc_factor = 0.5;
gcs.fc_limit = 16;
gcs.fc_master_slave = NO;
gcs.max_packet_size = 64500;
gcs.max_throttle = 0.25;
gcs.recv_q_hard_limit = 9223372036854775807;
gcs.recv_q_soft_limit = 0.25;
gcs.sync_donor = NO;
gmcast.listen_addr = tcp://0.0.0.0:4567;
gmcast.mcast_addr = ;
gmcast.mcast_ttl = 1;
gmcast.peer_timeout = PT3S;
gmcast.time_wait = PT5S;
gmcast.version = 0;
ist.recv_addr = 192.168.1.51;
pc.checksum = true;
pc.ignore_quorum = false;
pc.ignore_sb = false;
pc.linger = PT2S;
pc.npvo = false;
pc.version = 0;
protonet.backend = asio;
protonet.version = 0;
replicator.causal_read_timeout = PT30S;
replicator.commit_order = 3
```

Adding Nodes

To show the true strengths of this technology, we can add a third node to the cluster following the same steps when adding a second node (e.g.,

gamma). After confirmation in the error log that the node is correctly synchronized, schema and data are confirmed:

```
$ cd mysql
$ tail  data/`hostname`.err
120607 16:19:02 [Note] WSREP: 2 (gamma): State transfer from 0 (alpha) complete.
120607 16:19:02 [Note] WSREP: Shifting JOINER -> JOINED (TO: 75)
120607 16:19:02 [Note] WSREP: Member 2 (gamma) synced with group.
120607 16:19:02 [Note] WSREP: Shifting JOINED -> SYNCED (TO: 75)
120607 16:19:02 [Note] WSREP: Synchronized with group, ready for connections
$ bin/mysql -uroot -e "SHOW SCHEMAS"
+--------------------+
| Database           |
+--------------------+
| information_schema |
| mysql              |
| performance_schema |
| test               |
| test2              |
+--------------------+
5 rows in set (0.00 sec)
$ bin/mysql -uroot
gamma> PAGER md5sum
gamma> SELECT * FROM book3.numbers ORDER BY id;
bb39b97bfe7e28b8abdbf9b943b0cd3a  -
1048576 rows in set (0.34 sec)
gamma> NOPAGER
```

We can complete the test by repeating our example procedure and data
in a new test3 schema and confirming that the first two nodes receive all
data.

Additional Features

In addition to the already discussed features, several other features are
important for production use and implementation. These include the
following:

- Galera provides an independent arbitrator (garbd daemon) that
  operates as a dataless Galera node. The garbd node can help in
  detecting and dealing with network splits in an optimal way. A
  well-positioned garbd node can prevent split-brain situations.

- Galera supports SSL communications, which is important for added
  security, especially in cloud deployments. This is defined with
  the options socket.ssl_cert and socket.ssl_key. For the
  initial SST, additional precautions are necessary depending on the
  applicable method used.

- SST enables customizable methods for obtaining the initial dataset for a new node.

- Online rolling schema upgrades are possible by altering execution method from Total Order Isolation (TOI) to Rolling Schema Upgrade (RSU). While the default TOI method is predictable and guarantees data consistency, it does limit the cluster's high availability, e.g., during long running ALTER statements. There are several caveats for effective operation with this feature as the result of a blocking ALTER statement under normal MySQL operations.

Galera Cluster Implementation Recommendations

It is highly recommended that you run more than two Galera nodes in a production environment, or that you ensure you use a separate Galera Arbitrator. The `garbd` daemon is designed to avoid a split-brain situation with a minimum of two servers. More information can be found at http:// www.codership.com/wiki/doku.php?id=galera_arbitrator.

The `mysqld_safe` wrapper daemon is not the ideal manager for handing an automatic MySQL restart in a cluster situation. Future work is necessary here with your production environment to support various disaster situations.

Installation of MySQL and Galera should not be in a `/home/user` account on a production system as demonstrated in this working example. Applicable software release procedures and appropriate service startup and shutdown steps are also needed.

The FromDual Performance Monitor for MySQL (MPM) written by Oli Sennhauser provides monitoring and graphing of the important triggers of Galera Cluster for MySQL. These monitors are available with Zabbix, an open source monitoring tool. More information about MPM can be found at http://fromdual.com/mpm-0-9-is-out.

There is no information on when MySQL monitoring plugins for other available common monitoring will become available. Every production system should include adequate monitoring and alerting.

Percona XtraDB Cluster

Percona offers a MySQL server deployment with Galera automatically included. This provides the Percona Server software that includes additional instrumentation and performance patches and the XtraDB storage engine, which is a Percona variant of InnoDB. More details can be found at http://www.percona.com/software/percona-xtradb-cluster.

MariaDB Galera Cluster

Work is occurring to have support for Galera in MariaDB. More information can be found at the Monty Program Knowledge Base found at http://kb.askmonty.org/en/what-is-mariadb-galera-cluster/.

Galera Wrap-Up

The information in this chapter is only an introduction to Galera Cluster by the team at Codership. Details of server monitoring, performance analysis and tuning, arbitration management and handling node failures, recovery, and provisioning are important areas that require far greater explanation to appreciate the available features of this product. Additional information, including benchmarks, new features, presentations, and blogs, can be found at http://www.codership.com/.

Getting More Help

Galera provides a discussion mailing list for any questions or issues. Details can be found at http://codership.com/info/mailing-list.

Tungsten Replicator

Tungsten Replicator provides an extensive list of additional replication features to MySQL, including supporting seamless failover of MySQL servers, flexible filtering of operations, multi-master and multi-master to slave support (i.e., fan in), parallel replication, and much more.

In addition to MySQL replication, Tungsten Replicator can provide heterogeneous data management with other RDBMS and noSQL products, including data synchronization between MySQL and Oracle and vice versa.

Tungsten Replicator is available under the open source GNU GPL v2 license. Continuent, the creators of Tungsten Replicator, also provide commercial support with an enterprise offering. More information can be found at http://www.continuent.com/solutions/overview.

Features

There is a long list of possible features that can be discussed. In this section, which is an introduction to Tungsten Replicator, the following will be discussed and demonstrated:

- Master failover via slave promotion

- Bidirectional replication (e.g., active/active multi-master)

- Parallelization and replication prefetching for improved performance

- Complex topologies

With traditional MySQL replication, the version of a MySQL slave should be the same or greater than that of the master. With Tungsten Replicator, this limitation does not exist. It is possible to replicate from MySQL 5.5 to MySQL 5.0, for example. There are limitations to any features that are in the newer version of MySQL; however, Tungsten can handle the error condition gracefully and not interrupt replication from continuing.

NOTE   Tungsten Replicator has one significant benefit over other products. There is no change to the standard MySQL installation necessary. There are no custom or patched MySQL binaries to install or maintain. Tungsten Replicator works with your existing MySQL environment and can replicate between MySQL 4.1*, 5.0, 5.1, 5.5, and 5.6 as well as different flavors, including MySQL Community, MySQL Enterprise, MariaDB, and Percona Server.

References

The current version of Tungsten Replicator available at the time of this publication is 2.0.5. You can find additional information, including the most current version, at the following sites:

- **Product Page**   http://www.continuent.com/solutions/tungsten-replicator

- **Downloads**   http://tungsten-replicator.org

- **Documentation**   http://code.google.com/p/tungsten-replicator/w

---

*Tungsten supports replicating to MySQL 4.1, but not from it.

Prerequisites

Tungsten Replicator has a number of operating system, network, software, and MySQL prerequisites. These must be installed on all servers that will be used in the Tungsten cluster. The following steps are applicable for an Ubuntu/Debian operating system. Similar statements are available for Red Hat/CentOS/Oracle Linux distributions.

```
$ sudo apt-get install -y ruby
$ which ruby
$ ruby --version
$ which rsync
$ echo "p 'hello'" | ruby -ropenssl
$ sudo apt-get install openjdk-6-jre
$ java -version
$ uname -n
$ hostname --ip-address
```

CAUTION *An important prerequisite is that all hosts resolve to a correct IP address and not a 127.X.X.X loopback address. The* hostname --ip-address *command can be used to confirm this.*

If Tungsten is used for backup and restore management, sudo access without a password is also necessary.

More information on these prerequisites can be found at https://docs .continuent.com/wiki/display/TEDOC/System+Requirements.

Installation with Tungsten Sandbox

The easiest way to demonstrate the features of Tungsten Replicator is in a MySQL Sandbox environment. Refer to the MySQL Sandbox installation instructions in the appendix to configure the necessary Sandbox software first. The following steps will then install Tungsten Replicator and Tungsten Sandbox.

TIP *Tungsten Replicator is a complex product with several administration tools. The Tungsten Sandbox provides an easy way to evaluate and review these tools and the respective output. You can find a good cheat sheet for understanding the tungsten operations in comparison to MySQL replication. Details can be found at http://code.google.com/p/tungsten-replicator/wiki/Cheat_Sheet.*

```
$ cd $HOME/sandboxes
# Get Current version from http://bit.ly/tr20_builds
$ curl --silent -o tungsten-replicator.tar.gz https://s3.amazonaws.
com/files.continuent.com/builds/nightly/
tungsten-2.0-snapshots/tungsten-replicator-2.0.6-683.tar.gz
$ tar xvfz tungsten-replicator.tar.gz
$ rm -f tungsten-replicator.tar.gz
$ mv tungsten-replicator-* tungsten-replicator
$ cd tungsten-replicator
$ curl --silent -o tungsten-sandbox
  http://tungsten-toolbox.googlecode.com/files/tungsten-sandbox-2.0.11
$ chmod +x tungsten-sandbox
$ ./tungsten-sandbox --help
$ mkdir $HOME/tsb2
```

Finally, you can create a Tungsten cluster in a Tungsten Sandbox environment with a single command. The following command will create a master-master cluster:

```
$ cd $HOME/sandboxes/tungsten-replicator
$ mkdir -p $HOME/tsandboxes/master-master
$ ./tungsten-sandbox --topology bi-dir -l 12300 -r 10300
-t $HOME/tsandboxes/master-master -m 5.5.24 -p 7300 -d tsb-mm
```

The options specified relate to:

- **--topology**   The type of Tungsten topology. This includes `bi-dir`, `direct`, `star`, `all-masters`, `fan-in`, and `master-slave`.

- **-l**   The THL service port number.

- **-r**   The RMI service port number.

- **-t**   The full path to the Tungsten Replicator administration directory.

- **-m**   Refers to the MySQL version to be used.

- **-p**   Refers to the base port number for the MySQL nodes.

- **-d**   The relative path to the MySQL Sandbox installed MySQL topology.

TIP   If you add the `--verbose` option for Tungsten Sandbox, you will get more detailed information on the commands used to install the cluster.

You can get a full list of Tungsten Sandbox options with the help option:

```
$ ./tungsten-sandbox -h
```

There are two installed components of the new Tungsten Sandbox. The first are MySQL nodes, which are installed in `$HOME/sandboxes/tsb-mm` directory and operate like a regular sandbox environment having applicable tools to start, stop, and access MySQL. The second component is the Tungsten Replicator configuration, which is installed in `$HOME/tsandboxes/master-master` as specified by `-t`.

TIP If you receive an error when creating a Tungsten Sandbox, you may have created a port conflict with another MySQL Sandbox or Tungsten Sandbox installation. This can be easily confirmed by looking for any existing MySQL and Java processes that are running with $ `ps -ef | grep -e mysql -e java`.

Reviewing a Tungsten Replicator Environment

The following administration steps will give you an overview of some of the Tungsten Replicator functionality that can be used to review and administer a Tungsten cluster.

Overall Status of Cluster Services

```
$ cd $HOME/tsandboxes/master-master
./replicator_all status
#1
Tungsten Replicator Service is running (PID:31805).
#2
Tungsten Replicator Service is running (PID:32717).
```

The available options for `replicator_all` (a wrapper to the `replicator` command) are `start`, `stop`, `restart`, `condrestart`, `status`, `dump`, and `console`.

Important File Locations You can find the configuration files for each Tungsten node in the respective `db1` and `db2` sub-directories. For example, with `db1`:

```
$ cd $HOME/tsandboxes/master-master
$ cat db1/configs/tungsten.cfg
```

The `tungsten.cfg` file contains a JavaScript Object Notation (JSON) representation of the topology installed. This is also used by the installer tools to perform updates to the cluster configuration.

Additional configuration files can be found in `db1/releases/tung-sten-replicator/tungsten-replicator/conf`. The important files are

- **`wrapper.conf`**   This is the configuration for the Java instance and is used to assign resources or enable debugging.

- **`static-SERVICE-NAME.properties`**   This contains information for each service that is configured. There are currently over 200 settings.

Tungsten Sandbox provides a shortcut to examine the node configuration files:

```
$ cd $HOME/tsandboxes/master-master
$ ./db1/show_conf
```

Tungsten Replication supports three types of logs. These are the Master Relay Logs (MRL), the Transaction History Logs (THL), and the Service Logs. The Master Relay Logs are used when the master is extracting events from the MySQL server. The Transaction History Logs are used to store events after they are extracted. Finally the service logs are the replicator operating logs.

A very important feature of the THL is that Tungsten adds a global transaction ID when it extracts data from binary logs. This is a fundamental difference from native replication, as it allows seamless failover without manual inspection of the binary logs.

The service logs are:

```
$ cat db1/releases/tungsten-replicator/tungsten-replicator/log/trepsvc.log
$ cat db1/releases/tungsten-replicator/tungsten-replicator/log/user.log
```

When using Tungsten Sandbox there is also a shortcut to viewing the logs easily:

```
$ cd $HOME/tsandboxes/master-master
$ ./db1/show_log
```

It is important to understand and monitor all of these logs (MRL, THL, and Service) as they are one cause of additional diskspace usage. For example, to simulate an `expire_logs_days=4` you would set `replicator.store.thl.log_file_retention=4d` in the configuration file. More information on these logs and how to manage and configure usage

can be found at http://code.google.com/p/tungsten-replicator/wiki/
TRCAdministration#Managing_replicator_log_space.

Testing the Tungsten Sandbox Generally, you would first use the various administration tools to check and verify the operation of the cluster as later documented. Running the following included test script helps provide the following command examples with meaningful results to display:

```
$ cd $HOME/tsandboxes/master-master
./test_topology
# Testing topology bi-dir  with 2 nodes.
# Master nodes: [1 2] - Slave nodes: [1 2]
# node 1
ok - Tables from all masters
ok - Views from all masters
ok - Records from master #1
ok - Records from master #2
ok - Node #1-alpha online
ok - Node #1-bravo online
# node 2
ok - Tables from all masters
ok - Views from all masters
ok - Records from master #1
ok - Records from master #2
ok - Node #2-alpha online
ok - Node #2-bravo online
1..12
```

Details of Individual Node Servers You can view more information about the node servers in the given Tungsten cluster by looking at the services:

```
$ ./trepctl_all services    (also executed with ./services_all)
#1
Processing services command...
NAME            VALUE
----            -----
appliedLastSeqno: 8
appliedLatency  : 0.303
role            : master
serviceName     : alpha
serviceType     : local
started         : true
state           : ONLINE
NAME            VALUE
```

```
----                -----
appliedLastSeqno: 8
appliedLatency  : 1.211
role            : slave
serviceName     : bravo
serviceType     : remote
started         : true
state           : ONLINE
Finished services command...
#2
...
```

The Tungsten Toolbox (http://code.google.com/p/tungsten-toolbox/) also provides the following additional tools to help interpret the Tungsten status output:

- **simple_services**   This filters the output of trepctl services to produce a compact summary.

- **trepctl-progress**   Shows how much work a replicator has done and how much it needs to do to process its THL files.

To delve into more specifics for a given Tungsten node you can execute the following trepctl on an individual given node:

```
$ db1/trepctl -service alpha status
Processing status command...
NAME                    VALUE
----                    -----
appliedLastEventId    : mysql-bin.000002:0000000000001551;0
appliedLastSeqno      : 8
appliedLatency        : 0.303
clusterName           : default
currentEventId        : mysql-bin.000002:0000000000001551
currentTimeMillis     : 1340401306138
dataServerHost        : 127.0.0.1
extensions            :
latestEpochNumber     : 0
masterConnectUri      : thl://:/
masterListenUri       : thl://127.0.0.1:12300/
maximumStoredSeqNo    : 8
minimumStoredSeqNo    : 0
offlineRequests       : NONE
pendingError          : NONE
pendingErrorCode      : NONE
pendingErrorEventId   : NONE
pendingErrorSeqno     : -1
pendingExceptionMessage: NONE
resourcePrecedence    : 99
rmiPort               : 10300
role                  : master
seqnoType             : java.lang.Long
```

```
serviceName            : alpha
serviceType            : local
simpleServiceName      : alpha
siteName               : default
sourceId               : 127.0.0.1
state                  : ONLINE
timeInStateSeconds     : 2035.975
uptimeSeconds          : 2040.584
Finished status command...
```

Other syntax that should be reviewed includes

```
$ db1/trepctl -service alpha status -name tasks
$ db1/trepctl -service alpha status -name shards
$ db1/trepctl -service alpha status -name stores
```

The -name variants are best used to provide information for parallel replication or to provide information for huge row-based replication (RBR) transactions by providing details of the chunks processed. The output is not shown here due to space limitations. To see the full options of the Tungsten Replicator Control Utility, you can view the command help with:

```
$ db1/trepctl help
```

More information on the Tungsten Replicator Control Utility can be found at https://docs.continuent.com/wiki/display/TEDOC/The+Tungsten +Replicator+Control+Utility+%28trepctl%29.

Transaction History Logs (THL)   The Transaction History Logs (THL) hold all the data that is taken from the MySQL master binary logs and used by all Tungsten Replicators. The thl command can provide information about these logs, including:

```
db1/thl -service alpha info
INFO  thl.log.DiskLog Using directory '/home/user/tsandboxes/master-
master/db1/tlogs/alpha/' for replicator logs
INFO  thl.log.DiskLog Checksums enabled for log records: true
INFO  thl.log.DiskLog Using read-only log connection
INFO  thl.log.DiskLog Loaded event serializer class:
 com.continuent.tungsten.replicator.thl.serializer.ProtobufSerializer
INFO  thl.log.LogIndex Building file index on log directory:
 /home/user/tsandboxes/master-master/db1/tlogs/alpha
[ - main] INFO  thl.log.LogIndex Constructed index; total log files added=1
[ - main] INFO  thl.log.DiskLog Validating last log file:
 /home/user/tsandboxes/master-master/db1/tlogs/alpha/thl.data.0000000001
[ - main] INFO  thl.log.DiskLog Setting up log flush policy:
fsyncIntervalMillis=0 fsyncOnFlush=false
[ - main] INFO  thl.log.DiskLog Idle log connection timeout: 28800000ms
```

```
[ - main] INFO  thl.log.DiskLog Log preparation is complete
min seq# = 0
max seq# = 8
events = 8
```

The following option will list the details within the given log:

```
$ db1/thl -service alpha list -seqno 5
SEQ# = 5 / FRAG# = 0 (last frag)
- TIME = 2012-06-22 17:10:17.0
- EPOCH# = 0
- EVENTID = mysql-bin.000002:0000000000001003;0
- SOURCEID = 127.0.0.1
- METADATA = [mysql_server_id=101;unsafe_for_block_commit;
service=alpha;shard=test]
- TYPE = com.continuent.tungsten.replicator.event.ReplDBMSEvent
- OPTIONS = [##charset = UTF-8, autocommit = 1, sql_auto_is_null = 0,
foreign_key_checks = 1, unique_checks = 1, sql_mode = '', character_set_client =
 33, collation_connection = 33, collation_server = 8]
- SCHEMA =
- SQL(0) = DROP TABLE IF EXISTS TUNGSTEN_INFO.alpha, `test`.`v1` /* ... */

$ db1/thl -service alpha list -seqno 6
SEQ# = 6 / FRAG# = 0 (last frag)
- TIME = 2012-06-22 17:10:17.0
- EPOCH# = 0
- EVENTID = mysql-bin.000002:0000000000001137;0
- SOURCEID = 127.0.0.1
- METADATA = [mysql_server_id=101;unsafe_for_block_commit;
service=alpha;shard=test]
- TYPE = com.continuent.tungsten.replicator.event.ReplDBMSEvent
- OPTIONS = [##charset = UTF-8, autocommit = 1, sql_auto_is_null = 0,
foreign_key_checks = 1, unique_checks = 1, sql_mode = '',
character_set_client = 33, collation_connection = 33, collation_server = 8]
- SCHEMA =
- SQL(0) = create table test.t1(i int not null primary key, c char(20))
engine= innodb /* ___SERVICE___  = [alpha] */
...
```

The commands that can be performed with `thl` include `list`, `index`, `purge`, and `info`. More information about the Transaction History Log Utility can be found at https://docs.continuent.com/wiki/display/TEDOC/The+Transaction+History+Log+Utility+%28thl%29.

Tungsten Sandbox Cleanup The Tungsten Sandbox includes a number of working components. You can easily clean up all installed software with a single command. For example:

```
$ cd $HOME/tsandboxes/master-master
$ ./erase_tsandbox
```

Other Documentation Additional documentation can be found at http://code.google.com/p/tungsten-toolbox/wiki/TungstenSandbox. Detailed documentation for explaining how to install many different topologies of Tungsten Replicator can be found at http://code.google.com/p/tungsten-replicator/wiki/TungstenReplicatorCookbook. Details of administrative functions can be found at http://code.google.com/p/tungsten-replicator/wiki/TRCAdministration#Administration.

Other Tungsten Sandbox Examples

The following command will create a star Tungsten cluster:

```
$ mkdir -p $HOME/tsandboxes/star
$ cd $HOME/sandboxes/tungsten-replicator
$ ./tungsten-sandbox --topology star -l 12400 -r 10400 -n 5 --hub 3
-t $HOME/tsandboxes/star -m 5.5.24 -p 7400 -d tsb-star --verbose
```

The following command will create a fan-in cluster:

```
$ mkdir -p $HOME/tsandboxes/fan-in
$ cd $HOME/sandboxes/tungsten-replicator
$ ./tungsten-sandbox --topology fan-in -l 12500 -r 10500 -n 3 --fan-in
3 -t $HOME/tsandboxes/fan-in -m 5.5.24 -p 7500 -d tsb-fi --verbose
```

Be sure to repeat the Tungsten Replicator administration commands shown here to observe the difference in the various configurations.

Manual Tungsten Installation

The following steps will install a Tungsten Replicator configuration in the test virtual environment that is defined in the appendix. For the following examples the `alpha`, `beta`, and `gamma` servers will be used.

MySQL Setup

MySQL must first be installed and operating. Refer to the appendix for the basic installation of MySQL on the given server.

MySQL Configuration

Tungsten Replicator requires and recommends the following additional MySQL configuration settings:

```
# $HOME/mysql/etc/my.cnf
[mysqld]
server-id=51
```

```
log-bin=mysql-bin
default-storage-engine=InnoDB
# Recommended
innodb_flush_log_at_trx_commit=2
max_allowed_packet=48M
```

NOTE   *Tungsten relies on the MySQL binary log for replication. You should use the appropriate practices that best suit your business continuity needs and hardware capabilities, including configuring* sync_binlog *and* innodb_flush_log_at_trx_commit *appropriately.*

The MySQL instance can now be restarted:

```
$ cd $HOME/mysql
$ ./bin/mysqladmin shutdown
$ ./bin/mysqld_safe --defaults-file=etc/my.cnf &
$ tail -f data/`hostname`.err
```

These steps should be completed on all servers that you wish to include in the Tungsten cluster. In addition, a MySQL user with root-level privileges is necessary. This should be appropriately secured to minimize unauthorized access. There are no naming requirements on the username, i.e., tungsten is used here only for reference.

```
mysql> GRANT ALL ON *.* TO tungsten@'192.168.1.%' IDENTIFIED BY 'continuent'
    -> WITH GRANT OPTION;
```

Failure to do so will cause errors in installation, including:

```
ERROR >> alpha >> Unable to connect to the MySQL server using
root@alpha:3306 (WITH PASSWORD)
```

or

```
ERROR >> alpha >> The database user is missing some privileges or
the grant option.
Run 'mysql -u -p -h -e "GRANT ALL ON *.* to tungsten@alpha WITH GRANT OPTION"'
```

Tungsten Replicator Installation

The following steps will download Tungsten Replicator. Refer to the download link for the most current version available. You can also download regular daily builds from http://bit.ly/tr20_builds.

```
$ cd /tmp
$ wget http://tungsten-replicator.googlecode.com/files/
tungsten-replicator-2.0.5.tar.gz
```

```
$ tar xvfz tungsten-replicator*.tar.gz
$ rm -f tungsten-replicator*.tar.gz
$ mv tungsten-replicator-* tungsten-replicator
$ cd tungsten-replicator
```

Tungsten Replicator Master/Slave Setup

With the installation and operation of MySQL on the necessary servers, and the installation of Tungsten Replicator on the server, the following single command will configure the specified MySQL topology:

```
$ TUNGSTEN_HOME=$HOME/tungsten
$ MASTER=alpha
$ SLAVE1=beta
$ SLAVE2=gamma
$ ./tools/tungsten-installer \
    --master-slave --master-host=$MASTER \
    --datasource-user=tungsten --datasource-password=continuent \
    --datasource-log-directory=$HOME/mysql/data \
    --datasource-mysql-conf=$HOME/mysql/etc/my.cnf \
    --service-name=effectivemysql \
    --home-directory=$TUNGSTEN_HOME \
    --cluster-hosts=$MASTER,$SLAVE1,$SLAVE2 \
    --start-and-report
```

This takes a few moments to do all the necessary checking and verification:

```
INFO  >> alpha >> Getting services list
INFO  >> alpha >> ......
Processing services command...
NAME                 VALUE
----                 -----
appliedLastSeqno: 0
appliedLatency  : 0.832
role            : master
serviceName     : effectivemysql
serviceType     : local
started         : true
state           : ONLINE
Finished services command...
INFO  >> beta >> Getting services list
INFO  >> beta >> ..
Processing services command...
NAME                 VALUE
----                 -----
appliedLastSeqno: 0
appliedLatency  : 9.995
role            : slave
```

```
serviceName        : effectivemysql
serviceType        : local
started            : true
state              : ONLINE
Finished services command...
INFO  >> gamma >> Getting services list
INFO  >> gamma >> ..
Processing services command...
NAME                  VALUE
----                  -----
appliedLastSeqno:  0
appliedLatency   : 21.113
role             : slave
serviceName      : effectivemysql
serviceType      : local
started          : true
state            : ONLINE
Finished services command...
```

At this time you can delete the files downloaded for Tungsten Replicator, as these are now included at TUNGSTEN_HOME/tungsten/tungsten-replicator.

NOTE   *In this example, Tungsten was used to configure three servers with master/slave replication. Tungsten can also be installed in direct mode alongside existing MySQL replication, and a simple command can be used to take over from native replication on a running system.*

Tungsten Replicator Status Check

This is a MySQL master/slave topology managed by Tungsten Replicator. You can perform a few simple checks on the master:

```
$ export PATH=$HOME/tungsten/tungsten/tungsten-replicator/bin:$PATH
$ replicator status
Tungsten Replicator Service is running (PID:5843).
$ trepctl services
Processing services command...
NAME                  VALUE
----                  -----
appliedLastSeqno:  0
appliedLatency   : 1.024
role             : master
serviceName      : effectivemysql
serviceType      : local
started          : true
state            : ONLINE
```

```
Finished services command...
$ for H in `echo "alpha beta gamma"`; do echo "*** $H ***"; \
  trepctl -host $H status | grep applied; done
```

At this time we can repeat the replication example from the appendix. For example:

```
alpha> CREATE SCHEMA IF NOT EXISTS book3;
alpha> USE book3;
alpha> SOURCE fill_numbers.sql
```

While only a litmus test, we can confirm nothing obvious is wrong with the two slaves by comparing table results:

```
$ mysql -utungsten -p -halpha book3 -e "SELECT COUNT(*), SUM(id) FROM numbers"
+----------+--------------+
| COUNT(*) | SUM(id)      |
+----------+--------------+
|  1048576 | 549756338176 |
+----------+--------------+
$ mysql -utungsten -p -hbeta book3 -e "SELECT COUNT(*), SUM(id) FROM numbers"
+----------+--------------+
| COUNT(*) | SUM(id)      |
+----------+--------------+
|  1048576 | 549756338176 |
+----------+--------------+
$ mysql -utungsten -p -hgamma book3 -e "SELECT COUNT(*), SUM(id) FROM numbers"
+----------+--------------+
| COUNT(*) | SUM(id)      |
+----------+--------------+
|  1048576 | 549756338176 |
+----------+--------------+
```

Tungsten Replicator Testing

In order to show replication in various states of operation and verification and have a little fun, we can run an additional stored procedure that is a little more random and has a much longer execution time:

```
alpha> CREATE SCHEMA IF NOT EXISTS book3;
alpha> USE book3;
alpha> SOURCE rand_fill_numbers.sql
```

This will perform a modified version of the simple test case, randomizing data that is inserted and performing a large number of iterations:

```
$ for H in `echo "alpha beta gamma"`; do echo "*** $H ***";
  trepctl -host $H status | grep -e applied -e role -e stat; done
*** alpha ***
Processing status command...
```

```
appliedLastEventId      : mysql-bin.000002:0000000002402714;0
appliedLastSeqno        : 10638
appliedLatency          : 0.185
role                    : master
state                   : ONLINE
Finished status command...
*** beta ***
Processing status command...
appliedLastEventId      : mysql-bin.000002:0000000002403150;0
appliedLastSeqno        : 10640
appliedLatency          : 0.859
role                    : slave
state                   : ONLINE
Finished status command...
*** gamma ***
Processing status command...
appliedLastEventId      : mysql-bin.000002:0000000002403585;0
appliedLastSeqno        : 10642
appliedLatency          : 0.0
role                    : slave
state                   : ONLINE
Finished status command...
```

As you can see, the `appliedLastSeqno` shows work is occurring on the slaves that are online. The `appliedLatency` is an indication of slave lag. We can delve into the THL to identify the two SQL statements between the sequence numbers on the slaves by using the sequence number shown:

```
$ thl list -seqno 10641
SEQ# = 10641 / FRAG# = 0 (last frag)
- TIME = 2012-06-22 12:53:47.0
- EPOCH# = 0
- EVENTID = mysql-bin.000002:0000000002403395;0
- SOURCEID = alpha
- METADATA = [mysql_server_id=51;service=effectivemysql;shard=book3]
- TYPE = com.continuent.tungsten.replicator.event.ReplDBMSEvent
- OPTIONS = [##charset = UTF-8, autocommit = 1, sql_auto_is_null = 0,
foreign_key_checks = 1, unique_checks = 1, sql_mode = '',

character_set_client = 33, collation_connection = 33, collation_server = 8]
- SCHEMA = book3
- SQL(0) = INSERT INTO numbers (id)
      SELECT id +  NAME_CONST('counter',66148) FROM numbers
/*    SERVICE    = [effectivemysql] */

$ thl list -seqno 10642
SEQ# = 10642 / FRAG# = 0 (last frag)
- TIME = 2012-06-22 12:53:48.0
- EPOCH# = 0
- EVENTID = mysql-bin.000002:0000000002403585;0
- SOURCEID = alpha
- METADATA = [mysql_server_id=51;service=effectivemysql;shard=book3]
```

```
- TYPE = com.continuent.tungsten.replicator.event.ReplDBMSEvent
- OPTIONS = [##charset = UTF-8, autocommit = 1, sql_auto_is_null = 0,
foreign_key_checks = 1, unique_checks = 1, sql_mode = '',
character_set_client = 33, collation_connection = 33, collation_server = 8]
- SCHEMA = book3
- SQL(0) = DELETE FROM numbers LIMIT 6371 /* ___SERVICE___ = [effectivemysql] */
```

Replication Stoppage Verification

You can easily stop replication on a slave with:

```
$ trepctl -host gamma offline
```

The following verifies the stoppage:

```
$ trepctl -host gamma status
NAME                          VALUE
----                          -----
appliedLastEventId          : NONE
appliedLastSeqno            : -1
appliedLatency              : -1.0
pendingError                : NONE
pendingErrorCode            : NONE
...
state                       : OFFLINE:NORMAL
...
```

And to restart:

```
$ trepctl -host gamma online
```

Replication Failure Verification

We can simulate looking into a replication error on a slave with the follow-ing destructive command:

```
$ mysql -utungsten -p -hgamma book3 -e "DROP TABLE numbers";
```

A review of the Tungsten slave status shows:

```
$ trepctl -host gamma status
Processing status command...
NAME                         VALUE
----                         -----
appliedLastEventId         : NONE
appliedLastSeqno           : -1
appliedLatency             : -1.0
...
pendingError               : Event application failed: seqno=16268 fragno=0
message=java.sql.SQLException: Statement failed on slave but succeeded on master
pendingErrorCode           : NONE
pendingErrorEventId        : mysql-bin.000002:0000000003609171;0
pendingErrorSeqno          : 16268
```

```
pendingExceptionMessage: java.sql.SQLException: Statement failed on slave but
succeeded on master
                            TRUNCATE TABLE numbers /* ___SERVICE___ =
[effectivemysql] */
...
state                   : OFFLINE:ERROR
timeInStateSeconds      : 43.215
uptimeSeconds           : 168578.375
Finished status command...
```

As you can see, the `state` indicates an error and the `pendingError` related columns provide details of the failure. Following correction of the situation causing the error, you can restart the slave and verify the new state situation:

```
$ mysql -utungsten -p -hgamma book3 -e "CREATE TABLE numbers(id INT NOT NULL);"
$ trepctl -host gamma online
$ for H in `echo "gamma"`; do trepctl -host $H status | \
   grep -e applied -e role -e stat; done
Processing status command...
appliedLastEventId      : NONE
appliedLastSeqno        : -1
appliedLatency          : -1.0
role                    : slave
state                   : OFFLINE:ERROR
Finished status command...
Processing status command...
appliedLastEventId      : mysql-bin.000002:0000000003620196;0
appliedLastSeqno        : 16319
appliedLatency          : 0.0
role                    : slave
state                   : ONLINE
```

Replication Failover

The following steps are used to perform a failover in the example Tungsten Replicator environment:

- Confirm an operational cluster.
- Simulate a master failure.
- Verify the remaining cluster status.
- Select a new master.
- Fail over to new master.
- Verify cluster operations.

Verify Cluster   First, verify the state of the current master/slave cluster:

```
$ trepctl -host alpha heartbeat
$ for NODE in alpha beta gamma
do
   echo "#${NODE}"
   trepctl -host ${NODE} services | simple_services
done
#alpha
effectivemysql   [master]
seqno:           2  - latency:    0.101 - ONLINE
#beta
effectivemysql   [slave]
seqno:           2  - latency:    0.625 - ONLINE
#gamma
effcctivemysql   [slave]
seqno:           2  - latency:    0.994 - ONLINE
```

Simulate a Master Failure   The next step is to simulate some load on the master server with:

```
alpha> SOURCE rand_fill_numbers.sql
```

You can simulate a master server failure by taking the master server offline:

```
$ trepctl -host alpha offline
```

Verify Cluster   The next step is to confirm replication on the attached slaves is up to date based on the transaction logs stored on the slaves:

```
$ for NODE in beta gamma
do
  MAXSTORED=`trepctl -host $NODE status | grep maximumStoredSeqNo | \
  awk '{print $3}'`
  trepctl -host $NODE wait -applied $MAXSTORED
done
```

Identify New Master   Check the status of the remaining slave nodes to identify the most up-to-date server:

```
$ for NODE in beta gamma
do
  echo "#$NODE"
  trepctl -host $NODE services | simple_services
done
```

```
#beta
effectivemysql  [slave]
seqno:          620  - latency:  33.582 - GOING-ONLINE:SYNCHRONIZING
#gamma
effectivemysql  [slave]
seqno:          650  - latency:  25.289 - GOING-ONLINE:SYNCHRONIZING
```

From this output we can determine that the gamma server has the most current transaction sequence number and is the best candidate for the new master.

Perform Master Failover The master failover involves isolating the cluster nodes from operations, setting the role of the new master, and defining the new master for any slaves:

```
$ trepctl -host beta offline
$ trepctl -host gamma offline
$ trepctl -host gamma setrole -role master
$ trepctl -host gamma online
$ trepctl -host gamma services
$ trepctl -host beta setrole -role slave -uri thl://gamma
$ trepctl -host beta online
```

Verify Operational Cluster The final step of the failover process is to verify the state of the new cluster:

```
$ trepctl -host $node3 heartbeat
$ for NODE in beta gamma
do
  echo "#$NODE"
  trepctl -host $NODE services | simple_services
done
#beta
effectivemysql  [slave]
seqno:          651  - latency:   0.969 - ONLINE
#gamma
effectivemysql  [master]
seqno:          651  - latency:   0.427 - ONLINE
```

Recommended Configuration

Tungsten is a Java process, so understanding and managing the Java Virtual Machine (JVM) memory usage is important for optimal performance. Be sure to review the appropriate documentation and monitor JVM memory in your environment. It is recommended the JVM be configured with 1GB of RAM. The following are recommended THL settings:

- **bufferSize=128KB**   This is used for reads and writes from/to storage. This should never be less than the size of pages in persistent storage.

- **doCheckSum=true**   This enables checksums on records. This can have an impact on log performance but allows unambiguous detection of log record corruption.

- **fsyncOnFlush=true**   This performs a true fsync on disk write. This can be slow on storage with no battery backed write cache (BBWC) but required for crash-safe slaves.

- **logFileSize=100B**   This is the maximum number of bytes to write before rotating to a new log file.

  - Ensure at least 1GB in page cache.

  - Use `innodb_flush_method=O_DIRECT` if onboard with MySQL.

  - You should have 500M to 2GB free memory on the system for the OS page cache to improve parallel replication.

Alternative Tungsten Deployments

Tungsten Replicator provides for a variety of replication topologies that are not possible with native MySQL replication. One of these is the ability for a slave to have multiple masters, also referred to as fan-in replication.

Fan-In Replication

Fan-in replication, as shown in Figure 6-1, allows a MySQL instance to receive replication requests from multiple masters. When combined with appropriate filtering, this configuration can provide a centralized data warehouse of distribution data with no additional data manipulation or the common Extract, Transform, Load (ETL) step. With the advanced capabilities of Tungsten Replicator supporting different *RDBMS* and *NoSQL* products, it is possible for the fan-in instance to support data from varying sources.

Tungsten Sandbox includes a fan-in example that can be configured with a single command. The presentation at http://www.percona.com/live/mysql-conference-2012/sessions/build-simple-and-complex-replication-clusters-tungsten-replicator and blog post at http://mysql-replication-blog.blogspot.com/2011/12/testing-tungsten-fan-in-replication.html

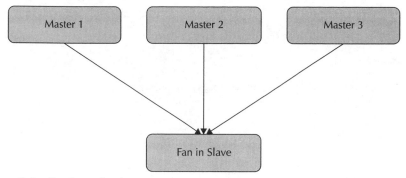

Figure 6-1 *Fan-in replication*

provide additional references for this type of deployment. The following
script provides a skeleton example.

```
#!/bin/bash

MASTER_HOSTS=(alpha beta)
FAN_IN_HOST=gamma
FAN_IN_DATASOURCE=${FAN_IN_HOST}
SERVICES=(alpha beta gamma)
SLAVE_SERVICES=(alpha beta)
TUNGSTEN_BASE=$HOME/installs/fan_in
TREPCTL=$TUNGSTEN_BASE/tungsten/tungsten-replicator/bin/trepctl
##
## First, we create a master service in each server
##
N=0
for HOST in ${MASTER_HOSTS[*]} ${FAN_IN_HOST}
do
./tools/tungsten-installer \
    --master-slave \
    --master-host=${HOST} \
    --cluster-hosts=${HOST} \
    --datasource-port=3306 \
    --datasource-user=tungsten \
    --datasource-password=secret \
    --home-directory=${TUNGSTEN_BASE} \
    --datasource-log-directory=/var/lib/mysql \
    --datasource-mysql-conf=/etc/my.cnf \
    --service-name=${SERVICES[$N]} \
    --start
    N=$(($N+1))
done

##
## After the remote masters are created,
## we create the corresponding slave services in the fan-in host
##
N=0
```

```
for HOST in ${MASTER_HOSTS[*]}
do
$TUNGSTEN_BASE/tungsten/tools/configure-service \
    -C \
    --quiet \
    --host=${FAN_IN_HOST} \
    --datasource=${FAN_IN_DATASOURCE} \
    --role=slave \
    --service-type=remote \
    --master-thl-host=${HOST} \
    --svc-start \
    --skip-validation-check=THLStorageCheck \
    --local-service-name=delta \
    --log-slave-updates=true \
    ${SERVICES[$N]}
    N=$(($N+1))
done

##
## Next, we test replication,
## by creating a different schema in each remote
## master, and collecting the results from the fan-in slave
##
N=0
for HOST in ${MASTER_HOSTS[*]}
do
    mysql -h${HOST} -utungsten -psecret -e \
    "DROP SCHEMA IF EXISTS ${SERVICES[$N]};" \
    "CREATE SCHEMA ${SERVICES[$N]};" \
    "USE ${SERVICES[$N]};" \
    "CREATE TABLE test_${SERVICES[$N]}(i int)" \
    "INSERT INTO test_${SERVICES[$N]} VALUES($N)"
    N=$(($N+1))
done
sleep 3

for SCHEMA in ${SLAVE_SERVICES[*]}
do
    mysql -v -h${FAN_IN_HOST} -utungsten -psecret ${SCHEMA} \
    -e "SELECT * FROM test_$SCHEMA"
done

##
## Finally, we show the replication summary using trepctl
##

for HOST in ${MASTER_HOSTS[*]} ${FAN_IN_HOST}
do
  $TREPCTL -host $HOST services | simple_services
done
exit 0
```

The following output is produced when run.

```
--------------
select * from test_alpha
--------------
+------+
| i    |
+------+
|    0 |
+------+
--------------
select * from test_beta
--------------
+------+
| i    |
+------+
|    1 |
+------+
alpha   [master]
seqno:            8  - latency:    0.232 - ONLINE
beta    [master]
seqno:            8  - latency:    0.316 - ONLINE
alpha   [slave]
seqno:            8  - latency:    1.279 - ONLINE
beta    [slave]
seqno:            8  - latency:    1.617 - ONLINE
delta   [master]
seqno:           90  - latency:    1.629 - ONLINE
```

Direct Replication Mode

Tungsten Replicator can be used in conjunction with MySQL replication in a production environment. The following script shows how a MySQL master/slave replication topology can use native MySQL replication, then have Tungsten Replicator take over for a period of time to reduce lag with parallel replication capabilities, and revert back to native MySQL replication.

```
#!/bin/sh
TUNGSTEN_BASE=$HOME/installs/direct
[ ! -d $TUNGSTEN_BASE ] && mkdir -p $TUNGSTEN_BASE
HOW_MANY_CHANNELS=$1
[ -z $HOW_MANY_CHANNELS ] && HOW_MANY_CHANNELS=5
TREPCTL=${TUNGSTEN_BASE}/tungsten/tungsten-replicator/bin/trepctl

MASTER="alpha"
SLAVE1="beta"
SLAVE2="gamma"
NUM_SLAVES="2"
```

```
##
## Installing native MySQL replication on the slaves
##
i=1
while [ $i -le ${NUM_SLAVES} ]
do
  SLAVE="slave${i}"
  mysql -h${SLAVE} -e "STOP SLAVE; " \
   "CHANGE MASTER TO MASTER_HOST='${MASTER}'," \
   "MASTER_PORT=3306, MASTER_USER='tungsten', MASTER_PASSWORD='secret'; " \
   "START SLAVE"
  i=`expr $i + 1`
done

##
## To test a direct slave with parallel replication, you should:
##   * create several database schemas
##   * start several dozen threads that update those databases concurrently
##   * stop the slaves for a few minutes, to accumulate some lag
##   * restart the slaves
##   * finally, let Tungsten Replicator take over on slave, with the command

./tools/tungsten-installer \
    --direct \
    --master-host=${MASTER} \
    --slave-host=${SLAVE2} \
    --master-user=tungsten \
    --master-mysql-conf=/etc/my.cnf \
    --slave-mysql-conf=/etc/my.cnf \
    --slave-user=tungsten \
    --master-password=secret \
    --slave-password=secret \
    --service-name=effectivemysql \
    --channels=${HOW_MANY_CHANNELS} \
    --home-directory=${TUNGSTEN_BASE} \
    --buffer-size=100 \
    --native-slave-takeover \
    --start-and-report

$TREPCTL status
$TREPCTL status -name shards
$TREPCTL status -name stores

mysql -h ${SLAVE2} -e 'SELECT * FROM tungsten_effectivemysql.trep_commit_seqno'

##
## To hand over replication back to MySQL native replication,
## do the following:
##   * check 'SHOW SLAVE STATUS\G' Should be stopped at the point where Tungsten
##     took over
##   * put the replicator offline (trepctl offline)
##   * check 'SHOW SLAVE STATUS\G' again. Should be updated to the latest
```

```
##      position used by Tungsten
##    * run 'START SLAVE', and the native replication will resume.
##
##  If you then put the replicator back online, it will take over again.
```

For more information see http://code.google.com/p/tungsten-replicator/ wiki/TRCBasicInstallation#Taking_over_replication_from_a_MySQL_ slave_in_direct_mode.

Unique Characteristics

You may not consider replication to be a disruptive technology; however, features of replication that can influence and support the changes occurring in the database and data store space, especially with managing larger and varying amounts of data, are disruptive.

Tungsten has some characteristics that set it apart uniquely from both MySQL and other third-party vendors, versions, flavors, patches, add-ons, etc.

1. Tungsten can replicate data to and from different disparate data sources, including Oracle, MongoDB, Postgres, and Vertica. That list, I am sure, will grow.

2. Tungsten runs on stock standard MySQL; no installation of modified MySQL necessary, no change to running software, installation procedures, monitoring, etc. Tungsten is an additional product that simply extends MySQL. Tungsten, of course, requires installation, management, monitoring, etc.

3. Tungsten allows for the fan in architecture. That is where a slave server can receive and manage information from multiple masters, including different products. This has just simplified the data warehouse process to a software installation and configuration process; no additional transformation or export/import necessary.

4. Tungsten Replicator can be installed in an existing MySQL replication environment and can be used to take over native replication with a simple command.

Continuent Tungsten

The commercial offering of Tungsten Replicator is called Continuent Tungsten. Some of the additional features in the enterprise version include

- Advanced installation for regular master/slave and multisite topologies.

- Database virtualization. A Tungsten cluster is seen and administered as a single database.

- Automatic failover (or manual failover with a single command when automatic is disabled).

- Automatic and manual recovery of failed slaves.

- Centralized management tool that includes backup and restore automation.

- Single command master switch with zero downtime.

- Transparent routing and connectivity that allow applications to see the cluster as a single server. No virtual IPs are necessary, even for cross-site switches.

Continuent also provides commercial 24/7 support for Tungsten. You can view a feature matrix at http://continuent.com/solutions/featurematrix.

Continuent Wrap-Up

This section only scratches the surface of the features and functionality of Tungsten Replicator. Indeed this product could easily have a full book for readers to understand and appreciate the depth. These examples are included to teach you to walk before learning to run with Tungsten. One of the true benefits and complexities of Tungsten is the amount of custom options for huge environments that replicate efficiently across global locations, providing parallelizing data flow and hot failovers of entire Tungsten clusters seamlessly. These features are available for a startup to the largest web properties around.

Get More Help

You can join the discussion group, and view and log any issues at http://tungsten-replicator.org.

SchoonerSQL

SchoonerSQL by Schooner Information Technology (recently acquired by SanDisk) provides a commercial synchronous MySQL replication solution using a modified version of InnoDB. The documented features include no loss of data, instance failover, and automated recovery capabilities. A SchoonerSQL solution can also include traditional MySQL replication for additional slaves. As a commerical product, there is no access to the software without a formal pre-sales process. A request to review the software for this book was not granted.

MySQL Replication Listener

The MySQL Replication Listener, available from https://launchpad.net/mysql-replication-listener, is an open source C++ library that can process a replication stream. This is a MySQL binary log API for capturing any data changes in MySQL. This can be used to read and decode information, and then custom code that can apply the data manipulation based on need, for example, populating a dedicated full text tool or synchronizing with a caching system. This tool can also be used to read and analyze the binary log.

This is a simple and extensible API that can use the network transport (i.e., a master server) or a file transport (i.e., a binary log file) to read and decode the replication events. Dr. Lars Thalmann and Dr. Mats Kindahl, two key members of the Oracle/MySQL replication team and co-authors of *MySQL High Availability* (O'Reilly, 2010), provide a more detailed explanation in the presentation "Binary Log API: A Library for Change Data Capture Using MySQL," obtained at http://www.oscon.com/oscon2011/public/schedule/detail/18785. A detailed example of how to use the API can be found at http://intuitive-search.blogspot.se/2011/07/binary-log-api-and-replication-listener.html.

MySQL in the Cloud

Two existing cloud product offerings extend traditional MySQL replication with synchronous replication options.

Amazon RDS for MySQL

Amazon RDS for MySQL provides for read replicas, which are traditional MySQL slaves using replication. RDS also provides a multi-AZ deployment where proprietary synchronous replication is used to provide a standby replica. Amazon RDS is also documented to automatically failover; however, this has not been tested for confirmation. While a read replica is available for general read access, a multi-AZ replica is not accessible before a failover. The *Effective MySQL: Backup and Recovery* book (McGraw-Hill, 2012) has a detailed section on the features and use of Amazon RDS for MySQL. Amazon RDS for MySQL is an established product offering with several years of general availability. More information is available at http://aws.amazon.com/rds/mysql/.

Google Cloud SQL

The Google cloud offering provides a proprietary synchronous replication configuration by default. There is no traditional asynchronous option. Google Cloud SQL does not provide any access to the synchronous copy and will also automatically manage failover without any need for human intervention. The *Effective MySQL: Backup and Recovery* book has a detailed section on the features and use of Google Cloud SQL. More information is available at https://developers.google.com/cloud-sql/.

Other Offerings

The MySQL ecosystem has included its share of new product offerings that pop up and claim to solve MySQL replication and scale out issues with various features. Many simply simulate the MySQL protocol, i.e., the communication that MySQL uses between client connectors and the MySQL kernel. This book is specifically designed for MySQL replication that is part of the core (and well established and stable) MySQL product. Reading about the problems these products are trying to solve is applicable when discussing replication. A few include (in alphabetical order) Clustrix (http://www.clustrix.com/), ScaleARC (http://www.scalearc.com/), ScaleDB (http://www.scaledb.com/), and Xeround (http://xeround.com/). No evaluation has been made for comparison with MySQL and what is stated at these respective company websites.

Conclusion

MySQL replication is a core component for designing scale out replication architectures. In this chapter we have discussed several commercial strength products and other features that extend traditional MySQL replication with many enterprise class features. As with many options, appropriate testing and verification in your unique environment are important to make an informed decision on what is most applicable in any given situation.

Examples and links in this chapter are available for download from http://EffectiveMySQL.com/book/replication-techniques.

7

MySQL Configuration Options

MySQL 5.6 now supports almost 400* configurable system variables. A number of these variables have a direct effect on how MySQL will operate when using replication. Understanding what system variables do and how they change the behavior of the MySQL server will help ensure that MySQL replication operates as expected.

---

* 391 in 5.6.5-m8, 319 in 5.5.24, 276 in 5.1.63, and just 239 in 5.0.95 for master servers. The count also changes depending on compile and startup options and if replication or plugins are enabled.

207

In this chapter we will discuss

- Binary logging variables
- Replication system variables
- Replication security variables
- New MySQL 5.6 variables
- Replication-specific grants, commands, and functions

About MySQL System Variables

Unless otherwise specified, all variables are available in MySQL 5.5, the current *GA* version. While every attempt has been made to document important and relevant MySQL 5.6 configuration variables, as a development release of MySQL these are subject to change. Always refer to the MySQL 5.6 documentation for current information at http://dev.mysql.com/doc/refman/5.6/en/server-system-variables.html.

This chapter does not discuss any variables that are part of any third-party products or MySQL variants mentioned during this book. The applicable sections describe references to the respective product documentation.

The MySQL reference manual is the best resource of information available. All replication-specific variables can be found at http://dev.mysql.com/doc/refman/5.5/en/replication-options-table.html.

Binary Logging

These initial variables are required settings for the configuration of MySQL binary logging, and are essential components when using MySQL replication:

- `server_id`   This mandatory variable is a unique number for the server within the current MySQL topology.
- `log_bin`   This enables the binary log and is mandatory for replication on the master host. This variable also defines the basename of the binary log files. The default file path is the data directory with a filename of the hostname + '-bin'.

- **`log_bin_index`**   This variable defines the name of the index that holds a list of all current binary logs. This will default to the `log_bin` basename with an `.index` extension.

- **`binlog_format`**   This variable controls the type of binary logging. The value of STATEMENT, the default, logs the actual SQL statement to the binary log. The value of ROW will log changed data blocks to the binary log. The value of MIXED will choose the most applicable method for the given statement necessary to ensure data consistency. This option can be specified on a per session level, for example, with SET SESSION.binlog_format = ROW.

- **`binlog_row_image`** (5.6)   This variable alters the amount of data block information that is used when `binlog_format` is ROW. The value of `full`, the default, logs full before and after row images. The values of `minimal` and `blob` alter the columns used in the before and after images to reduce disk space and network bandwidth.

- **`binlog_do_db` & `binlog_ignore_db`**   These variables on the master host limit which statements are logged to the binary log based on the specified database name, preceded by a USE qualifier. Multiple database values can be specified using multiple lines in the `my.cnf`. For example:

```
#my.cnf
[mysqld]
binlog_do_db = book3
binlog_do_db = mysql
```

CAUTION   *Use of `binlog_do_db` and `binlog_ingnore_db` can make a binary log unusable in a point in time recovery of a full primary database. These options are also incomplete, as they require all SQL to be preceded by an applicable USE, and do not handle cross-schema joins as you would expect.*

- **`binlog_cache_size`**   This cache is used to hold changes that are to be written to the binary log during a transaction. Increasing this value for very large transactions can possibly increase performance.

- **`binlog_stmt_cache_size`**   This variable specifies the size of the cache for the binary log to hold non-transactional statements during transactions on a per client basis. There may be a benefit to increasing this value using large non-transactional statements.

- `binlog_row_event_max_size` This variable represents the maximum size of a row-based binary log event.

- `max_binlog_size` This is the maximum size of the binary log file before a new file is created. This defaults to and can be a maximum of 1GB. It is possible the resulting file may be larger, as binary logs contain completed transactions. The FLUSH BINARY LOGS command will also dynamically close the current binary log and create a new file.

- `expire_logs_days` This variable defines the number of days binary log files are retained. Files older than the number of days are removed (similar in operation to a PURGE MASTER LOGS command) when a new binary log file is created. A check is performed to confirm no connected slave server is currently using a binary log that is being purged. There is no check for any slaves that may not be connected.

- `sync_binlog` This variable defines when the binary log file is physically synced to disk. The value is the number of statements executed. The best durability is a value of 1, meaning at the worst case only one transaction could be lost in a system failure with appropriate redundancies. The default is 0, which delegates to the operating system to manage the sync. With an applicable *RAID* controller card and Battery Backed Write Cache (BBWC), this hardware feature may provide the same level of durability as a value of 1.

- `log_bin_basename` **(5.6)** This new variable defines the complete path to the binary log. In previous versions the `log_bin` variable was used to define the enabling of the binary log (e.g., ON) and an optional basename in the configuration. This basename was never visible with SHOW GLOBAL VARIABLES. The following shows the `log-bin` variable defined in MySQL Sandbox for versions 5.5 and 5.6, and shows the corresponding values represented by SHOW GLOBAL VARIABLES to demonstrate the new `log_bin_basename` variable.

For MySQL 5.5:

```
$ cd $HOME/sandboxes/rsandbox_5_5_24
$ grep log-bin master/my.sandbox.cnf
log-bin=mysql-bin
mysql55> SHOW GLOBAL VARIABLES LIKE  'log_bin%'\G
```

```
*************************** 1. row ***************************
Variable_name: log_bin
        Value: ON
*************************** 2. row ***************************
Variable_name: log_bin_trust_function_creators
        Value: OFF
```

For MySQL 5.6

```
$ cd $HOME/sandboxes/rsandbox_5_6_5
$ grep log-bin master/my.sandbox.cnf
log-bin=mysql-bin
```

Note that the configuration is identical to MySQL 5.5; however, there is now the `log_bin_basename` variable:

```
mysql56> SHOW GLOBAL VARIABLES LIKE  'log_bin%'\G
*************************** 1. row ***************************
Variable_name: log_bin
        Value: ON
*************************** 2. row ***************************
Variable_name: log_bin_basename
        Value: /home/user/sandboxes/rsandbox_5_6_5/master/data/mysql-bin
*************************** 3. row ***************************
Variable_name: log_bin_index
        Value: /home/user/sandboxes/rsandbox_5_6_5/master/data/mysql-bin.index
*************************** 4. row ***************************
Variable_name: log_bin_trust_function_creators
        Value: OFF
```

- **`binlog_rows_query_log_events` (5.6)**   This new variable is used to provide additional row-based logging information with the binary log and can be used for debugging purposes. One example is the representation of the actual SQL statement when using row-based replication:

```
master> CREATE SCHEMA IF NOT EXISTS book3;
master> USE book3;
master> DROP TABLE IF EXISTS bl_events;
master> CREATE TABLE bl_events (ID INT NOT NULL);
master> SET SESSION binlog_format=ROW;
master> FLUSH BINARY LOGS;
master> SHOW BINARY LOGS;
master> SET SESSION binlog_rows_query_log_events=ON;
master> INSERT INTO bl_events VALUES(1),(2),(3);
master> SET SESSION binlog_rows_query_log_events=OFF;
master> INSERT INTO bl_events VALUES(1),(2),(3);
master> SHOW BINLOG EVENTS IN 'mysql-bin.000009';
+-----+---------------+-------------------------------------------------
| Pos | Event_type    |Info
+-----+---------------+-------------------------------------------------
|   4 | Format_desc   |Server ver: 5.6.5-m8-log, Binlog ver: 4
| 120 | Previous_gtids |B9A8FDE1-B4A3-11E1-921D-B499BAF75D68:1-9
```

```
| 187 | Gtid         |SET @@SESSION.GTID_NEXT= 'B9A8FDE1-B4A3-11E1-
| 231 | Query        |BEGIN
| 300 | Rows_query   |# INSERT INTO bl_events VALUES(1),(2),(3)
| 359 | Table_map    |table_id: 72 (book3.bl_events)
| 408 | Write_rows   |table_id: 72 flags: STMT_END_F
| 452 | Xid          |COMMIT /* xid=75 */
| 479 | Gtid         |SET @@SESSION.GTID_NEXT= 'B9A8FDE1-B4A3-11E1-
| 523 | Query        |BEGIN
| 592 | Table_map    |table_id: 72 (book3.bl_events)
| 641 | Write_rows   |table_id: 72 flags: STMT_END_F
| 685 | Xid          |COMMIT /* xid=77 */
+-----+--------------+----------------------------------------------
```

The previous example also shows the GTID-specific binary log entries. If `gtid_mode` is not enabled, this output will not be displayed. The full list of columns for SHOW BINLOG EVENTS can be seen with \G. For example:

```
master> SHOW BINLOG EVENTS IN 'mysql-bin.000009'\G
*************************** 1. row ***************************
  Log_name: mysql-bin.000009
       Pos: 4
Event_type: Format_desc
 Server_id: 1
End_log_pos: 120
      Info: Server ver: 5.6.5-m8-log, Binlog ver: 4
...
```

- **binlog_order_commits** (5.6)   This group commit variable determines the order of committed transactions to support parallel operations.

- **binlog_max_flush_queue_time** (5.6)   This group commit variable determines how many milliseconds to keep reading transactions from the flush queue before proceeding.

- **binlog_flush_log_at_timeout** (5.6)   This variable determines when to flush the binary log every N seconds.

This is not a complete list of possible variables for binary logs. See http://dev.mysql.com/doc/refman/5.6/en/replication-options.html for detailed information of these replication options.

MySQL Replication

These variables affect the way MySQL replication behaves. Whether a slave host is set to only replicate certain databases, skip certain errors, and/or is set up in a unique chain topology, it is important to know how the following will affect your setup:

- `relay_log` The relay logs hold replicated database changes retrieved from the master binary log and written with the I/O thread. If not specified, this file path will default to the MySQL data directory, the server hostname, and the MySQL port.

- `relay_log_index` This variable defines the name of the relay log index that holds the names of all the relay logs available. The default filename is the `relay_log` variable value with the extension `.index`.

- `replicate_do_db & replicate_ignore_db` These variables are used to filter which recorded master binary log statements are applied on the slave. Their use is much like `binlog_do_db` and `binlog_ignore_db` options on the master host. For multiple database values, specify the options multiple times. There are similar `replicate-` options for tables and for wildcard database/table matching.

CAUTION   *The `replicate_do_db` and `replicate_ingnore_db` can cause errors, as they require all SQL to be preceded by an applicable USE and do not handle cross-schema joins as you would expect.*

- `slave_skip_errors` Replication error codes can be skipped automatically when specified with this variable. Normally, replication will stop when the SQL thread encounters an error; however, this variable will cause the SQL thread to skip those errors listed in the variable value. It is rarely a good idea to specify a value for `slave_skip_errors`, because there is no accountability of the occurrences of these silent errors, which will generally lead to data drift and/or loss of data integrity. The format of the value for this variable is a comma separated list of MySQL error numbers.

- `slave_exec_mode` There are two valid values for `slave_exec_mode`, IDEMPOTENT and STRICT. This variable is used for replication conflict resolution and error checking. If the value is set to IDEMPOTENT (default for NDB), the slave will not error out during duplicate key or no key found errors. The IDEMPOTENT value is useful with a system that is set up in a multi-master or circular replication fashion. When the value is set to STRICT, the default, replication will stop on duplicate key and no key found errors.

- `log_slave_updates`   When defined and binary logging is enabled on a slave, all replicated changes from the SQL thread are also written to the slave server binary log. This option is used to chain multiple nodes together through replication. For example, if you have three servers (A, B, and C) and want to connect them in a chain you would use `log_slave_updates` on B. B would replicate from A, and C from B, forming a chain, (A -> B -> C).

- `relay_log_purge`   This variable controls how the relay log files are purged. The default of 1 specifies that the relay log files are removed when they are no longer needed for applying replication events. A value of 0 retains the log files.

- `read_only`   This variable defines that the slave will not accept DML or DDL statements other than those applied by the replication slave SQL thread. The exception is a user with SUPER privilege will override this setting.

- `skip_slave_start`   By default, when a slave server starts, an implied SLAVE START occurs. With this variable specified, the slave is not automatically started and must be performed manually with START SLAVE.

- `sync_relay_log`, `sync_relay_log_info`   These variables control how frequently a file sync is performed on the respective relay log and relay log info file. The number represents the name of executed SQL statements to apply before action. The default is 0; the safest durability setting is 1.

- `report_host`   This optional variable provides a string for the slave that is reported with SHOW SLAVE HOSTS on the master.

- `slave-max-allowed-packet` (5.6)   This new variable defines the maximum allowed packet size for the slave SQL and I/O threads.

- `relay-log-recovery` (5.6)   This new variable, when enabled (disabled by default), will discard any unprocessed slave relay log events that have not been applied and will initiate obtaining the events from the master.

This is not an exhaustive list of all replication-related variables. Full details can be found at http://dev.mysql.com/doc/refman/5.6/en/replication-options-slave.html.

Semisynchronous Replication

A new feature in MySQL 5.5 is the ability to define semisynchronous replication. This is an improvement on classic asynchronous replication, as the master server waits for a confirmation from a slave that the event has been received and recorded on a different server before returning a success indicator to the calling client. The following semisynchronous variables will only be visible following the installation of the necessary plugins as described in Chapter 3. These variables control master/slave semisynchronous operation.

On the master:

- `rpl_semi_sync_master_enabled` When set to ON, semisynchronous replication may be initiated by the master. At least one slave must also have the corresponding variable set to ON for semisynchronous replication to become operational. The SHOW GLOBAL VARIABLES LIKE 'rpl_semi%' can be used to confirm and monitor semisynchronous replication.

- `rpl_semi_sync_master_timeout` The master will wait a default of 10,000 milliseconds for a response from any slave configured to use semisynchronous replication before the master will revert to asynchronous replication and return a response to the client. This can be set to a lower value if applicable.

- `rpl_semi_sync_master_wait_no_slave` This value controls how the master will wait for a timeout from one or more slaves before reverting to asynchronous replication. The default value is ON.

- `rpl_semi_sync_master_trace_level` This defines the level of debugging logging. The allowed values are 1 (general level logging), 16 (detailed level logging), 32 (network wait logging), and 64 (function level logging).

On the slave:

- `rpl_semi_sync_slave_enabled` When set to ON, semisynchronous replication on the slave is possible.

- **`rpl_semi_sync_slave_trace_level`** This defines the level of debugging logging. The allowed values are 1, 16, 32, and 64.

NOTE MySQL will disable semisynchronous replication and revert automatically to asynchronous replication when any error occurs or slow network overhead exceeds the timeout, so slave servers can continue to operate. This may lessen your high availability requirements. Adequate monitoring of MySQL status variables and the MySQL error log is very important to determine this situation and rectify accordingly.

Refer to Chapter 3 for the use and demonstration of these variables in conjunction with loading the necessary plugins. More information can also be found in the MySQL Reference Manual at http://dev.mysql.com/doc/refman/5.5/en/replication-semisync.html.

Security

Support for SSL communication with MySQL has been around since version 4.0.0 (October 2001). In a recent survey of over 1000 people at the 2012 Percona Live MySQL conference keynote, less than 1 percent indicated using SSL. The need to use SSL is more prevalent today with the use of cloud services. To improve the future adoption of improved security, starting with MySQL 5.6, starting a slave without SSL will produce a warning. These variables define SSL usage for securing client/server and replication stream communications:

- **`ssl`** This variable states that the MySQL server permits SSL connections. This option does not state that connections require SSL. See the GRANT command described later.

- **`ssl-ca`** This variable is used to identify the Certificate Authority (CA) certificate file.

- **`ssl-cert`** This identifies the server public key file. This is used in client authentication with the CA certificate.

- **`ssl-key`** This identifies the server private key file that is used for confirmation of provided security credentials from the client.

TIP Ensure that you also adequately secure on the file system appropriate access to the SSL certificate files defined with these options.

The GRANT command is used to ensure user connections requiring secure communication using SSL are defined with the REQUIRE SSL syntax. This syntax also enables additional SSL attributes, including X509, ISSUER, SUBJECT, and CIPHER, to further limit SSL authorization. See http://dev.mysql.com/doc/refman/5.5/en/grant.html for the full range of syntax options.

Chapter 3 provides a detailed example of the setup and use of SSL in MySQL.

Related SSL variables not described here include `skip-ssl`, `ssl-capath`, `ssl-cipher`, and `ssl-verify-server-cert`. For more information see http://dev.mysql.com/doc/refman/5.5/en/secure-basics.html.

MySQL Server Variables

The MySQL server has a number of general variables that can affect MySQL replication or are recommended with certain tools that are associated with MySQL replication:

- `have_dynamic_loading` This variable defines if the dynamic execution of plugins is supported, for example, when using the semisynchronous plugin.

- `auto_increment_increment` This variable defines the increment value that is used for an AUTO_INCREMENT column in a table. The default value is 1. This is applicable in a multi-master environment when it is beneficial to change (for example, to 2). When combined with `auto_increment_offset`, this can ensure no possible collision detection for an auto increment primary key if writing to multiple servers. This is a global setting for all tables in a given instance. More information can be found in Chapter 4.

- `auto_increment_offset` This variable defines the starting value of an AUTO_INCREMENT column for a table. The default value is 1. As described with `auto_increment_increment`, this variable is used in multi-master environments to manage uniqueness in MySQL topology of auto incrementing primary key value.

- `default_storage_engine` This variable defines the storage engine that is used when not specified with the CREATE TABLE statement. The default (from MySQL 5.5) and recommended value is InnoDB, which is a transactional storage engine. The historical value is MyISAM. For more information about MySQL storage engines, see http://dev.mysql.com/doc/refman/5.5/en/storage-engines.html.

- `max_allowed_packet`   This defines the maximum size of a communication packet of MySQL information that can be sent from a client to a MySQL server.

- `bind_address`   By default, MySQL will accept network TCP/IP communication on the defined port for all system IP addresses. Use `bind_address` to limit communications to an individual IP address. When set to localhost, or the loopback address (e.g., 127.0.0.1), communication to the database is only possible on the server. This option accepts any IPv4 or IPv6 address.

InnoDB Variables

- `innodb_flush_log_at_trx_commit`   This variable defines the level of durability for InnoDB log transactions when they are written. The default value of 1 will write and flush every log transaction to disk. This is the safest method for durability. A common setting based on business needs and an appropriate RAID controller is a value of 2. This writes all transactions to disk; however, it only flushes to disk approximately once per second. The final permissible value is 0, which will only write and flush approximately once per second.

- `innodb_locks_unsafe_for_binlog`   This variable controls how InnoDB manages row level locking for operations on a range of rows. The default value is 0 (or disabled), which means the normal algorithm involves setting appropriate exclusive index-row and gap locking for operations. This is a difficult concept to describe in a few words. For a detailed description and examples refer to http://dev.mysql.com/doc/refman/5.5/en/innodb-parameters.html#sysvar_innodb_locks_unsafe_for_binlog.

- `innodb_autoinc_lock_mode`   This value controls the locking mode that is used for generating auto increment values in InnoDB tables. This option supports three values: 0, which represents traditional mode; 1, the default, which represents consecutive mode; and 2, which represents interleaved mode. A detailed description is at http://dev.mysql.com/doc/refman/5.5/en/innodb-auto-increment-handling.html.

- `innodb_doublewrite` This variable defines if the InnoDB doublewrite buffer is enabled. The default is ON. This provides a level of crash recovery as updated data pages are first written to disk sequentially before they are applied in place. Setting this value to OFF can affect durability in a disaster recovery situation.

- `innodb_support_xa` This variable, which is enabled by default, provides support for an XA two-phase commit with InnoDB. If disabled, this can result in a different order of transactions being written to the binary log than the commit order. It is recommended that you disable this for a slave due to the single threaded nature of replication to improve performance.

MySQL 5.6 Features

In addition to some of the mentioned 5.6 variables in common replication sections already described, these variables are new for various 5.6 replication features.

Universally Unique Identifier (UUID)

- `server_uuid (5.6)` This is a server generated unique identifier. This is maintained in a separate configuration file, `auto.cnf`, in the MySQL `datadir`. This value is automatically generated by the MySQL server and should not be modified. This information is used by MySQL slaves to identify the master.

More information can be found at http://dev.mysql.com/doc/refman/5.6/en/replication-options.html#sysvar_server_uuid.

Crash-Safe Slaves

- `master-info-repository` When defined as TABLE, this variable will move logging of the slave log's master status from the `master.info` file to the `mysql.slave_master_info` table.

- `relay-log-info-repository`   When defined as TABLE, this variable will move logging of the slave relay log information from the `relay-log.info` file to the `mysql.slave_relay_log_info` table.

Additional details can be found at http://dev.mysql.com/doc/refman/5.6/en/replication-options-binary-log.html#option_mysqld_master-info-repository.

Replication Checksums

- `binlog_checksum`   When this option is set to CRC32 (currently the only possible value), the master will write a checksum for each event into the binary log.

- `master_verify_checksum`   When set to ON the master host will examine checksums that were written to the binary log when reading from the binary log to send events to a slave.

- `slave_sql_verify_checksum`   When set to ON the slave host will examine and verify checksums when reading the relay log.

Additional details can be found at http://dev.mysql.com/doc/refman/5.6/en/replication-options-binary-log.html#option_mysqld_binlog-checksum.

Multi-Threaded Slaves

- `slave_parallel_workers`   This is the number of slave worker threads that can be used for parallel execution of replication events on the slave. This requires that `relay_log_info_repository` has a value of TABLE.

Global Transaction Identifier (GTID)

- `gtid-mode`   When set to ON, this option defines that GTIDs are enabled on the server. GTID operations are only possible when this option is enabled on all master and slave servers.

- `disable-gtid-unsafe-statements`   When enabled, this option will prevent any SQL statements that cannot be logged safely in a transaction. This includes using non-transactional storage engine tables CREATE TEMPORARY TABLE and CREATE TABLE ... SELECT at this time.

Additional variables not discussed include `gtid_done`, `gtid_owned`, `gtid_lost`, and `gtid_next`. You can find more information on these variables at http://dev.mysql.com/doc/refman/5.6/en/replication-options-gtids .html.

User Privileges

In addition to the available MySQL configuration variables, there are some replication-specific privileges that can be specified with the GRANT command:

- GRANT REPLICATION SLAVE is required for retrieving binary log events to be applied in replication. This is the user specified in the CHANGE MASTER TO command.

- GRANT REPLICATION CLIENT is required for using SHOW MASTER STATUS, SHOW SLAVE STATUS, and SHOW BINARY LOGS (statement privilege since 5.6).

The SUPER privilege is required for SET SQL_LOG_BIN and SET SQL_SLAVE_SKIP_COUNTER commands. A user that has the SUPER privilege will also bypass the `read_only` variable that is used for MySQL slave data integrity.

TIP   Application users should only ever have SELECT, INSERT, UPDATE, and DELETE on database objects in the respective application database only. Some other privileges for views and routines may be necessary if required; however, CREATE, DROP, ALTER, and SUPER should never be assigned to an application user accessing MySQL. That is the role of a different and separate DBA account with restricted host access.

More information on the individual GRANT command options can be found at http://dev.mysql.com/doc/refman/5.6/en/grant.html.

SQL Commands and Functions

Throughout this book there have been a large number of SQL statements specifically for MySQL replication use in addition to the common *DDL* and *DML* SQL commands. These have included the following.

Binary Log Statements

- SHOW MASTER STATUS
- SHOW MASTER | BINARY LOGS
- SHOW BINLOG EVENTS
- PURGE MASTER | BINARY LOGS
- FLUSH BINARY LOGS
- FLUSH [MASTER] LOGS (deprecated and removed in 5.6; use RESET MASTER)
- RESET MASTER
- SHOW PLUGINS (5.1)
- SET SESSION SQL_LOG_BIN

CAUTION   *While MASTER or BINARY keywords can be interchanged in SHOW LOGS and PURGE LOGS, FLUSH BINARY LOGS and FLUSH MASTER LOGS perform two very different options, the latter being very destructive.*

Replication Statements

- CHANGE MASTER TO
- START SLAVE [SQL THREAD | IO_THREAD] [UNTIL ...]
- STOP SLAVE [SQL THREAD | IO_THREAD]
- FLUSH SLAVE (deprecated and removed in 5.6; use RESET SLAVE)
- RESET SLAVE
- SHOW SLAVE STATUS
- SHOW SLAVE HOSTS
- SHOW RELAYLOG EVENTS (5.5)
- SET GLOBAL SLAVE_SKIP_SQL_COUNTER

For more information see http://dev.mysql.com/doc/refman/5.6/en/sql-syntax-replication.html   and   http://dev.mysql.com/doc/refman/5.6/en/show.html.

Replication Related Functions

In addition, there are some replication-specific functions that can be used in SQL statements:

- MASTER_POS_WAIT() (since 3.23)
- UUID() (5.6)
- UUID_SHORT() (5.6)
- GTID_SUBSET() (5.6)
- GTID_SUBSTRACT() (5.6)

For more information see http://dev.mysql.com/doc/refman/5.6/en/miscellaneous-functions.html.

Conclusion

As stated at the beginning of the chapter, there are a large number of different MySQL configuration variables. The number of configurable MySQL variables has increased with new versions. It is important to know how a MySQL server has been configured and load tested in order to provide the best performance, reliability, and data integrity, especially with new versions. The correct settings for your individual system can only be determined by understanding the load and business needs of your unique system. Benchmarking should be an integral part of system management and evaluation for new MySQL versions.

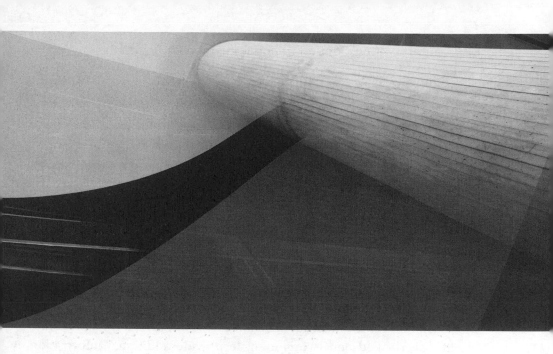

8

Monitoring Replication

Monitoring MySQL is an essential requirement for a functioning production environment, and replication is a key component to most situations. Knowing if a replication server has failed is a crucial part of database administration. A MySQL administrator should have the right tools in place to help identify replication issues, both proactive and reactively. In this chapter we will discuss the following:

- The types of monitoring needed
- Important information to monitor
- Available monitoring products

Types of Monitoring

Traditional monitoring tools provide common features, including a graphical interface recording historical information and providing comparative analysis between servers for a given timeframe. Alerting capabilities may be part of monitoring software or an additional product. The following sections will discuss many of the common tools available.

MySQL Configuration

Any level of monitoring should also record important configuration information, both via the MySQL configuration file and current runtime configuration that can be modified dynamically. Monitoring a change of state is often overlooked and is important to provide additional information when understanding some observed condition. The following is an example script that monitors these conditions and reports any detected changes:

```
$ cat check_mysql_config.sh
#!/bin/sh
#
# Name:    check_mysql_config
# Purpose: Check the current MySQL my.cnf and runtime configuration
#          for any changes.
# Author:  Effective MySQL  http://effectivemysql.com
#
LOG_DIR="${HOME}/log"   # Change appropriately
MY_CNF="/etc/my.cnf"

SCRIPT_NAME=`basename $0 | sed -e "s/.sh$//"`

[ -z `which mysqladmin 2>/dev/null` ] && \
  echo "ERROR: mysqladmin not in PATH." && exit 1
[ ! -s "${HOME}/.my.cnf" ] && \
  echo "ERROR: No MySQL authentication available." && exit 1
[ -z "${LOG_DIR}" ] && echo "ERROR: LOG_DIR is not defined." && exit 1
[ ! -d "${LOG_DIR}" ] && mkdir -p ${LOG_FILE}
[ -z "${MY_CNF}" ] && echo "ERROR: MY_CNF is not defined." && exit 1
[ ! -s "${MY_CNF}" ] && echo "ERROR: MySQL Configuration file '${MY_CNF}' not
found." \
    && exit 1
[ -z "${TMP_DIR}" ] && TMP_DIR="/tmp"

LOG_FILE="${LOG_DIR}/${SCRIPT_NAME}.log"
CURRENT_CNF="${LOG_DIR}/my.cnf.runtime"
CURRENT_CNF_FILE="${LOG_DIR}/my.cnf.current"

TMP_FILE="${TMP_DIR}/${SCRIPT_NAME}.tmp.$$"
```

```
DIFF_FILE="${TMP_DIR}/${SCRIPT_NAME}.diff.$$"

DATE_TIME=`date +%Y%m%d.%H%M%S`
mysqladmin variables  > ${TMP_FILE}

[ ! -s "${CURRENT_CNF}" ] && \
  echo "${DATE_TIME} No running configuration recorded, creating." \
>> ${LOG_FILE} && cp ${TMP_FILE} ${CURRENT_CNF}
[ ! -s "${CURRENT_CNF_FILE}" ] && \
  echo "${DATE_TIME} No my.cnf recorded, creating." >> ${LOG_FILE} && \
  cp ${MY_CNF} ${CURRENT_CNF_FILE}

diff -U 0 ${CURRENT_CNF_FILE} ${MY_CNF} > ${DIFF_FILE}
if [ -s "${DIFF_FILE}" ]
then
  echo "${DATE_TIME} WARN: A difference has been detected" >> ${LOG_FILE}
  cat ${DIFF_FILE} >> ${LOG_FILE}
  cp ${MY_CNF} ${CURRENT_CNF_FILE}
  CHANGES="Y"
fi

diff -U 0 ${CURRENT_CNF} ${TMP_FILE} > ${DIFF_FILE}
if [ -s "${DIFF_FILE}" ]
then
  CHANGES="Y"
  echo "${DATE_TIME} WARN: A difference in config has been detected" \
>> ${LOG_FILE}
  cat ${DIFF_FILE} >> ${LOG_FILE}
  cp ${TMP_FILE} ${CURRENT_CNF}
fi

[ -z "${CHANGES}" ] && \
  echo "${DATE_TIME} INFO: No changes detected" >> ${LOG_FILE}
#[ ! -z "${CHANGES}" ] && \
# echo "Do something to alert a change has occurred"
rm -f ${TMP_FILE} ${DIFF_FILE}
exit 0
```

This script should be modified to include an appropriate alert, for example, an email when a change is detected. This should be defined as a scheduled job run with a regular frequency.

TIP   A common mistake is to make a dynamic change to a MySQL global variable and not record this change in the MySQL configuration file that is read during a MySQL restart.

Applying the same principle of detecting change, the MySQL error log and other system configuration files that can affect MySQL operations should also be monitored appropriately.

Monitoring Granularity

In a production environment the information recorded with general monitoring does not identify issues that occur with a much finer granularity. In many situations, replication monitoring requires a granularity of a few seconds to detect important conditions, including replication lag or failed replication threads. For example, if replication lag was monitored every five minutes, then the reported value may always be zero (0) or a smaller number. By using the example procedure defined in the appendix, lag can easily be more; however, if this all occurred within the five minute period there would be no indication. There is no maximum lag for the last five minutes available unless it is captured with a more real-time monitoring implementation. Also waiting up to five minutes to know if a MySQL slave has stopped processing may be unacceptable. Developing a simple dashboard to display information is an important feature for proactive administration.

Important MySQL Information

This section does not contain any new information that has not already been discussed in previous chapters. It is important to combine information from various primary sources and from all MySQL instances in a given topology to get a complete picture of an operational environment. This section outlines what information should be included in your applicable system and database monitoring.

MySQL Error Log

The MySQL error log will report information about the state of replication, including when this started, stopped, or produced an error. The following is a sample of the information, warning, and error messages possible:

```
120709 11:32:27 [Note] Start binlog_dump to master_thread_id(1)
 slave_server(101), pos(mysql-bin.000009, 712)
120709 11:32:27 [Note] Start binlog_dump to master_thread_id(2)
 slave_server(102), pos(mysql-bin.000009, 712)
120709 11:32:27 [Note] Semi-sync replication initialized for transactions.
120709 11:32:27 [Note] Semi-sync replication enabled on the master.
120709 11:32:27 [Note] Slave I/O thread: connected to master 'rsandbox@127.0.0.1
:12630',replication started in log 'mysql-bin.000009'
at position 712
120709 11:32:28 [Warning] Slave SQL: If a crash happens this configuration
```

```
does not guarantee that the relay log info will be consistent, Error_code: 0
120709 11:32:28 [Note] Slave SQL thread initialized, starting replication in
log 'mysql-bin.000008' at position 446, relay log './mysql_sandbox12631-
relay-bin.000019' position: 648
120709 11:32:28 [ERROR] Slave SQL: Error executing row event: 'Cannot
execute statement: impossible to write to binary log since statement is in
row format and BINLOG_FORMAT = STATEMENT.', Error_code: 1666
120709 11:32:28 [Warning] Slave SQL: ... The slave coordinator and worker
threads are stopped, possibly leaving data in inconsistent state. A restart
should restore consistency automatically, although using non-transactional
storage for data or info tables or DDL queries could lead to problems. In
such cases you have to examine your data (see documentation for details).
Error_code: 1753
```

Chapter 2 provides more information on the different types of error messages you may encounter and suitable resolution techniques.

Detecting a change of the MySQL error log size is a basic monitoring step that should be implemented, regardless if you are using replication.

SHOW MASTER STATUS

MySQL replication requires a master with binary logging enabled. Details of the current binary log file and position are obtained with the SHOW MASTER STATUS command. Additional information on the underlying binary logs used and available on the master can be found with the SHOW BINARY LOGS command. Combined with the log_bin and log_bin_basename (5.6) variables, the underlying filesystem files defined by these variables can be verified independently from any SQL statements.

TIP Detecting no change in the binary log size, or a change significantly greater or less than the average expected (generally for the given time of day) over a short sampling period is an additional monitoring step that can preempt a problem. The monitoring for a lack of volume change is just important to indicate a potential problem in a production system.

SHOW SLAVE STATUS

This SQL command is the primary source of slave replication information. As discussed in several chapters, the thread status via Slave_IO_Running and Slave_SQL_Running are the most important columns of information to monitor. The Seconds_Behind_Master is also important to monitor if replication is lagging, or is improving or worsening over time. These slave status variables were detailed in Chapter 2.

It is important to understand that in some situations, these threads may not be running for a reason, for example, a backup process or a schema change that has stopped a thread intentionally. Applicable monitoring needs to account for these situations and not automatically report an error.

SHOW GLOBAL STATUS

Certain replication information can be obtained via SHOW GLOBAL STATUS. This includes information about binary log settings and usage, including replication heartbeat. Commencing in MySQL 5.5, semisynchronous replication information is obtained from SHOW GLOBAL STATUS.

NOTE   The information from SHOW GLOBAL STATUS can also be retrieved via the INFORMATION_SCHEMA.GLOBAL_STATUS table.

Semisynchronous Replication (5.5)

A new feature with MySQL 5.5, semisynchronous replication can only be monitored via MySQL status variables. MySQL can also elect to move between asynchronous and semisynchronous replication without any additional notification. The status value to monitor is different between the master and the slave:

```
master> SHOW STATUS LIKE 'Rpl_semi_sync_master_status';
+---------------------------------------------+----------+
| Variable_name                               | Value    |
+---------------------------------------------+----------+
| Rpl_semi_sync_master_status                 | ON       |
+---------------------------------------------+----------+
```

CAUTION   This is a new MySQL status variable that may not be included in many of the monitoring products available.

```
slave> SHOW STATUS LIKE 'Rpl_semi_sync_slave_status';
+---------------------------------------------+-------+
| Variable_name                               | Value |
+---------------------------------------------+-------+
| Rpl_semi_sync_slave_status                  | ON    |
+---------------------------------------------+-------+
```

The full list of status variables on the master for semisynchronous replication is

```
master> SHOW STATUS LIKE 'Rpl_semi_sync%';
```

```
+-------------------------------------------+----------+
| Variable_name                             | Value    |
+-------------------------------------------+----------+
| Rpl_semi_sync_master_clients              | 1        |
| Rpl_semi_sync_master_net_avg_wait_time    | 321      |
| Rpl_semi_sync_master_net_wait_time        | 58540232 |
| Rpl_semi_sync_master_net_waits            | 182303   |
| Rpl_semi_sync_master_no_times             | 2        |
| Rpl_semi_sync_master_no_tx                | 3106     |
| Rpl_semi_sync_master_status               | ON       |
| Rpl_semi_sync_master_timefunc_failures    | 0        |
| Rpl_semi_sync_master_tx_avg_wait_time     | 377      |
| Rpl_semi_sync_master_tx_wait_time         | 65273713 |
| Rpl_semi_sync_master_tx_waits             | 172914   |
| Rpl_semi_sync_master_wait_pos_backtraverse| 11       |
| Rpl_semi_sync_master_wait_sessions        | 0        |
| Rpl_semi_sync_master_yes_tx               | 182306   |
+-------------------------------------------+----------+
```

TIP   *If you use semisynchronous replication with multiple slaves, a change of the*
`Rpl_semi_sync_master_clients` status variable can detect a potential
problem within the replication topology.

Meta Files

MySQL includes a number of files that contain important information about the configuration and operation of slave replication. These are

- datadir/master.info
- datadir/relay_log.info

master.info

The contents of `master.info` for MySQL 5.6 using the MySQL Sandbox example defined in the appendix are

```
$ more master.info
23
mysql-bin.000009
712
127.0.0.1
rsandbox
rsandbox
12630
60
0
```

```
0
1800.000

0
b9a8fde1-b4a3-11e1-921d-b499baf75d68
86400

0
```

These lines are

1. Number of lines in file

2. Current master binary log file

3. Current master binary log position

4. Master host

5. Master username

6. Master password

7. Master port

8. Master connection retry time

9. SSL enabled

10. SSL CA

11. SSL CA Path

12. SSL Certificate

13. SSL Cipher

14. SSL Key

15. SSL Verify Certificate

16. Heartbeat

17. Master Bind Address

18. Replicate Ignore Server IDs

19. Master UUID

20. Master Retry Count

21. SSL Certificate Revocation List (CRL)

22. SSL CRL Path

23. GTID Position enabled

This is similar to the information set with the CHANGE MASTER TO statement.

relay_log.info

The contents of `relay_log.info` for MySQL 5.6 using the MySQL Sandbox example defined in the appendix are

```
$ cat relay-log.info
6
./mysql_sandbox12631-relay-bin.000019
648
mysql-bin.000008
446
0
3
3
3
```

These lines are

1. Master ID

2. Current relay log file

3. Current relay log position

4. Current master binary log

5. Current master binary log position

6. SQL Delay

7. Number of slave workers

Meta Tables

Starting with MySQL 5.6, important replication information can be recorded in meta tables rather than underlying files. As mentioned in Chapter 3, the new server variables `master-info-repository` and `relay-log-info-repository` can be used to control the location of information. A value to TABLE instead of the default FILE will store replication metadata in two tables instead of the traditional files (`master.info` and `relay-log.info`). For example:

```
slave> SELECT * FROM mysql.slave_master_info\G
*********************** 1. row ***********************
          Master_id: 2
```

```
        Number_of_lines: 22
        Master_log_name: bin-log.000005
         Master_log_pos: 317
                   Host: master
              User_name: repl
          User_password: clearpassword
                   Port: 3306
          Connect_retry: 10
            Enabled_ssl: 0
                 Ssl_ca:
             Ssl_capath:
               Ssl_cert:
             Ssl_cipher:
                Ssl_key:
 Ssl_verify_server_cert: 0
              Heartbeat: 1800
                   Bind:
      Ignored_server_ids: 0
                   Uuid: b1467eac-b431-11e1-8f35-001b245c2ae9
            Retry_count: 86400
                Ssl_crl:
            Ssl_crlpath:
slave> SELECT * FROM mysql.slave_relay_log_info\G
*********************** 1. row ***********************
              Master_id: 2
        Number_of_lines: 6
         Relay_log_name: /var/lib/mysql/relay-bin.000009
          Relay_log_pos: 273
        Master_log_name: bin-log.000005
         Master_log_pos: 317
              Sql_delay: 0
      Number_of_workers: 0
```

These tables contain information that matches the results of information found with SHOW MASTER STATUS and SHOW SLAVE STATUS. The use of tables enables easier manipulation using standard SQL commands.

Monitoring Products

As you saw in the previous section, the type of replication information that can be monitored will assist you in determining which type of monitoring product is the right one for your environment. A number of technologies listed in this section are generic monitoring products and include the ability, either natively or with additional plugins, to monitor MySQL. An existing monitoring product may already exist in your organization, requiring only the addition of MySQL specific metrics and alerts.

The following tables list the common monitoring tools used in the industry for MySQL monitoring.

Dedicated Monitoring Products

MySQL Enterprise Monitor	http://www.mysql.com/products/enterprise/monitor.html
MySQL Performance Monitor	http://www.fromdual.ch/mysql-performance-monitor
Kontrolbase	http://kontrollsoft.com/software-kontrollbase
MONyog MySQL Monitor	http://www.webyog.com/
Jet Profiler for MySQL	http://www.jetprofiler.com/

System Monitoring Products

Cacti	http://www.cacti.net/ Plugin: http://www.percona.com/downloads/percona-monitoring-plugins/
Nagios	http://www.nagios.org/
Zenoss	http://www.zenoss.com/ Plugin: http://community.zenoss.org/docs/DOC-3501
Munin	http://munin-monitoring.org/ Plugin: https://github.com/kjellm/munin-mysql/
Hyperic	http://www.hyperic.com/ Plugin: http://support.hyperic.com/display/hyperforge/MySQL
Ganglia	http://ganglia.sourceforge.net/
Zabbix	http://www.zabbix.com/
Big Brother	http://bb4.com/
DBTuna	http://www.dbtuna.com/
Oracle Enterprise Manager	http://oracle.com/enterprisemanager Plugin: http://www.pythian.com/news/mysql-plugin-for-oracle-grid-control/

Other Commercial System Monitoring Products

IBM Tivoli Monitoring	http://www-01.ibm.com/software/tivoli/products/monitor/ Plugin: https://www-304.ibm.com/software/brandcatalog/ismlibrary/details?catalog.label=1TW10TM2S
HP Openview	http://www.openview.hp.com/
CA Unicenter	http://www.ca.com/us/infrastructure-management.aspx

Many monitoring products require a working Linux/Apache/MySQL/PHP (LAMP) stack to correctly operate. It is recommended to use a different system for monitoring MySQL severs. There are several client GUI development tools that can perform some level of real-time monitoring, for example, MySQL Workbench; however, this is impractical in a production situation. Additional runtime graphical display commands that can be useful include

- Mytop http://jeremy.zawodny.com/mysql/mytop/
- mtop http://mtop.sourceforge.net/
- InnoTop http://code.google.com/p/innotop/

The Implementation of Monitoring

An important decision when choosing a monitoring product may be due to how information is collected. There are two implementations, using an agent or agentless. When a product uses an agent, a version of software is installed and configured on every MySQL server. When configured, the agent will communicate with a central repository of information that is used for the graphical display of information. The agent may retain information when the central repository is unavailable for later processing. An agentless monitoring product uses a centralized mechanism to poll the necessary MySQL servers for information and records the results at that time. There are advantages and disadvantages with both methods.

MySQL Enterprise Monitor

MySQL Enterprise Monitor (MEM) is the commercial MySQL monitoring product that is included with a MySQL subscription. With this solution you can continuously monitor your MySQL instances and be alerted to potential problems before a higher impact event occurs. All threshold limits within each monitor are configurable, but have a specified default value associated to monitoring types. This means you can toggle a threshold on an alert to fit into the expected behavior of your system.

Replication Advisors Within MEM

MEM comprises the Enterprise Dashboard web interface and the MEM agent for each MySQL instance. After you have installed the Enterprise server and the agent(s) you will be able to assign advisors to a particular server or group of servers within the Enterprise Dashboard. The following is a list of replication-related advisors that are available with MEM version 2.3:

- Binary Log File Count Exceeds Specified Limit
- Binary Log Space Exceeds Specified Limit
- INSERT ON DUPLICATE KEY UPDATE Bug May Break Replication
- Slave Detection of Network Outages Too High
- Slave Error: Unknown or Incorrect Time Zone
- Slave Execution Position Too Far Behind Read Position
- Slave Has Been Stopped
- Slave Has Experienced a Replication Error
- Slave Has Login Accounts with Inappropriate Privileges
- Slave Has Problem Communicating with Master
- Slave Has Stopped Replicating
- Slave I/O Thread Not Running
- Slave Not Configured as Read Only
- Slave Relay Log Space Is Very Large
- Slave Relay Logs Not Automatically Purged
- Slave SQL Thread Not Running
- Slave SQL Thread Reading from Older Relay Log Than I/O Thread
- Slave Too Far Behind Master
- Slave Waiting to Free Relay Log Space
- Slave Without REPLICATION SLAVE Accounts

As you can see there are advisors that include information on performance, errors, lag, security, and optimal configuration. You can also develop your own custom advisors.

In addition to these replication advisors you will be able to see all replication topologies, what server is replicating from where, and other replication metadata like binary log and position. Replication topologies are automatically mapped out for you when the agent reports information to MEM. All servers in a replicated set are assigned to a default group name within the Dashboard. The group name can be changed to something more meaningful in your environment.

Cacti

Cacti is an open source graphing system that uses the common Round Robin Database (RRD) format for data storage and graphing functionality. Cacti is a polling-based monitoring system, not agent based like MySQL Enterprise Monitor. Polling a system is accomplished when the `poller.php` script is run. This script is included in the default Cacti installation. This script will gather SNMP and connectivity information for all of the servers configured within Cacti and then send out SNMP requests to those servers. The response back from your servers is then recorded and graphed within Cacti. This can lead to scaling problems depending on the quantity of servers you are monitoring and the number of data points you are trying to graph.

By default Cacti does not have alerting capabilities, but is very useful for visualizing the current and past state of your system. This means that you will be able to see system activity after it is polled within the Cacti GUI but will not be able to receive alerts. To harness the true power of Cacti you will need to use the Plugin Architecture. There are many plugins for Cacti that could be addressed here; however, one of the most important is `thold`. More information about Cacti can be found at http://cacti.net.

Alerting with `thold`

If you require alerting for your system the `thold` plugin for Cacti offers threshold alerts based off Cacti graphs. Adding this plugin previously required the installation of the Plugin Architecture (PIA). Starting with Cacti version 0.8.8a, the PIA is included in the default Cacti code base, making it easier to work with all of the Cacti plugins. More information on the `thold` plugin can be found at http://docs.cacti.net/plugin:thold. This plugin has a prerequisite of the `settings` plugin to also be installed. More information can be found at http://docs.cacti.net/plugin:settings.

NOTE   A full list of plugins can be found at http://docs.cacti.net/plugins.

Cacti Graph Templates

Cacti comes with 33 default graph templates. These templates are for monitoring server characteristics like CPU, disk, memory, network, process count, and logged in user count. This system information is good when monitoring MySQL servers; however, it does not provide detailed behavior of `mysqld` itself. Graphing information specifically related to MySQL can be gathered by installing additional cacti graphing templates. Percona provides a popular version of MySQL monitoring plugins. These are available from http://www.percona.com/downloads/percona-monitoring-plugins/.

First you will need to download the latest version of the templates and make sure they are on your computer and also on the Cacti server. The Cacti server will need to access the scripts, while you will need to import the templates through your web browser by selecting the file from your computer:

```
$ wget http://www.percona.com/redir/downloads/percona-monitoring-
plugins/percona-monitoring-plugins-1.0.1.tar.gz
$ tar xzvf percona-monitoring-plugins-1.0.1.tar.gz
$ cd percona-monitoring-plugins-1.0.1/
```

Notice there are two directories: one for the Cacti templates and the other for Nagios plugins. We are interested in the cacti directory for this example.

```
$ ls -l
COPYING
Changelog
cacti
nagios
```

There are multiple templates in the cacti directory you can install, including mysql, mongo, redis, and apache just to name a few. The general process for installation is to copy the data-gathering script into the scripts directory of Cacti and then import the templates via the web interface.

On the server that hosts the Cacti installation you will need to copy the PHP scripts into the Cacti installation script directory. In this case Cacti has been installed in /var/www/html/cacti/ and the cacti scripts directory is /var/www/html/cacti/scripts.

```
$ sudo cp percona-monitoring-plugins-1.0.1/cacti/scripts/ss_get_mysql_stats.php \
/var/www/html/cacti/scripts/
```

Now that the scripts are in place on the Cacti server you will need to log into the Cacti Console and import the MySQL templates by navigating to Console | Import Templates in your browser. In the "Import Template from Local File" section of the page, you can choose a file from your local computer. In this case we want to import the MySQL template file named cacti_host_template_percona_mysql_server_ht_0.8.6i-sver1.0.1.xml.

NOTE   *Full details about how to install and configure the templates can be found at http://www.percona.com/doc/percona-monitoring-plugins/cacti/installing-templates.html.*

In this chapter we are most interested in monitoring replication. Contained in the newly imported templates is the Percona MySQL Replication GT template. The items graphed are

- slave_lag
- Slave_open_tmp_tbls
- Slave_rtd_trnsctns
- slave_stopped

The MySQL Replication graph displays the status of the SQL replication thread and replication delay. If you are using `pt-heartbeat` on the MySQL topology you will be able to use the information in the heartbeat table to populate this graph; otherwise, `Seconds_Behind_Master` from SHOW SLAVE STATUS is used. If you are using `pt-heartbeat` and would like to use that metadata to populate the graph, you will need to define the `$heartbeat` variable in the `ss_get_mysql_stats.php` script.

MySQL Performance Monitor (MPM)

Created and maintained by Oli Sennhauser at FromDual, MPM is an open source monitoring solution based on Zabbix. This solution provides all the necessary modules to monitor and report MySQL performance metrics. In addition, MPM has preconfigured monitoring support for additional third-party storage engines and Galera for MySQL. FromDual also offers Monitoring As A Service (MAAS) to remove the burden from existing resources.

See http://www.fromdual.com/mysql-performance-monitor for more information and http://www.slideshare.net/shinguz/mysql-monitoring-with-zabbix for a good presentation on usage.

Poor Man's Replication Monitor

An extremely inexpensive way to monitor replication would be to use a simple Linux shell script. Giuseppe Maxia wrote a great article on this titled "Refactored again: poor man's MySQL replication monitor." See http://datacharmer.blogspot.com/2011/04/refactored-again-poor-mans-mysql.html. The example script described in the article checks replication is running, if the slave is replicating from the intended master, and if the slave host is lagging behind. If there is an error or multiple errors an email is sent out to a designated recipient reporting the replication issue.

Troubleshooting Replication Incidents

A good practice for administrators is to have a checklist when trying to determine the cause of a replication issue when an alert has been generated. Table 8-1 shows a list that you can use as an aid when troubleshooting MySQL replication.

This is not an exhaustive checklist; however, it provides a template to be used and enhanced accordingly for your environment and business needs.

Step	Checked	What to Check?
1		Check the MySQL error log on the master for any recent errors, either related to or not related to replication.
2		Check the master to ensure `log_bin` is enabled and verify the SHOW MASTER STATUS information.
3		Ensure the master and *all* slave hosts have a unique `server-id` and `server-uuid`.
4		Ensure the master replication user has the correct privileges for replication.
5		Check to see if the slave(s) are connected to the master with the SHOW PROCESSLIST command.
6		Check the MySQL error log on the slave(s) for any recent errors, either related to or not related to replication.
7		Check to see if the slave is running with SHOW SLAVE STATUS\G.
8		Ensure you are using the correct master connection information on the slave. This is set with the CHANGE MASTER TO statement.

9		Ensure you can connect to the master host from the slave using the `mysql` CLI and with telnet, for example:
		CLI:
		`$ mysql -urepl -psomepassword -hmaster -P3306`
		The master information (host, user, and port) can be obtained from the SHOW SLAVE STATUS command. The password can be obtained from the `master.info` file, or all information can be found in the `mysql.slave_master_info` table when configured.
		You can also confirm MySQL port access with telnet:
		`$ telnet master 3306`

10		Check the firewall rules to ensure the MySQL port is not being filtered. The `nmap` command can be used to determine TCP/IP access to the master. For example: `$ nmap -p 3306 master`
11		If a slave is no longer running and has an error caused by a SQL statement, check your data on the slave and determine if you can skip the error or fix the data on the slave.

Table 8-1 *Replication Checklist*

Conclusion

There are many ways to manually monitor MySQL replication. This chapter has outlined some of the tools that a database administrator can use and implement to provide automation of applicable monitoring. This is a practical and time-saving requirement for any environment, from one server to thousands of servers.

Monitoring technologies can help identify performance problems and provide a history of information monitored for comparison and evaluation. You should evaluate and test some of the monitoring strategies outlined to determine which best fits your business. Implementing monitoring should be a process of continual improvement to minimize the time for regular maintenance operations.

Examples and links in this chapter are available for download from http://EffectiveMySQL.com/book/replication-techniques.

Appendix
A MySQL Replication
Test Environment

Throughout this book, *Effective MySQL: Replication Techniques in Depth,*
many examples require a working environment of a master instance and at
least one slave instance to demonstrate the output shown. There are several
ways to create an appropriate MySQL environment if you do not have access
to the necessary hardware and software. The following setups are used for
the demonstrations in this book and can be easily created to reproduce all
the examples. Some advanced examples in this book do require additional
operating system configuration, for example, dedicated IP addresses.

Manual Steps to Configure MySQL Replication

It is very easy to set up MySQL replication, even on a single machine for testing purposes. In summary, the following steps are needed for replication configuration between a master server and a slave server:

- Set up two new MySQL instances. These will be represented as the master and the slave.

- Define binary logging with the `log-bin` configuration option, and a unique server ID with `server-id` on the master instance. This will require a MySQL instance restart.

- Obtain the master binary log position with the SHOW MASTER STATUS command.

- Create a new MySQL user on the master instance with host access from the second instance and with the REPLICATION SLAVE privilege.

- Define a unique server ID with `server-id` on the slave. This will require a MySQL instance restart.

- Configure replication on the slave instance with the CHANGE MASTER TO command, including the details of the master instance, the new MySQL user, and the master instance binary log position.

- Start replication on the slave instance with the SLAVE START command and verify with the SHOW SLAVE STATUS command.

The MySQL Reference Manual provides detailed instructions on how to configure replication at http://dev.mysql.com/doc/refman/5.5/en/replication-howto.html.

When running multiple instances of MySQL on a single machine, the following configuration information must be different between the instances:

- MySQL data directory (`datadir`)
- MySQL socket file (`socket`)
- Port (`port`) or IP address (`bind-address`)

TIP   *It is a common practice to run multiple instances of MySQL on a single machine by changing the MySQL communication port. Alternatively, by configuring multiple IP addresses on the server and using the* bind-address *configuration option, you can run multiple MySQL instances on a single server and use the default port of 3306 for all instances, which can simplify many commands that use the default port.*

Using MySQL Sandbox

Created by long time MySQL community advocate and hacker Giuseppe Maxia, the MySQL Sandbox (http://mysqlsandbox.net/) is an essential tool for any database administrator. As the name implies, this tool enables you to create a gated sandbox of MySQL with various versions and replication topologies all on a single server. This open source tool is written in Perl. With a single command you can create the following working environments in a few seconds:

- Single sandboxes
- Standard replication
- Circular replication
- Multiple sandboxes (same version)
- Multiple sandboxes (different versions)

Throughout this book we discussed several tools that can be tested and confirmed in a MySQL Sandbox environment.

MySQL Sandbox Installation

The following steps will install MySQL Sandbox on your Linux or Mac system:

```
$ sudo cpan MySQL::Sandbox
```

This step will install or upgrade MySQL Sandbox. If this is the very first usage of cpan on this system, you will be prompted for some default configuration that is saved for later usage.

Alternatively, you can install MySQL Sandbox directly from source with the following:

```
$ cd /tmp
$ curl --silent -o MySQL-Sandbox.tar.gz \
  https://launchpadlibrarian.net/91596901/MySQL-Sandbox-3.0.25.tar.gz
$ tar xvfz MySQL-Sandbox.tar.gz
$ cd MySQL-Sandbox-*
$ perl Makefile.PL
$ make
$ make test
$ sudo make install
$ make_sandbox --help
$ cd ..
$ rm -rf MySQL-Sandbox*  # Optionally cleanup temporary installation files
```

CAUTION   You should always refer to https://launchpad.net/mysql-sandbox for the current version of MySQL Sandbox to download with the `curl` *command.*

Both of these options for installation require the `make` command. You can verify this is on your system and in your current PATH with the command:

```
$ which make
```

If this does not return the path to the binary (for example, `/Applications/Xcode.app/Contents/Developer/usr/bin/make` on MAC OS X), you may require additional software to be installed to use MySQL Sandbox.

TIP   For Mac OS X users, you will need to install Xcode from https://developer .apple.com/xcode or from your operating system installation DVD for either installation steps of MySQL Sandbox. Unfortunately, there is no simple command line interface to obtain and install this software without using the Apple App Store, which requires an account to log in, even though the software is free. In addition you need to install the Command Line Utilities to address various make complication errors. These are installed from within Xcode with the menu option under Preferences | Downloads | Components.

MySQL Software Releases

MySQL Sandbox does not include the MySQL software it installs. You can obtain the MySQL software to install from http://dev.mysql.com/downloads for many different operating systems and architectures. The following steps install MySQL 5.0, 5.1 GA, 5.5 GA, and 5.6 DMR software binaries for further testing using a generic Linux 64-bit software release. You should refer to the respective software downloads page at http://dev.mysql.com/ downloads for the current point release of each version. The links provided here are from the Effective MySQL website only to ensure a level of automation when repeating these installation steps, because direct download links from the various mirror sites can easily become unavailable as newer point releases are released.

```
$ mkdir -p $HOME/opt/mysql
$ cd $HOME/opt/mysql
$ curl-o mysql-5.0.95-linux-x86_64-glibc23.tar.gz
    http://effectivemysql.com/downloads/mysql-5.0.95-linux-x86_64-glibc23.tar.gz
$ curl-o mysql-5.1.63-linux-x86_64-glibc23.tar.gz
    http://effectivemysql.com/downloads/mysql-5.1.63-linux-x86_64-glibc23.tar.gz
$ curl -o mysql-5.5.24-linux2.6-x86_64.tar.gz
    http://effectivemysql.com/downloads/mysql-5.5.24-linux2.6-x86_64.tar.gz
$ curl -o mysql-5.6.5-m8-linux2.6-x86_64.tar.gz
    http://effectivemysql.com/downloads/mysql-5.6.5-m8-linux2.6-x86_64.tar.gz
$ for F in $HOME/opt/mysql/mysql-5*.tar.gz ; \
  do make_sandbox --export_binaries $F ; done
$ rm -rf */mysql-test */sql-bench */man */docs
```

TIP   *For scripting purposes, add the* `--silent` *option to the* `curl` *command to remove the interactive display of the download progress.*

The following MD5 values are provided to ensure the software matches original MySQL download versions:

```
$ md5sum mysql*.gz
749120f0d9715a387b9dccb552e8c59a  mysql-5.0.95-linux-x86_64-glibc23.tar.gz
594ea37fcd9f29a9e3eddf38e7288e3f  mysql-5.1.63-linux-x86_64-glibc23.tar.gz
a9364f4c352c92c163b93106d56df463  mysql-5.5.24-linux2.6-x86_64.tar.gz
47404074376165599f8a152f8ed08d97  mysql-5.6.5-m8-linux2.6-x86_64.tar.gz
```

CAUTION   *You should always check the MySQL Downloads page and use the appropriate mirrors to obtain the current point release of each MySQL applicable MySQL version you wish to test.*

Replication Setup with MySQL Sandbox

There are several different MySQL Sandbox commands to create various types of configurations. The following simple command will create a MySQL master and two slaves configuration:

```
$ make_replication_sandbox 5.5.24
installing and starting master
installing slave 1
installing slave 2
```

```
starting slave 1
.. sandbox server started
starting slave 2
.. sandbox server started
initializing slave 1
initializing slave 2
replication directory installed in $HOME/sandboxes/rsandbox_5_5_24
```

This has installed a working MySQL replication topology into the $HOME/sandboxes/rsandbox_5_5_24 directory. The MySQL instances are also started by default. A number of files and subdirectories exist here:

```
$ cd $HOME/sandboxes/rsandbox_5_5_24
$ ls -l
total 60
-rwxr-xr-x 1 uid gid    302 May 21 16:33 check_slaves
-rwxr-xr-x 1 uid gid    465 May 21 16:33 clear_all
-rwxr-xr-x 1 uid gid    785 May 21 16:33 initialize_slaves
-rwxr-xr-x 1 uid gid    171 May 21 16:33 m
drwxrwxr-x 4 uid gid   4096 May 21 17:42 master
drwxrwxr-x 4 uid gid   4096 May 21 17:18 node1
drwxrwxr-x 4 uid gid   4096 May 21 20:14 node2
-rwxr-xr-x 1 uid gid    220 May 21 16:33 restart_all
-rwxr-xr-x 1 uid gid     56 May 21 16:33 s1
-rwxr-xr-x 1 uid gid     56 May 21 16:33 s2
-rwxr-xr-x 1 uid gid    420 May 21 16:33 send_kill_all
-rwxr-xr-x 1 uid gid    612 May 21 16:33 start_all
-rwxr-xr-x 1 uid gid    287 May 21 16:33 status_all
-rwxr-xr-x 1 uid gid    390 May 21 16:33 stop_all
-rwxr-xr-x 1 uid gid    405 May 21 16:33 use_all
```

The MySQL instances and individual configuration can be found in the master, node1, and node2 directories. All other files are convenience utilities for managing the sandbox environment. The individual filenames describe the different purposes, including starting, stopping, connecting, and checking the sandbox environment.

NOTE *When creating a new MySQL Sandbox replication environment the respective MySQL instances will be started. To stop these instances, use the* stop_all *command found in the applicable directory. You can use the* start_all *command to launch the MySQL instances following a shutdown or reboot of the host machine.*

References

MySQL Sandbox is an open source product released under the GNU GPL v2. More information is available from the following sites:

- **Product Home**   http://mysqlsandbox.net/
- **Code Download**   https://launchpad.net/mysql-sandbox/+download
- **Perl CPAN package**   http://search.cpan.org/
  perldoc?MySQL::Sandbox
- **Cookbook**   http://search.cpan.org/~gmax/MySQL-Sandbox-3.0.25/
  lib/MySQL/Sandbox/Recipes.pm

Using Virtual Servers

There are many different virtualization products available that can support running a virtual environment on a single server. The following steps show how to set up a dedicated MySQL server environment using VirtualBox.

VirtualBox Installation

VirtualBox is an open source product that can be downloaded from https://www.virtualbox.org/. This runs on multiple operating systems, including Mac OS X, Microsoft Windows, Linux, and Solaris. Refer to the website for specific instructions on installation with your operating system at http://www.virtualbox.org/manual/ch02.html.

Following the installation of the virtualization tool on your machine, referred to as the host, you also need to install an operating system to operate a virtual host. This is also known as a guest. For this demonstration we will be using the Ubuntu Server 12.04 LTS 64-bit operating system available from http://www.ubuntu.com/download/server. Detailed instructions for configuration of a virtual server can be found at https://www.virtualbox.org/manual/ch03.html.

As part of the installation process you will be required to specify a username. There is no restriction to what this must be. For demonstration purposes in this book, the username will be "user."

VirtualBox Configuration

After installing and configuring a new virtual host, one setting is necessary for use in the examples throughout this book. Under the settings for the virtual host, select Network and enable Adapter 2, as shown in Figure A-1. This should be configured to attach to a bridged adapter. The name should

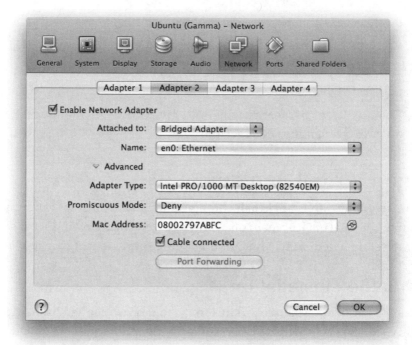

Figure A-1   *Virtual Box Network Adapter 2 configuration*

also match your applicable network device on your host. Adapter 1 should remain enabled as a NAT Adapter.

MySQL Replication Environment

For this book, the following environment of three servers is used:

- Server 1 is called `alpha`, and has an IP address of 192.168.1.51
- Server 2 is called `beta`, and has an IP address of 192.168.1.52
- Server 3 is called `gamma`, and has an IP address of 192.168.1.53

The IP addresses can be defined at your discretion. It is recommended you use the same C class as your host machine and internal network, i.e., the 192.168.1. portion should be configured to match your own network. The following configuration is repeated for each new VirtualBox guest host that is created. VirtualBox also enables you to easily create one guest host and use the clone option.

Virtual Host Configuration

The following steps are necessary to configure the default Ubuntu Server installation to match the needs for the examples.

Sudo Privileges

To automate many commands in the examples for this book, removing the password requirements when executing the sudo command will remove unnecessary complexity. The following steps will grant the user this privilege:

```
$ echo `id -un`"   ALL=NOPASSWD: ALL" > /tmp/mysql
$ chmod 440 /tmp/mysql
$ sudo chown root:root /tmp/mysql
$ sudo mv /tmp/mysql /etc/sudoers.d
```

Hostname

For each instance we set the hostname by changing this in the /etc/hostname file:

```
$ sudo vi /etc/hostname
```

The contents of this file should look like:

```
$ cat /etc/hostname
alpha
```

The contents of this file should reflect alpha, beta, and gamma, respectively.

DNS Hosts

In order to refer to the server hostnames in all examples, the following values are added to each virtual server hosts file:

```
$ sudo /etc/hosts
```

The contents of this file should look like this for all virtual servers:

```
$ cat /etc/hosts
127.0.0.1    localhost
192.168.1.51    alpha
192.168.1.52    beta
192.168.1.53    gamma
```

In addition, the default installation will create an entry for the default hostname at 127.0.[01].1. This line in the hosts file must be removed.

TIP   *If you use your host machine to execute any commands, it is highly recommended you add these entries to the host machine's respective hosts file. This will vary depending on your operating system.*

Server IP Address

In order to be able to reference hosts in a reproducible fashion, each virtual server must be defined with a static IP address rather than a dynamic DHCP IP address. This is specified in the network interfaces file by adding entries for `eth0` and `eth1`:

```
$ sudo vi /etc/network/interfaces
```

The contents of this file should look like:

```
$ cat /etc/network/interfaces
# The loopback network interface
auto lo
iface lo inet loopback

# Adapter 1
auto eth0
iface eth0 inet dhcp

# Adapter 2
auto eth1
iface eth1 inet static
address 192.168.1.51
netmask 255.255.255.0
network 192.168.1.1
broadcast 192.168.1.255
```

The address value should represent the corresponding value for each virtual server. All other information remains unchanged.

NOTE   *If you clone a guest virtual server to create a new virtual server, be sure to select the option to create a new MAC address for each network device.*

The preceding network definition relies on the virtual network adapter name in the guest server to be `eth0` and `eth1`. These are the default values for the first two network adapters, and when you create your first guest instance this should operate without incident.

Adjusting Cloned Virtual Hosts

If you choose to clone your first guest virtual server to avoid repeating these steps, it is likely the virtual server will not correctly define `eth0` and eth1. This is due to the change of MAC address, which is necessary to operate multiple virtual hosts concurrently. To address this problem, you must correctly reference the MAC address to the virtual adapter name in the /etc/udev/rules.d/70-persistent-net.rules file. Generally, this involves removing older entries that match eth0 and eth1, and updating the following entries with the correct name. For reference purposes, the format of this file follows. The ATTR{address} value should match the MAC address defined in the Network tab of your guest virtual server for Adapter 1 (NAT) and Adapter 2 (Bridged Adapter), respectively. The NAME value should match eth0 and eth1, respectively:

```
$ cat /etc/udev/rules.d/70-persistent-net.rules
# PCI device 0x8086:/sys/devices/pci0000:00/0000:00:03.0 (e1000)
SUBSYSTEM=="net", ACTION=="add", DRIVERS=="?*",
 ATTR{address}=="08:00:27:58:24:dc", ATTR{dev_id}=="0x0",
ATTR{type}=="1",
KERNEL=="eth*", NAME="eth0"
# PCI device 0x8086:/sys/devices/pci0000:00/0000:00:08.0 (e1000)
SUBSYSTEM=="net", ACTION=="add", DRIVERS=="?*",
ATTR{address}=="08:00:27:d4:5f:91", ATTR{dev_id}=="0x0",
ATTR{type}=="1",
KERNEL=="eth*", NAME="eth1"
```

CAUTION   *If you clone your guest virtual server, it is likely that internally the virtual adapter name will not match expectations and networking will not be correctly configured. A manual change to the mapping on the guest operating system will be required.*

Additional network reference information can be found at https://help .ubuntu.com/12.04/serverguide/network-configuration.html.

MySQL Installation

The following steps will manually install MySQL 5.6 on each virtual server that has just been created. Any MySQL version can be installed by changing the appropriate value on the first line to a matching source MySQL binary file as described in the MySQL Sandbox section:

```
$ MYSQL_TAR="mysql-5.6.5-m8-linux2.6-x86_64.tar.gz"
$ cd
$ sudo apt-get update
$ sudo apt-get install libaio1    # This is only needed for MySQL 5.6
$ rm -f $HOME/.my.cnf
$ wget http://effectivemysql.com/downloads/${MYSQL_TAR}
$ md5sum ${MYSQL_TAR}
```

```
$ tar xvfz ${MYSQL_TAR}
$ rm -f ${MYSQL_TAR}
$ mv mysql-5* mysql
$ cd mysql
$ ./scripts/mysql_install_db
$ ./bin/mysqld_safe &
$ sleep 3
$ tail data/`hostname`.err
```

The output of the MySQL error log should be verified to confirm that MySQL successfully started:

```
120615 12:32:41 [Note] /home/user/mysql/bin/mysqld: ready for connections.
Version: '5.6.5-m8'  socket: '/tmp/mysql.sock'  port: 3306  MySQL Community
 Server (GPL)
```

A second sanity check can also be performed:

```
$ ./bin/mysql -e "SELECT VERSION()"
+-----------+
| VERSION() |
+-----------+
| 5.6.5-m8  |
+-----------+
```

NOTE   *For demonstration purposes MySQL installation is performed using the applicable binary tar to easily support multiple MySQL versions. The software is installed in the home directory of the current user for simplicity only. These steps are for testing purposes only and do not reflect a suitable practice for a production deployment.*

The following step will help to secure the MySQL installation. During this step you are asked to specify a `root` password for the MySQL instance. This value is also used in a subsequent configuration file. For demonstration purposes this value is "passwd"; however, any value can be specified if configured appropriately in the subsequent step:

```
$ ./bin/mysql_secure_installation
# Follow the prompts
$ ./bin/mysql -uroot
ERROR 1045 (28000): Access denied for user 'root'@'localhost'
(using password: NO)
$ HOSTNAME=`hostname`
$ echo "[client]
user=root
password=passwd
[mysql]
prompt='${HOSTNAME}> '" > $HOME/.my.cnf
$ ./bin/mysql -e "SELECT VERSION()"
```

NOTE *For demonstration purposes in this book the* root *MySQL user is used, and a configuration file is created for simplicity of password authentication. In a production environment, appropriate procedures to match your business needs should be implemented accordingly.*

The final steps help in command pathing and basic configuration to enable tools and replication configuration happen unaided:

```
$ echo "export MYSQL_HOME=\$HOME/mysql
export PATH=\$MYSQL_HOME/bin:\$PATH" > /tmp/mysql.sh
sudo mv /tmp/mysql.sh /etc/profile.d/
. /etc/profile.d/mysql.sh
$ mysql -e "GRANT ALL ON *.* TO root@'192.168.1.%' \
  IDENTIFIED BY 'passwd' WITH GRANT OPTION"
$ cd $HOME/mysql
$ mkdir etc
$ SERVER_ID=` grep address /etc/network/interfaces | cut -d. -f4`
$ echo "[mysqld]
server-id=${SERVER_ID}
log-bin" > etc/my.cnf
$ mysqladmin shutdown
$ mysqld_safe --defaults-file=$HOME/mysql/etc/my.cnf &
$ sleep 2
$ tail data/`hostname`.err
```

These steps have not completed the replication setup. Each virtual server has MySQL running and configured to support being used in a MySQL replication topology. The MySQL utilities described in Chapter 4 are used to complete the necessary steps. Alternatively, the manual instructions defined in this appendix may be used to complete the setup.

Testing and Verifying MySQL Replication

The following simple test can be used to show MySQL replication (and lag) in operation. Also from Giuseppe, the following simple procedure produces a repeating and increased statement duration that demonstrates replication lag using the default MySQL asynchronous replication. This requires two separate terminal sessions.

In one terminal session perform the following command to monitor MySQL replication in action using the MySQL Sandbox setup previously described:

```
$ cd $HOME/sandboxes/rsandbox_5_5_24
$ ./restart_all
$ while [ : ] ; do date; ./s1 -e "SHOW SLAVE STATUS\G" | \
  grep Seconds; sleep 1; done
```

In a different terminal session run the following commands:

```
$ cd $HOME/sandboxes/rsandbox_5_5_24
$ ./m
#http://datacharmer.blogspot.com/2006/06/filling-test-tables-quickly.html
CREATE SCHEMA IF NOT EXISTS book3;
USE book3
DROP TABLE IF EXISTS numbers;
CREATE TABLE numbers (id INT NOT NULL PRIMARY KEY);
DELIMITER $$
DROP PROCEDURE IF EXISTS fill_numbers $$
CREATE PROCEDURE fill_numbers()
DETERMINISTIC
BEGIN
  DECLARE counter INT DEFAULT 1;
  TRUNCATE TABLE numbers;
  INSERT INTO numbers VALUES (1);
  WHILE counter < 1000000
  DO
        INSERT INTO numbers (id)
        SELECT id + counter
        FROM numbers;
        SELECT COUNT(*) INTO counter FROM numbers;
        SELECT counter;
  END WHILE;
END $$
DELIMITER ;
CALL fill_numbers();
```

This SQL statement will produce the following output. Depending on your hardware this may take 20 seconds or longer to complete:

```
...
+----------+
| counter |
+----------+
|  131072 |
+----------+
1 row in set (1.11 sec)
+----------+
| counter |
+----------+
|  262144 |
+----------+
1 row in set (2.09 sec)
+----------+
| counter |
+----------+
|  524288 |
+----------+
```

```
1 row in set (4.10 sec)
+----------+
| counter  |
+----------+
| 1048576  |
+----------+
1 row in set (7.83 sec)
```

The result from the initial monitoring terminal shows MySQL in operation and that replication lag is present:

```
...
Sun May 20 20:11:06 EDT 2012
        Seconds_Behind_Master: 0
Sun May 20 20:11:07 EDT 2012
        Seconds_Behind_Master: 1
Sun May 20 20:11:08 EDT 2012
        Seconds_Behind_Master: 1
Sun May 20 20:11:09 EDT 2012
        Seconds_Behind_Master: 2
Sun May 20 20:11:10 EDT 2012
        Seconds_Behind_Master: 3
Sun May 20 20:11:11 EDT 2012
        Seconds_Behind_Master: 4
Sun May 20 20:11:12 EDT 2012
        Seconds_Behind_Master: 5
Sun May 20 20:11:13 EDT 2012
        Seconds_Behind_Master: 0
Sun May 20 20:11:14 EDT 2012
        Seconds_Behind_Master: 6
Sun May 20 20:11:16 EDT 2012
        Seconds_Behind_Master: 8
Sun May 20 20:11:17 EDT 2012
        Seconds_Behind_Master: 9
Sun May 20 20:11:18 EDT 2012
        Seconds_Behind_Master: 10
Sun May 20 20:11:19 EDT 2012
        Seconds_Behind_Master: 0
```

You can also monitor MySQL replication in real time with the SHOW SLAVE STATUS command. The following watch syntax provides an online display that does not translate into print:

```
$ cd $HOME/sandboxes/rsandbox_5_5_24
$ watch --interval=1 --differences \
'mysql --defaults-file=node1/my.sandbox.cnf -e "SHOW SLAVE STATUS\G"'
```

When using MySQL Sandbox you can simplify this syntax using the convenience command for connecting to the slave:

```
$ watch --interval=1 --differences  './s1 -e "SHOW SLAVE STATUS\G"'
```

MySQL Sandbox also provides a quick command for viewing and monitoring a subset of replication information:

```
$ ./check_slaves
slave # 1
              Master_Log_File: mysql-bin.000002
          Read_Master_Log_Pos: 5308
            Slave_IO_Running: Yes
           Slave_SQL_Running: Yes
          Exec_Master_Log_Pos: 5059
slave # 2
              Master_Log_File: mysql-bin.000002
          Read_Master_Log_Pos: 5308
            Slave_IO_Running: Yes
           Slave_SQL_Running: Yes
          Exec_Master_Log_Pos: 5059
```

NOTE *The true replication delay is not* `Seconds_Behind_Master`. *This value is an indication of the current system time with the time the current statement was executed on the master. It is possible that no statements have since physically occurred, and replication will be in sync with the completion of the running statement, which may be a few seconds, when a value of hundreds is reported. This value is a good indication that the slave has not yet completed executing all available statements in the replication stream.*

Conclusion

These are just two simple examples of how to create a suitable MySQL replication environment for testing purposes.

Examples and links in this chapter are available for download from http://EffectiveMySQL.com/book/replication-techniques.

Index

GET YOUR FREE SUBSCRIPTION TO *ORACLE MAGAZINE*

Oracle Magazine is essential gear for today's information technology professionals. Stay informed and increase your productivity with every issue of *Oracle Magazine*. Inside each free bimonthly issue you'll get:

- Up-to-date information on Oracle Database, Oracle Application Server, Web development, enterprise grid computing, database technology, and business trends

- Third-party news and announcements

- Technical articles on Oracle and partner products, technologies, and operating environments

- Development and administration tips

- Real-world customer stories

If there are other Oracle users at your location who would like to receive their own subscription to *Oracle Magazine*, please photocopy this form and pass it along.

Three easy ways to subscribe:

① Web
Visit our Web site at **oracle.com/oraclemagazine**
You'll find a subscription form there, plus much more

② Fax
Complete the questionnaire on the back of this card
and fax the questionnaire side only to **+1.847.763.9638**

③ Mail
Complete the questionnaire on the back of this card
and mail it to **P.O. Box 1263, Skokie, IL 60076-8263**

ORACLE

Want your own FREE subscription?

To receive a free subscription to *Oracle Magazine*, you must fill out the entire card, sign it, and date it (incomplete cards cannot be processed or acknowledged). You can also fax your application to +1.847.763.9638. Or subscribe at our Web site at oracle.com/oraclemagazine

O **Yes, please send me a FREE subscription *Oracle Magazine***.   O **No.**

O From time to time, Oracle Publishing allows our partners exclusive access to our e-mail addresses for special promotions and announcements. To be included in this program, please check this circle. If you do not wish to be included, you will only receive notices about your subscription via e-mail.

O Oracle Publishing allows sharing of our postal mailing list with selected third parties. If you prefer your mailing address not to be included in this program, please check this circle.

If at any time you would like to be removed from either mailing list, please contact Customer Service at +1.847.763.9635 or send an e-mail to oracle@halldata.com. If you opt in to the sharing of information, Oracle may also provide you with e-mail related to Oracle products, services, and events. If you want to completely unsubscribe from any e-mail communication from Oracle, please send an e-mail to: unsubscribe@oracle-mail.com with the following in the subject line: REMOVE [your e-mail address]. For complete information on Oracle Publishing's privacy practices, please visit oracle.com/html/privacy/html

X _____

signature (required)   date

name   title

company   e-mail address

street/p.o. box

city/state/zip or postal code   telephone

country   fax

Would you like to receive your free subscription in digital format instead of print if it becomes available? O Yes O No

---

YOU MUST ANSWER ALL 10 QUESTIONS BELOW.

① WHAT IS THE PRIMARY BUSINESS ACTIVITY OF YOUR FIRM AT THIS LOCATION? (check one only)

- ☐ 01 Aerospace and Defense Manufacturing
- ☐ 02 Application Service Provider
- ☐ 03 Automotive Manufacturing
- ☐ 04 Chemicals
- ☐ 05 Media and Entertainment
- ☐ 06 Construction/Engineering
- ☐ 07 Consumer Sector/Consumer Packaged Goods
- ☐ 08 Education
- ☐ 09 Financial Services/Insurance
- ☐ 10 Health Care
- ☐ 11 High Technology Manufacturing, OEM
- ☐ 12 Industrial Manufacturing
- ☐ 13 Independent Software Vendor
- ☐ 14 Life Sciences (biotech, pharmaceuticals)
- ☐ 15 Natural Resources
- ☐ 16 Oil and Gas
- ☐ 17 Professional Services
- ☐ 18 Public Sector (government)
- ☐ 19 Research
- ☐ 20 Retail/Wholesale/Distribution
- ☐ 21 Systems Integrator, VAR/VAD
- ☐ 22 Telecommunications
- ☐ 23 Travel and Transportation
- ☐ 24 Utilities (electric, gas, sanitation, water)
- ☐ 98 Other Business and Services _____

② WHICH OF THE FOLLOWING BEST DESCRIBES YOUR PRIMARY JOB FUNCTION? (check one only)

CORPORATE MANAGEMENT/STAFF
- ☐ 01 Executive Management (President, Chair, CEO, CFO, Owner, Partner, Principal)
- ☐ 02 Finance/Administrative Management (VP/Director/ Manager/Controller, Purchasing, Administration)
- ☐ 03 Sales/Marketing Management (VP/Director/Manager)
- ☐ 04 Computer Systems/Operations Management (CIO/VP/Director/Manager MIS/IS/IT, Ops)

IS/IT STAFF
- ☐ 05 Application Development/Programming Management
- ☐ 06 Application Development/Programming Staff
- ☐ 07 Consulting
- ☐ 08 DBA/Systems Administrator
- ☐ 09 Education/Training
- ☐ 10 Technical Support Director/Manager
- ☐ 11 Other Technical Management/Staff
- ☐ 98 Other

③ WHAT IS YOUR CURRENT PRIMARY OPERATING PLATFORM (check all that apply)

- ☐ 01 Digital Equipment Corp UNIX/VAX/VMS
- ☐ 02 HP UNIX
- ☐ 03 IBM AIX
- ☐ 04 IBM UNIX
- ☐ 05 Linux (Red Hat)
- ☐ 06 Linux (SUSE)
- ☐ 07 Linux (Oracle Enterprise)
- ☐ 08 Linux (other)
- ☐ 09 Macintosh
- ☐ 10 MVS
- ☐ 11 Netware
- ☐ 12 Network Computing
- ☐ 13 SCO UNIX
- ☐ 14 Sun Solaris/SunOS
- ☐ 15 Windows
- ☐ 16 Other UNIX
- ☐ 98 Other
- ☐ 99 None of the Above

④ DO YOU EVALUATE, SPECIFY, RECOMMEND, OR AUTHORIZE THE PURCHASE OF ANY OF THE FOLLOWING? (check all that apply)

- ☐ 01 Hardware
- ☐ 02 Business Applications (ERP, CRM, etc.)
- ☐ 03 Application Development Tools
- ☐ 04 Database Products
- ☐ 05 Internet or Intranet Products
- ☐ 06 Other Software
- ☐ 07 Middleware Products
- ☐ 99 None of the Above

⑤ IN YOUR JOB, DO YOU USE OR PLAN TO PURCHASE ANY OF THE FOLLOWING PRODUCTS? (check all that apply)

SOFTWARE
- ☐ 01 CAD/CAE/CAM
- ☐ 02 Collaboration Software
- ☐ 03 Communications
- ☐ 04 Database Management
- ☐ 05 File Management
- ☐ 06 Finance
- ☐ 07 Java
- ☐ 08 Multimedia Authoring
- ☐ 09 Networking
- ☐ 10 Programming
- ☐ 11 Project Management
- ☐ 12 Scientific and Engineering
- ☐ 13 Systems Management
- ☐ 14 Workflow

HARDWARE
- ☐ 15 Macintosh
- ☐ 16 Mainframe
- ☐ 17 Massively Parallel Processing

- ☐ 18 Minicomputer
- ☐ 19 Intel x86(32)
- ☐ 20 Intel x86(64)
- ☐ 21 Network Computer
- ☐ 22 Symmetric Multiprocessing
- ☐ 23 Workstation Services

SERVICES
- ☐ 24 Consulting
- ☐ 25 Education/Training
- ☐ 26 Maintenance
- ☐ 27 Online Database
- ☐ 28 Support
- ☐ 29 Technology-Based Training
- ☐ 30 Other
- ☐ 99 None of the Above

⑥ WHAT IS YOUR COMPANY'S SIZE? (check one only)

- ☐ 01 More than 25,000 Employees
- ☐ 02 10,001 to 25,000 Employees
- ☐ 03 5,001 to 10,000 Employees
- ☐ 04 1,001 to 5,000 Employees
- ☐ 05 101 to 1,000 Employees
- ☐ 06 Fewer than 100 Employees

⑦ DURING THE NEXT 12 MONTHS, HOW MUCH DO YOU ANTICIPATE YOUR ORGANIZATION WILL SPEND ON COMPUTER HARDWARE, SOFTWARE, PERIPHERALS, AND SERVICES FOR YOUR LOCATION? (check one only)

- ☐ 01 Less than $10,000
- ☐ 02 $10,000 to $49,999
- ☐ 03 $50,000 to $99,999
- ☐ 04 $100,000 to $499,999
- ☐ 05 $500,000 to $999,999
- ☐ 06 $1,000,000 and Over

⑧ WHAT IS YOUR COMPANY'S YEARLY SALES REVENUE? (check one only)

- ☐ 01 $500, 000, 000 and above
- ☐ 02 $100, 000, 000 to $500, 000, 000
- ☐ 03 $50, 000, 000 to $100, 000, 000
- ☐ 04 $5, 000, 000 to $50, 000, 000
- ☐ 05 $1, 000, 000 to $5, 000, 000

⑨ WHAT LANGUAGES AND FRAMEWORKS DO YOU USE? (check all that apply)

- ☐ 01 Ajax
- ☐ 02 C
- ☐ 03 C++
- ☐ 04 C#
- ☐ 13 Python
- ☐ 14 Ruby/Rails
- ☐ 15 Spring
- ☐ 16 Struts
- ☐ 05 Hibernate
- ☐ 06 J++/J#
- ☐ 07 Java
- ☐ 08 JSP
- ☐ 09 .NET
- ☐ 10 Perl
- ☐ 11 PHP
- ☐ 12 PL/SQL
- ☐ 17 SQL
- ☐ 18 Visual Basic
- ☐ 98 Other

⑩ WHAT ORACLE PRODUCTS ARE IN USE AT YOUR SITE? (check all that apply)

ORACLE DATABASE
- ☐ 01 Oracle Database 11g
- ☐ 02 Oracle Database 10g
- ☐ 03 Oracle9i Database
- ☐ 04 Oracle Embedded Database (Oracle Lite, Times Ten, Berkeley DB)
- ☐ 05 Other Oracle Database Release

ORACLE FUSION MIDDLEWARE
- ☐ 06 Oracle Application Server
- ☐ 07 Oracle Portal
- ☐ 08 Oracle Enterprise Manager
- ☐ 09 Oracle BPEL Process Manager
- ☐ 10 Oracle Identity Management
- ☐ 11 Oracle SOA Suite
- ☐ 12 Oracle Data Hubs

ORACLE DEVELOPMENT TOOLS
- ☐ 13 Oracle JDeveloper
- ☐ 14 Oracle Forms
- ☐ 15 Oracle Reports
- ☐ 16 Oracle Designer
- ☐ 17 Oracle Discoverer
- ☐ 18 Oracle BI Beans
- ☐ 19 Oracle Warehouse Builder
- ☐ 20 Oracle WebCenter
- ☐ 21 Oracle Application Express

ORACLE APPLICATIONS
- ☐ 22 Oracle E-Business Suite
- ☐ 23 PeopleSoft Enterprise
- ☐ 24 JD Edwards EnterpriseOne
- ☐ 25 JD Edwards World
- ☐ 26 Oracle Fusion
- ☐ 27 Hyperion
- ☐ 28 Siebel CRM

ORACLE SERVICES
- ☐ 28 Oracle E-Business Suite On Demand
- ☐ 29 Oracle Technology On Demand
- ☐ 30 Siebel CRM On Demand
- ☐ 31 Oracle Consulting
- ☐ 32 Oracle Education
- ☐ 33 Oracle Support
- ☐ 98 Other
- ☐ 99 None of the Above